The
Corporate
University
Handbook

The Corporate University Handbook

Designing, Managing, and Growing a Successful Program

Mark Allen, Ph.D.
Editor

American Management Association

New York • Atlanta • Brussels • Buenos Aires • Chicago • London • Mexico City
San Francisco • Shanghai • Tokyo • Toronto • Washington, D.C.

Special discounts on bulk quantities of AMACOM books are available to corporations, professional associations, and other organizations. For details, contact Special Sales Department, AMACOM, a division of American Management Association, 1601 Broadway, New York, NY 10019.
Tel.: 212-903-8316. Fax: 212-903-8083.
Web site: www.amacombooks.org

This publication is designed to provide accurate and authoritative information in regard to the subject matter covered. It is sold with the understanding that the publisher is not engaged in rendering legal, accounting, or other professional service. If egal advice or other expert assistance is required, the services of a competent professional person should be sought.

Library of Congress Cataloging-in-Publication Data

Allen, Mark, 1959–
    The corporate university handbook : designing, managing, and growing a successful program / Mark Allen
        p.   cm.
Includes bibliographical references and index.
    ISBNs: 9780814407110 (HC) and 9780814420270 (PB)
    1. Employer-supported education.   2. Employees—Training of.   I. Title.
    HF5549.5.T7 A469   2002
    658.3'1243—dc21   2002004852

Printing number

10 9 8 7 6 5 4 3 2 1

Contents

Part 2: Managing a Corporate University

Part 3: International Perspectives

The
Corporate
University
Handbook

Introduction

What Is a Corporate University, and Why Should an Organization Have One?

Mark Allen

In the beginning, there were universities. Maybe not at the very beginning, but by medieval times, the antecedents of modern universities were taking shape in Europe. In the New World, colleges sprang up in colonial times, before there was a United States of America. Corporations came later. The corporate model for American commerce developed in the nineteenth century and was well established by the turn of the twentieth century.

So how did universities and corporations come together to form corporate universities? Was there a master plan, or was it a serendipitous you-got-your-chocolate-on-my-peanut-butter sort of accident? The answer is a little bit of both, as the rapid proliferation of corporate universities over the past two decades is not a revolution in workplace education; it is merely the next step in an evolutionary process that had been unfolding for a half-century.

This book will examine the phenomenon of corporate universities in all of its forms. Corporate university managers, consultants, and observers, representing all aspects of corporate university operations, have contributed chapters describing the various dimensions of this rapidly growing trend.

Corporate university veterans from some of America's largest and most respected organizations share their experiences. Consultants and educators who have worked with numerous corporate universities—from

1

start-ups to large, thriving organizations—relate tales of what they have learned. International authors describe the corporate university phenomenon in Europe, Asia, and Australia. *The Corporate University Handbook* is designed to provide practical, hands-on information to the professionals who work daily within a corporate university, to the educators and consultants who contribute to corporate university success, and to the executives and managers who are charged with planning, developing, and creating new corporate universities.

The first part of the book deals with the design of corporate universities. Mike Morrison kicks off the section by addressing the launch of a corporate university from the ground up by relating his very personal tale of getting the University of Toyota started. Then Jim Moore examines different funding models for corporate universities based on his experience at Sun Microsystems' SunU. The topic of organizational structures for corporate universities is addressed by Karen Barley, who has consulted with and provides examples from numerous corporate universities. Motorola University's Tom McCarty then writes about how to use a corporate university as a strategic lever. I conclude the section by examining the options for partnerships that corporate universities can engage in.

Managing a corporate university is the subject of Part 2. The section begins with a look at best practices in corporate universities. This chapter is authored by Robert Fulmer, who has worked with thousands of executives in dozens of companies and provides the findings from several research studies on best practice corporate universities. Linda Lewis of Charles Schwab writes about how to integrate the training function into a corporate university. The role of technology in corporate education is described by distance learning expert Brandon Hall. Laree Kiely discusses various options for evaluation and measurement in corporate universities, while Matt Barney of Motorola wraps up the section by presenting ROI models.

Part 3 provides international perspectives on corporate universities. Annick Renaud-Coulon delivers the results of her research on the corporate university experience in Europe. Ian Dickson, from Deakin University in Australia, describes corporate university activities in Australia and Asia. I conclude the book with a look ahead at the future of corporate universities.

Defining Corporate Universities

Before we can discuss all of these various aspects of corporate universities, it would be useful to define the beast. However, a simple, widely accepted definition has been elusive. I will provide several possible definitions while working toward arriving at a single definition that will serve as a guideline for the rest of this book.

One author has estimated that there are currently more than two thousand corporate universities in the United States alone.[1] Although there is no definition associated with that estimate, it does bring up the question of how to know whether an entity should be included in the count. In order to address that question, let's use the example of an organization I recently worked with.

This was a large division of a *Fortune* 500 company. One day, someone in the marketing department read an article about corporate universities and decided that the organization should have one. He brought the idea to his managers, who quickly endorsed it. The first thing he did was come up with a name for the corporate university. This was followed quickly by the design of a logo. Once you've got a logo, you pretty much have to have T-shirts. After several months, the corporate university had a name, a logo, some T-shirts, and a budget. What it didn't have was any staff devoted to corporate education, any dedicated place for its operation, or any educational programs whatsoever. Yet the hundreds of employees at this organization said that they had a corporate university and believed that they had a corporate university. I have no idea whether that organization was included in Jeanne Meister's estimate, but there are many stories of training departments that are magically transformed into corporate universities overnight by virtue of nothing more than a name change.

This brings us to one possible definition of a corporate university: Any entity that calls itself a corporate university is a corporate university. If, in fact, there are two thousand corporate universities in America, I believe that many of them are small entities that call themselves corporate universities but either do little in the way of corporate education or are merely training departments that have undergone a name change. While this definition might get us to two thousand corporate universities in the United States, it does not go very far in satisfying our curiosity about corporate universities. It is not very descriptive, and it does little to clarify the concept.

We can also look to the literature for definitions of corporate universities. An article in 1983 provided the first detailed research on corporate universities (which were then called *corporate colleges*). The authors of this study defined a corporate college as an institution "offering postsecondary degrees which was initially established by an entity, profit or nonprofit,

3

whose primary mission was something other than granting collegiate degrees."[2] This definition is a bit too restrictive, as it limits corporate colleges to those institutions that offer degrees. As I will explain later in this introduction, this definition would apply to only a small handful of corporate universities today.

Nearly two decades ago, the Carnegie Foundation for the Advancement of Teaching published the first book on corporate universities (which the author also referred to as *corporate colleges*). That book defined corporate colleges as educational entities that "were all started by incorporated organizations whose first purpose was not education."[3] While this definition can be helpful—for example, it would rule out the Apollo Group's University of Phoenix, which is both a corporation and a university, but is not a corporate university, since its primary business is education—it also does not provide much description of the goals and activities of a corporate university. Any corporation's training department would qualify as a corporate university under this definition.

Four Levels of Corporate Universities

The question of whether a training department should be considered a corporate university is worthy of examination. One method of defining a corporate university would be to examine the scope of activities undertaken. I have identified four levels of activity that corporate universities may engage in:

1. Training only
2. Training plus managerial and/or executive development
3. Courses offered for academic credit
4. Courses offered that lead to an academic degree

At one end of the spectrum are corporate universities that are simply training departments. They exist to provide job-specific training to employees. The next level of corporate universities provides management and executive development courses in addition to training. While "training" focuses on skills that are necessary for specific tasks, "development" refers to education that is designed to modify "core parts of the executive and his/her behavior."[4]

Level 3 corporate universities offer courses that can be taken for academic credit—credit that can be transferred or applied to an academic degree. Because of the stringent and bureaucratic requirements for receiving accreditation, few corporate universities are entering the business of offering transferable credit. Those that wish to offer their employees courses for credit typically do so in partnership with traditional accredited universities. In these cases, the course credit comes from the partner institution, not the corporate university.

Level 4 corporate universities offer degree programs at the baccalaureate or master's level. To be considered at this level, a corporate university must offer accredited degrees. As discussed in the Conclusion, the MGM Grand Hotel's University of Oz offers programs leading to the Th.D. degree (Doctor of Thinkology). While this degree is quite prestigious within the walls of MGM Grand, it is not an accredited degree, and therefore the university would not qualify for level 4 status.

While many in traditional institutions of higher education have either feared or reviled corporate universities for poaching on their turf, the truth is that very few corporate universities offer degree programs or aspire to do so. In 1985, N. P. Eurich identified eighteen such institutions and predicted that the number would grow rapidly. In fact, a more recent study went in search of corporations throughout the United States and Canada that offer degrees and was able to identify only five that definitely met the criteria, with a possible seven others that broadly met some of the criteria.[5] This was fewer institutions than Eurich identified in 1985, and these twelve accounted for a total of less than eleven thousand students. So traditional institutions can rest easy—corporate universities are not trying to poach on their degree-granting turf.

Why do so few corporate universities offer degrees? There are several reasons, but the most important is the difficulty in obtaining accreditation. There are many time-consuming obstacles to overcome in order to achieve accreditation, and while traditional institutions of higher education need to hurdle these obstacles (both to gain eligibility for federal funds and to gain general respect), corporate universities do not. In fact, corporations that want their employees to earn degrees can send them directly to traditional colleges. Of course, many corporate universities exist because of dissatisfaction with the offerings of traditional colleges. Those corporations that want a more specialized or customized program can get one in partnership with a college that is willing to customize its curricula and be flexible with regard to delivery. An increasing number of colleges are demonstrating a willingness to enter into such partnerships (as will be discussed in Chapter 5), so corporate universities are finding that it is unnecessary for them to establish their own degree programs.

Another reason why there are so few level 4 institutions is that when a corporate university reaches this level, it has a tendency to spin off from its parent organization, at which point it is no longer a corporate university. One of the earliest examples of a corporate university is Northrop University. Needing well-trained workers for the rapidly growing aviation industry, Northrop Aviation created this university in the 1940s. The university grew in size and scope over several decades and was spun off from the parent company and became an independent, not-for-profit university. Northrop University continued to offer programs in aviation but expanded to include a school of business offering MBA degrees and a law school. It became a fully accredited, degree-granting institution that was completely independent of Northrop Aviation. The increasingly competitive higher education marketplace forced Northrop University to close its doors in the 1990s.

The Arthur D. Little School of Management is another example of a corporate university that began offering degrees and was later spun off from its parent. Founded in 1964 as an integral part of its consulting company parent, the Arthur D. Little School of Management began offering degrees in 1973.[6] Gradually, the school moved away from being a training ground for employees of Arthur D. Little and started recruiting students from outside the company. It gained an impressive international reputation, and its Master of Science in Management program came to be fully accredited. After many years of operating as a part of Arthur D. Little, the school is now an independent, not-for-profit organization. Like so many children that have grown up, the school has moved out of its parent's headquarters and has taken up residence at Boston College. The school still maintains a relationship with Arthur D. Little, but in fact it is more closely allied with Boston College, where it maintains its facilities and with which it shares resources.

So clearly an organization does not have to issue degrees to be considered to be a corporate university, although most people would agree that an entity that merely conducts job training is not a true corporate university, even if that training is quite extensive. I think an organization should at least conduct management and executive development (in addition to training) to qualify as a corporate university. But does meeting this qualification definitely make an institution a corporate university? I think that offering management and executive development is a necessary minimum criterion, but that it is not sufficient to automatically earn an institution the designation of corporate university. In order to be a true corporate university, something more is needed.

The Link to Organizational Strategy

That extra something is a clear tie to company strategy. One theme that will emerge in many of the chapters of this book is that the best corporate universities are those that exist to help the company meets its goals. Every organization exists for a reason, and that reason is usually articulated in a mission statement. Most well-run organizations develop strategic plans designed to help the organization fulfill its mission. Having a corporate university should not be viewed as a goal of an organization—it is a means of helping the organization to achieve its goals.

When viewed in this way, a corporate university can be a powerful tool for helping organizations get where they need to be. Motorola's Tom McCarty in Chapter 4 refers to corporate universities as being "strategic levers."

In fact, recent attempts in the literature to define corporate universities have all, in one form or another, asserted that the feature that most defines a corporate university is its connection to its parent organization's strategy. As Martyn Rademakers and Nicoline Huizinga state, "What makes corporate universities 'corporate,' one can argue, is their link with strategy, which brings up the question of how strongly corporate university programs are related to corporate strategy."[7] These authors identify three stages of corporate university development: operational, tactical, and strategic. It is interesting to note that they do not refer to these designations as three different types of corporate universities; rather, they call them three developmental stages of corporate universities. So a corporate university might not start out with a clear link to company strategy, but it may be working its way toward that stage as it evolves.

A more recent article specifically addressed the issue of defining corporate universities.[8] Five corporate university professionals were interviewed and were asked to provide their definitions of a corporate university. Most of these included some tie to organizational strategy and goals.

One definition was provided by Jim Moore, the former director of SunU, who is the author of Chapter 2 of this book. Moore defined a corporate university as "a central organization serving multiple constituencies that helps the organization to develop the employee capabilities required for successes.''[9] This definition is instructive because it focuses on the corporate university's role in developing employee capabilities. There are numerous tools that an organization may use to help it achieve its goals—products, services, finances, etc.—but the corporate university is the tool that helps the organization meet its goals through its people.

Motorola University's Tom McCarty, who contributed Chapter 4 of this book, is also quoted in the article. His definition is, "The corporate university is the organization responsible for managing the learning processes and knowledge assets of the corporation for the purpose of increasing total shareholder value of the corporation.''[10] The important part of this definition is that it assigns to the corporate university the tasks of "managing the learning process and knowledge assets of the corporation." While not mentioning employees as specifically as Moore's definition did, this phrasing recognizes that learning is both an individual and an organizational activity. This definition also implies that organizations have knowledge assets; these are often in the heads of individual employees but also may exist independently of the employees (in databases, documents, etc.). McCarty ascribed an important role to the corporate university in giving it responsibility for this knowledge management function in addition to the traditional role of employee education.

However, there is one part of McCarty's definition that I would not include in a blanket definition of corporate universities: the focus on shareholder value. As a matter of fact, I think the word *corporation* does not belong in the definition of a corporate university. The corporate university concept has been effectively utilized in many organizations that are not corporations and do not exist for the purpose of making a profit or creating shareholder value. Numerous government agencies, municipalities, hospitals, and other not-for-profit organizations have successful corporate universities. The fact that these organizations are not corporations should in no way disqualify them from having corporate universities in the sense in which the term is commonly used. Because Motorola is an organization focused on shareholder value, it makes sense that Motorola University's role is to help increase shareholder value. However, not all organizations have this focus. Therefore, for many corporate universities, the "increasing shareholder value" part of the definition should be replaced with wording that more accurately reflects the organization's mission.

A New Definition

So from all of this, can we cobble together a definition that is both descriptive and comprehensive? The key descriptors of a corporate university are that it is an educational organization, that it provides a variety of functions, and that these functions are clearly and strategically linked to the organization's goals and mission. Based on all of the foregoing, I offer this as a definition of a corporate university:

> A corporate university is an educational entity that is a strategic tool designed to assist its parent organization in achieving its mission by conducting activities that cultivate individual and organizational learning, knowledge, and wisdom.

To deconstruct this definition into its component parts, I think it is essential to first characterize a corporate university as an educational entity, since education is the primary function of any university, corporate or traditional. This definition clearly states that a corporate university is strategic, while adding that it is a tool (one of many at an organization's disposal) to help its parent organization achieve its mission. The clear tie to the organizational mission is important here, as it emphasizes the strategic nature of corporate universities in meeting the overarching goals of the parent organization. And the word *organization* recognizes that the parent need not be a corporation, need not be in the business of making money, and may be in any industry (perhaps even education—couldn't a university have a corporate university?).

The definition also has the corporate university "conducting activities." The nonspecific nature of this phrase is intentional—there are many possible activities, ranging from classroom learning to distance learning, to executive development, succession planning, knowledge management, strategic hiring and orientation, and many other possible activities. What ties them together is that they are all designed to cultivate individual and organizational learning, knowledge, and wisdom.

This last phrase first acknowledges that the primary focus of the corporate university is on the individual, but it additionally recognizes that organizations also learn and that the ultimate beneficiary of the activities of the corporate university is the organization.

Finally, the definition refers to "learning, knowledge, and wisdom," three words that should probably be defined. *Learning* refers to change. Individuals change, both internally and in their behaviors, when they undergo learning. This description can also apply to organizational learning. *Knowledge* refers to specific facts, procedures, and skills that can be possessed by an individual or an organization (and that are typically acquired through the change process called learning). The highest rung on the ladder is *wisdom*, the ability to effectively apply knowledge to organizational goals. Remember, the whole purpose of a corporate university is to support the organization's mission. The achievement of learning that is not applied to organizational goals is not a successful outcome of a corporate university. Employees and organizations must have the wisdom to effectively apply their learning and knowledge to meeting organizational goals in order for corporate universities to be effective.

It is important to note that under this definition, training is certainly a viable corporate university activity. However, a training department by itself typically would not qualify as a corporate university because its activities usually do not have a direct strategic link with the organization's mission and rarely are designed to cultivate organizational learning, knowledge, and wisdom.

Why Have a Corporate University?

I have spoken to many people who have come across the concept of the corporate university and have asked them whether the model is appropriate for their organization. Based on the foregoing definition, there is really only one reason to have a corporate university: to help an organization achieve its mission. Every organization has a mission, but there are a variety of ways of trying to achieve that mission. So while the goal of helping an organization achieve its mission can apply to virtually any entity, is the corporate university the right tool for every organization? For many, the answer is yes, but not for all.

Since a corporate university exists to assist in developing individual and organizational learning, knowledge, and wisdom, the first criterion must be that the organization have a good number of individuals (it is true that organizations learn, but organizational learning happens first inside the individuals that make up the organization). While there is no critical mass or specific head count that qualifies an organization as being appropriate for having a corporate university, it is clear that the concept applies best to those organizations that are very dependent on their employees and on those employees' knowledge and skills. While this applies to increasing numbers of organizations in the so-called knowledge economy, it is not true of all organizations. Certainly very small organizations and those that are more reliant on automated technology than on human labor might not be appropriate candidates for a corporate university.

The size of the organization is clearly not the primary determinant of its eligibility for having a corporate university. While having a corporate university would not make sense for an organization with only three or four employees, I have seen some relatively small organizations (with only a few hundred employees) successfully apply the concept.

Some organizations have become so successful at running a corporate university that members of outside organizations have requested that their members be allowed to attend. This often starts with related organizations—suppliers, customers, and other strategic partners. It frequently makes sense for a corporate university to provide education to its partners—the organization's goals can better be met if its partners are well educated.

Often, this evolves to the point where the corporate university's offerings are so much in demand that many outsiders, even those with no relationship to the organization, ask to attend. Some corporate universities have acquiesced to this demand and allow or encourage outsiders to attend their programs, or even aggressively sell attendance to outsiders. Disney University is one such example. High-quality brochures trumpet Disney University's many offerings and encourage anyone who is willing to pay to attend these programs. Once a corporate university starts making money selling education, is it disqualified from being a true corporate university? Not necessarily. While Disney University aggressively markets its offerings, the sale of these programs is not its primary purpose. Its main purpose is still the education of Disney employees.

Saturn University is another corporate university that sells seats in its programs to outsiders. However, this is indirectly consistent with its mission, as Saturn University uses the revenue from outside participants to support its primary mission of educating Saturn associates.

Conclusion

I have often heard the phrase "the corporate university phenomenon." Yes, corporate universities can certainly be viewed as a phenomenon. They can also be described as a concept. Some people have even described corporate universities as a process, as opposed to a physical entity.

While it is true that corporate universities can be thought of in all of these ways, for the purposes of this book, my fellow authors and I view corporate universities as actual entities that exist to perform some very real functions. Using the definition given previously as a guideline, we provide information designed to assist professionals in actual corporate universities to perform the very important work that lies before them. We encourage you to read this book for information as well as for more practical purposes. We hope we can provide advice and insight that will help you define, understand, and perform your jobs, and we hope you enjoy the book.

Designing a Corporate University

1

Creating a Corporate University: Diary of a Launch

Mike Morrison

The University of Toyota, headquartered in Torrance, California, was officially approved by Toyota Motor Sales, USA, Inc., in 1998. The university was one of several corporate initiatives that emerged from Toyota's New Era Group, whose charter was to design strategies that would enhance Toyota's competitiveness in the new millennium. The University of Toyota is a distinct business unit independent of the human resource and organizational development departmental functions. Built on the values of trust, respect, integrity, commitment, and enthusiasm, the University of Toyota has a stated mission "to continuously improve associate and dealer performance through lifelong learning." This is accomplished through two colleges: the College of Dealer Education and Development and the College of Associate Education and Development. The university now serves the global Toyota organization. This chapter is an account of our beginnings at the University of Toyota—a tale intended both to tell the story of our journey and to provide some guidance to those who are on the verge of or already in the process of creating a corporate university.

Journal Entry, December 1, 1998

We've officially been a university for several months now, but I'm beginning to get nervous. I have a fairly clear vision of the university's future, and I want to move forward quickly. Yes, we have a mission statement and a set of values—our brochures say so! My point here is that these things, while they all sound right and are directionally good, were all born out of the need to internally market the launch of the University of Toyota. They aren't known by my staff, so they certainly aren't shared. Part of my challenge is that we're so new that we don't even know each other—a challenge that is heightened by the fact that we're housed in a number of locations around the company and around the country.

As I think about it, I need to get my arms around a number of things:

❏ A strategy to move us beyond a centralized training function to a unique corporate university organization
❏ A means of building a true team and organizing my staff
❏ A strategy for identifying and structuring our real "centers of excellence"
❏ A means of organizing and aligning our current and future curricula to ensure quality service to our "customers"
❏ A way to transform our loose collection of courseware into well-purposed, well-integrated curricula
❏ Some way to give my team input into and ownership of our direction and my vision
❏ As the bottom line, a shared understanding of who we are (individually and as a team), what our strengths are, where we're headed, and how we're going to get there

In short, I need a plan for the future.

Journal Entry, December 15, 1998

I have decided to bring the entire team together for a three-day off-site strategic planning session immediately following the New Year. I need a plan to make those three days as productive and engaging as possible. I have thirty people reporting to me, so it'll be no easy challenge. In my mind, I have three primary objectives:

1. Build a collectively designed vision of the future for the College of Associate Education and Development
2. Develop an initial curriculum direction and integration strategy
3. Enhance teamwork and camaraderie

I realize that I need to enlist some independent help. I set a full-day design meeting with a consulting partner. We'll have to meet over the holiday when Toyota is "dark."

Journal Entry, December 29, 1998

Today was a good day. Design day. Good meeting. I'm fairly confident that our agenda will work. Design Challenge #1 was to create a mechanism to immediately focus the energy of the team on the issues that will define and determine our success as a corporate university—some creative way to elicit input in a positive way with an eye toward finding out what's possible.

Our creative device: a fictitious "*Wall Street Journal*-like" newspaper exposé set three years in the future (see Figure 1-1), with the various issues embedded. This will enable us to construct a master list of critical success factors. Additionally, it will serve as a visioning exercise, as the assignment will be to rewrite the headline and first paragraph of the article—in essence, to paint the picture of the future. As I see it, we have to overcome a number of critical, potentially crippling obstacles.

First, we need to transform ourselves from a loose-knit, decentralized provider of corporate training and education to a cohesive provider of performance improvement solutions with the ability to design, develop, and deliver interventions that will have impact. The focus on lifelong learning and performance improvement is what will elevate us to university status, beyond being merely a catalog of courses.

Second, we will have to overcome the fairly entrenched notion that we have no new capability, only a new name. We need to be the provider

17

Figure 1-1.

Corporate Obituaries

The University of Toyota Calls It Quits

Requiem for a Noble Concept

"University" Means More Than Training

BY I. M. ACARBUFF

Staff Reporter of THE WALL STREET REVIEW

TORRANCE, California (Jan. 4, 2001) — Less than three years since an auspicious launch, the much ballyhooed University of Toyota has closed its doors. Toyota Motor Sales today officially announced the initiative a failed corporate experiment — noble in intent, sound in concept, but lacking in execution.

The lofty founding values, espousing trust, respect, commitment, integrity, and enthusiasm, never sustained the path-breaking launch that captured the envy of the industry. In the end, it was merely a functional department offering "traditional" training courses and events.

Not for lack of talent and support, however. "We had the makings of a real breakthrough success," states Richard Chitty, Vice President and leader of the University. "From the beginning through to the end, we never lacked expertise, funding, facilities, or recognition."

"We never really escaped the notion that we were anything more than a dressed-up internal training organization," avers Mike Morrison, Dean of the Associate Division. "We suffered from an inability to deliver performance improvement advice and programs that advanced the levels of knowledge, skill, and attitude to client groups in a timely manner in response to market shifts and customer requirements. In short, we couldn't compete with external providers. We had a short window of opportunity, and we missed it."

A closer look at the demise of the University revealed a lack of clear vision. As one insider states, "We never really got a sense of who we were, what we were about. The focus on corporate fire-fighting took precedence over a real long-term strategy backed up by a good communication process. I don't see how you can align and allocate your resources if you don't have a firm handle on these things."

As a result, the University never fully operationalized its overall goal of improving corporate performance. Risk-taking and group decision-making gave way to meeting the "urgent" demands and playing it safe. Managers reported being so busy responding to day-to-day operational requirements that they had no time for innovative new thinking. The "cutting edge" was replaced with "cutting budgets," as returns on investment failed to show positive results. Courses overlapped and were even duplicated.

Curricula were developed that had no clear application to business results. While clients demanded customized, just-in-time training tailored to their specific and immediate needs, the University delivered "traditional training programs." The programs appeared to be on track with consistently high "level one" scores. It wasn't long before credibility had eroded and internal clients either returned to the external vendors that they had relied on in the past – or withdrew their participation.

"The University had every opportunity to establish a clear and steady direction, with the financial commitment, technological innovation, and leadership to support it," discloses one internal client. "Watching them struggle, we got the feeling that they could and would be a potent force if they could get it all together."

Clearly, the disconnect was between a long-term strategy built on meeting client requirements and the short-term necessity to offer training. "We didn't have one strategy," says one manager. "We had at least three. And they were all incompatible."

The fallout left University staff asking: "What do we really stand for? What are our priorities?" Toward the end, political maneuvering and defection occurred as the inevitable became clear in the minds of University staffers.

The life and times of the University of Toyota are not a new story. The reality is that most corporate universities fail to meet the lofty expectations they were established under. "Many times, a corporate university will simply fail to align itself around the real business needs of the organization," states Bob Thurow, author of *Why Training Fails*.

To be sure, the University had many "wins." New training was built, an impressive catalogue of course offerings was developed, and new delivery systems were implemented capitalizing on emerging technology and distance learning concepts. From senior leaders down to the entry level management trainees, all levels enthusiastically participated in initial programs.

As one executive lamented, "It's not like they didn't have a fair chance."

But in the end, training and catalogues do not a university make.

* * * *

of choice. In effect, we will be competing with independent vendors. Our products and services must be world-class.

Finally, we need to ensure that we are able to link strategically to the business goals and objectives of Toyota. By that I mean that we need to show our impact on business results.

The general process for the meeting is shown in Figure 1-2. The meeting is designed to be highly interactive and self-directed, with several facilitators, including myself.

Journal Entry, January 4, 1999

Day One of the off-site meeting is in the can, and it was successful. As I expected, we had to overcome some initial skepticism. But by the end of

Figure 1-2.

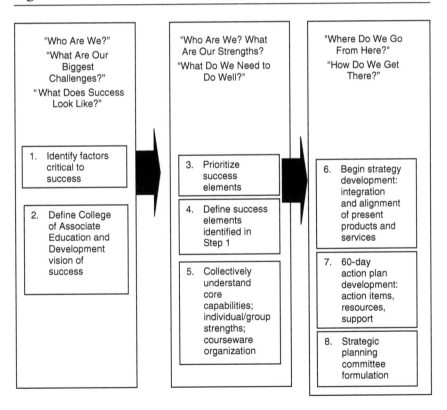

the day, I sensed a growing feeling of unity. We split the larger group into rounds of five, and teamwork grew as people got to know one another.

The fictitious article worked! The team identified a number of factors, all of which address my own concerns:

- ❏ *Clarity in values.* What are we? Who are we? What are our beliefs, our norms? Does our mission statement capture our purpose fully? What does "lifelong learning" mean? What do we bring to the party to add value?

- ❏ *Shared vision.* What is our picture of the future? What are our goals? What does it look like when we meet those goals? How do we treat one another? How does our mission support Toyota's?

- ❏ *Client focus.* Whom are we serving? At what levels? Are we responding to their requirements? How are we serving them now? How should we be serving them? How are we structured to serve them? Are we aligned correctly to do so? What are their real and perceived needs? How do we assess those needs?

- ❏ *Unified strategy.* How do we achieve our mission/vision? What are our priorities? What are our core competencies, our centers of excellence? What are our products and services? What are our curricula and courses? How and where are we aligned and integrated?

- ❏ *Alignment with business results.* What are the business goals of the College of Associate Education and Development? Are we aligned correctly? Are the goals achievable?

- ❏ *Operational consistency.* How does our work get done? What are our core processes (e.g., efficient communication)?

- ❏ *Measure of success in performance improvement.* How will we know if we're successful? What evidence is needed? How do we hold ourselves accountable?

The rewritten story is worthy of capturing (see Figure 1-3).

Journal Entry, January 5, 1999

Day Two down . . . and a long one at that. But it was highly productive: We prioritized and defined our output from Day One, and we began to get a real sense of our curricula.

Figure 1-3.

"THE UNIVERSITY OF TOYOTA—LEADING THE WAY!"

Celebrating Corporate Learning Breakthroughs

Proof that a corporate university means more than "training"

(January 4, 2001)

If it were any company other than Toyota, we'd be amazed at the success of its new university. Less than three years since its celebrated launch, the University of Toyota has widened its influence to include all of global Toyota, and outside clients as well. The sound concept of putting performance improvement first has paid big dividends for Toyota.

By anchoring itself solidly to corporate values, having a clear vision, and tenaciously linking to business needs, the University of Toyota has captured the envy of the industry by providing anything but traditional training courses and events. It has redefined the concept of lifelong learning and established a clear path for all Toyota associates to increase their impact both professionally and personally.

The group came to the consensus that really only two primary success element categories existed: (1) values/mission/vision and (2) a unified strategy addressing client focus, operational efficiency, and personal development (see Figure 1-4).

The next step was to define these elements. Having already agreed on the vision of our future, the group unanimously agreed that our purpose, or mission, was in fact as we had stated already:

> *"To continuously improve associate performance through lifelong learning."*

21

Figure 1-4.

It remains my personal goal to arrive at a unique definition of lifelong learning, far beyond something that simply means "continuous study." Our unique identity will hinge on a conceptual model that ties our purpose and values to our products and services.

The group also confirmed that our stated values—*trust, respect, integrity, commitment,* and *enthusiasm*—provided the principles to which we could turn in making critical decisions.

The more detailed work revolved around defining the three pillars of a unified strategy. The first element of that strategy, client focus, was defined as encompassing seven key components:

1. Clear client definition (divisions, business units, audiences)
2. Clear needs definition (via consultative assessment)
3. A clear performance improvement process and plan (consulting model)
4. Courseware aligned with desired Toyota business results
5. World-class delivery (methods, materials, faculty)
6. Measurement (evaluation at all levels)
7. Catalyst for strategic alliances (become a true partner in performance)

The second strategic element, operational efficiency, was defined around five tenets:

1. Effective communication (internal communication, external communications, shared meetings, full utilization of available technology)

2. Technology systems (delivery systems, registration, tracking, measurement)

3. Curriculum development (quality standards)

4. Self-directed learning environment

5. Consistent/rigorous project management

The third strategic element, personal development, focused on ensuring our performance improvement capability. This meant developing our skills related to consulting, consultative selling, project management, needs assessment, business updates, learning technology, process consulting, and facilitation.

It remained to get a sense of where our individual and group strengths were, and how we should begin to think about organizing our courses.

The group completed course descriptions for more than seventy-five current courses. Forms detailing the course name, audience, content, vendor support, delivery system, evaluation, and other factors for each course were posted around the room, arranged according to client and business unit. Individual "talent" sheets were also completed by individuals and posted, in an effort to communicate and identify expertise.

At the end of the day, I gave a presentation that offered my suggestions for aligning what I thought should be our core capabilities. I proposed ten core capability centers, or "centers of excellence":

❑ Leadership

❑ Market focus

❑ Management

❑ Citizenship

❑ Technology

❑ Teamwork

❑ Diversity

❑ Functional expertise

❏ Continuous improvement
❏ Consulting

This set us up for the final day.

Journal Entry, January 6, 1999

The final day was a home run. We spent the majority of the day conducting a significant gap analysis, alignment, and integration exercise. The challenge would be turning the great ideas into action.

First, current courses were mapped to the ten core capability areas to identify gaps and begin the process of integration and alignment. This was done by rearranging the course descriptions, moving them from client/business units to the ten core capability areas. This allowed a visual display of the product/service deficiencies and the general lack of integration and consistency in the core areas.

We then assigned two of the ten capability areas to each of the five teams. We charged each team with the task of identifying the current and ideal states of their designated core capability areas, in an effort to assess gaps and needs.

I was impressed with the teams' output. The visions for the various centers of excellence were well thought out and are worth noting here; they are given in Figure 1-5.

The real work then began—developing sixty-day action items focused on the team-developed gap analyses and "ideal states" and identifying the support and resources needed to accomplish those action items.

At the end of the day, we had ten 60-day action plans—a lot of work to do and not a lot of time to do it. This begged the question, Who would implement these plans?

The need for a strategic planning team consisting of one point person for each area of core capability was apparent. The team would be charged with integration, alignment, and curriculum review, much like a true university planning committee. I explained the requirements and requested that volunteers respond to me personally within twenty-four hours.

Our launch meeting concluded with the team members sharing personal reflections with the large group. Based on the heartfelt affirmations

Figure 1-5.

Leadership
Currently, we have little in the way of depth in this area. We have some outside speaker forums, but no continuum of curriculum to progress through. Ideally, we want to develop our associates at all levels as leaders. Elements of a well-designed curriculum might entail such things as a six-month consulting assignment in Japan and other TMC locations, a succession/development plan available on database for all associates, a system for sharing "lessons learned," sending executives to outside programs, building development assignments for leaders at all levels, and designing an organizational communication plan.

Market Focus
We currently have a basic, general customer satisfaction orientation in this area, but market focus is neither a top priority nor consistent throughout the organization. There is some top-level manager exposure through some of the speaker series we have implemented. Ideally, though, we need to make our internal and external customers central to all activities. This could include ideas such as requiring core market-focused courses for all associates now and in the future, quarterly competitive updates, developing associates as Toyota ambassadors, understanding individual contributions to the bottom line and selling cars, and requiring customer experience of all associates. To encourage customer focus, we should make strategic thinking a part of all leadership/management interventions and utilize a variety of media to communicate market focus.

Management
Currently, our offerings in this area are isolated to specific audiences (divisions/departments). Ideally, we would have a well-supported management development continuum. This might mean rewarding individual contributors and renaming "lateral moves," creating self-directed performers by providing development assignments, providing "value-added" learning opportunities for each associate, and providing support tools for development plans.

Citizenship
While we have a number of courses in this area, we need a more integrated curriculum. Ideally, we need to understand areas of our organization that are removed from the headquarters campus. This might mean tours of dealerships, plants, ports, regional offices, and parts distribution centers. We should have a central philosophy regarding teamwork. One thought is to design a buddy system—"the Sensei Program"—which would entail professionally trained volunteers from the organization, trained at the university, acting as personal buddies/sponsors for a one-year period. The Sensei Program would be a fully integrated orientation process that would brings all associates to a baseline level of knowledge, skill, and attitude.

Figure 1-5. (continued)

Functional Expertise

We currently have a non-standardized curriculum in this area. Training and development is supported but not embraced by management, skill sets are not clearly defined, and training is fragmented across the organization. Additionally, we experience a loss of productivity and momentum as a result of associate turnover. Ideally, though, we would build a revelant, timely, task-specific curriculum with mentoring and support of a standardized knowledge system database—resulting in associates performing specific duties within standards, as defined by the organization, department, or manager. Core areas should be: Sales, Finance, Collections, Marketing, Credit, Operations, HR, Insurance, Planning, Administration, Claims, Warranty, Distribution, Legal, Merchandising, Data, Pricing, and Facilities. The best strategy would be to help the business units create their own functional expertise through process management, standardized work, and job instruction—providing line managers with tools to select appropriate subject matter experts and training trainers to be subject matter experts.

Teamwork and Diversity

Currently, we have very little in these areas. Ideally, we would have courses built around team problem solving, team visioning, coaching/mentoring, understanding and managing diversity, facilitating the change process, building an entrepreneurial environment, and international/cultural awareness.

Continuous Improvement

Although we have a number of courses in this area—it is, after all, part of our unique heritage as a company—we have room to expand. Ideally, we should build depth in areas such as process reengineering, developing alliances externally and internally, internal benchmarking, developing talent, personal communication skills, consulting skills, negotiation, project management, business insight, industry expertise, customer service, product knowledge, career development, and personal effectiveness (time management, creative thinking, and personal assessment).

Figure 1-5. **(continued)**

Technology
Right now there's a lack of awareness; people don't know what's available, where we're at, or even what technology can do for them. We haven't yet identified a core skill set, and competencies by position have not been identified. We're challenged also by logistics. Ideally, though, all of these items would be turned around. We need a Toyota-wide audience that is aware of the strategic use of technology. We need to develop courses for both Internet and intranet use, supported by registration/tracking to facilitate skill gap identification, preassessment/measurement, and communication (database, chat rooms, e-mail, newsgroups, message boards, listserve). We need to build depth in areas such as e-commerce strategy. And we need state-of-the-art delivery—virtual classrooms, just-in-time, case-based, e-courses, etc.

Consulting
While we have no capability in this area currently, ideally this center of excellence would provide access to insights, ideas, and best practices. It is a potential profit center, with both internal and external clients. Utilizing a "virtual" business model (deploying a network of top consulting talent operating under the University of Toyota name and brand), the consulting function would be at once a "think tank" (independent studies, projects, publishing, leading-edge knowledge providers) and an expert practitioner.

---

offered by each team member, I am confident that the next sixty days will bring us much closer to my envisioned future for the University of Toyota.

Journal Entry, March 1999

Things have been moving incredibly fast. In two short months, we have completed the first attempt at our organizational structure and fleshed out the implementation of our performance improvement approach. We have also started to think about how best to internally market the university.

We have decided to organize ourselves around six key centers of excellence, down from the original ten. Given the realities of the broader organization, these centers have a hybrid focus—a mix of subject matter, function, and audience. I plan to have an associate dean for each center.

These plans are not carved in stone by any means, but this is what we're thinking:

- ❏ *Center for the Toyota Way*—to provide learning that helps each Toyota associate become a Toyota advocate and citizen for life.
- ❏ *Center for Management Effectiveness*—to provide learning that enables managers to better mobilize people and resources and to align them with the business goals of the organization in the most productive manner.
- ❏ *Center for Personal and Professional Effectiveness*—to provide the learning needed for associate self-discovery in the areas of both personal and professional development.
- ❏ *Center for Technology Learning*—to provide learning that helps all associates maintain, update, and expand their current personal computer skills, with the goals of ensuring not only personal and professional productivity, but also future employability.
- ❏ *Center for Automotive Business Operations*—to provide a broad base of knowledge in all areas of automotive business operations, including corporate operations such as marketing, sales, service and parts, and customer service as well as retail operations.
- ❏ *Center for Executive Leadership*—to provide learning that helps our executives and high-potential managers prepare themselves to lead our organization into new ways of thinking and new ways of doing business.

We have identified each major business unit within the Toyota organization, and we have decided to assign a business unit liaison to each unit. This is our strategy for achieving both a client focus and a performance improvement approach.

Business unit liaisons have two primary functions: (1) they serve as the primary resource contact for associates who wish to take advantage of our curricula; and (2) they serve as performance improvement consultants, assisting the business units in systematically analyzing problems and determining how education and development can support their key business goals. This is in keeping with our philosophy that a corporate university must transcend the traditional notion of corporate training and education—it must focus on performance improvement and consulting, rather than just filling training requests. Additionally, it further one of our fundamental goals: to align education and development with the strategic goals and objectives of the various Toyota business units.

This requires a consultative approach, which looks like this:

❏ We will assist in the definition and diagnosis of a business problem, evaluate various alternatives, and recommend a performance improvement strategy.

❏ If the solution is education, we will assess the business need, validate the training request, and determine which educational solution will most effectively aid in attaining the stated business objectives.

❏ If the solution exists within the curriculum of one of our centers, enrollment will follow. If no courseware presently exists, the development of a customized program will be considered.

❏ If the assessment of a business need calls for custom education and development solutions, we will assist in determining the best course of action and implementation. If the solution requires special subject matter expertise, the business unit liaison will aid in the identification, screening, selection, and assignment of the needed consultative expertise or resource.

Journal Entry, Fall 2001

I ran across my 1999 launch diary today. *Wow!* It's hard to believe that the university is approaching three years old. We've come so far in that time, and I guess I'm so close to it that I didn't notice. It's like looking at a three-year-old photograph of yourself and comparing it with the image in the mirror.

In short, we have surpassed the headline we wrote in our January 1999 off-site meeting. I guess that shows the power of envisioning the future. In the three years since our launch, we have grown not only in size, but in concept. Our strong alliance with the Gallup Organization has dramatically influenced the way we think about improving performance. In fact, we have made great progress in becoming a strengths-based organization. In short, strengths theory is, just as it sounds, a proven idea that says that world-class performance is born out of a focus on inherent personal talents and strengths, not out of well-roundedness. This is contrary to the conventional education and training approach, which would have you work primarily on overcoming weaknesses and let strengths take care of themselves.

But I'm getting ahead of myself. Let me back up. It looks as if my last entry was March 1999. I will provide the epilogue to that entry here.

First, while we still have six centers of excellence, they are profoundly different. The realities of the broader needs of the Toyota organization have helped us shape our internal structure. The six centers now look like this:

- ❏ *Center for the Toyota Way*—focusing on broad foundational knowledge, including the rich company history, heritage, culture, and methods.
- ❏ *Center for Strengths Management*—focusing on identifying, selecting, motivating, developing, and leveraging individual and team talents.
- ❏ *Center for Personal and Professional Development*—focusing on personal growth, interpersonal communication, and technology-related skills.
- ❏ *Center for Executive Leadership*—focusing on high-priority strategic issues, knowledge sharing, and development of opportunities for Toyota managers and officers.
- ❏ *Center for Automotive Business Operations*—focusing on targeted development of regional/field personal and management trainees.
- ❏ *Center for Toyota/Lexus Financial Services Learning*—focusing on knowledge and skills specific to the Toyota/Lexus Financial Services organization.

Through these centers, we now have a comprehensive curriculum of a global nature, encompassing nearly a thousand course offerings.

To tick off some of our other accomplishments:

- ❏ Our marketing engine is driven by a cutting-edge electronic mail mechanism linked to our own university Web site, where associates can browse, search, and enroll.
- ❏ Our strategic alliances with a number of providers of learning content continue to strengthen and broaden our capability.

❑ Our performance improvement efforts have evolved to even higher levels of strategic importance, as the university is now helping our parent corporation in Japan to define, launch, communicate, and educate the global Toyota community on the principles of *The Toyota Way.*

❑ We now publish two free value-added periodicals. One is intended for external audiences and features provocative thoughts centered on lifelong learning. The other is intended for our internal Toyota audience and focuses on learning-centered management strategies.

Finally, and perhaps most importantly, we have redefined the notion of lifelong learning. It is this, and perhaps this alone, that truly sets us apart. We look at lifelong learning as a deeper, continuous journey beyond simply knowledge and skills—one that has five key markers to define the path:

1. *Lead with your strengths.* Leverage unique individual and team talents, work around weaknesses, and leverage the talents of others. In short, find and work within natural power zones.

2. *Serve others.* Move beyond ego, meet the great needs of others, foster positive feelings, share talents to the highest benefit of others. In short, practice servant leadership.

3. *Engage fully.* Take intelligent risks, seek new challenges, and get well connected. In short, be proactive, positive, and purposeful.

4. *Think big.* Creatively add value, solve problems systematically, question conventional wisdom where appropriate, and embrace appreciative inquiry. In short, leverage human ingenuity.

5. *Envision the future.* Paint the picture of tomorrow, set compelling goals, be action-oriented, and knock down barriers that may impede progress. In short, make the vision reality.

Our entire curriculum—each and every course—is aligned with at least one of these central, universal strategies. This is who we are, and this is lifelong learning.

Postscript: Lessons Learned

It occurs to me that I have learned quite a bit over the course of the last three years. The clarity of the vision increases daily. Would I do it differently if I had the chance? Maybe. It has taken three years to arrive at the five precepts of lifelong learning, but those are my lessons learned!

Here's what I mean and here is my advice to others embarking on the process of launching a corporate university:

- ❏ *Lead with your strengths.* In terms of launching a corporate university, stick to your competencies and outsource the rest. The strengths of my team were (and are) in management and administration, not in curriculum design, development, or delivery. As a university, we fully leverage the talents of our strong strategic partners.

- ❏ *Serve others.* We recognized early on that our own interests in education and development—i.e., new technology and delivery, offerings we thought provocative, etc.—were not nearly as important as the ability to meet the great needs of clients.

- ❏ *Engage fully.* We have never been satisfied, and "good enough" never is. Our content is as dynamic as the ability of our partners to shift and change with us. We continually drive for mastery, and "fast pilot" is one of our hallmarks. Is it a risk not to wait for consensus? Sure, but it's an intelligent risk, and a risk that allows us to lead the organization "from the middle," as it were.

- ❏ *Think big.* We reinvented the concept of lifelong learning, and it became the driving force behind everything we do. It has become our brand—and brands have no equity without trust, and no power without distinction.

- ❏ *Envision the future.* We never wanted to be a "catalog." We wanted to be more, much more. We set big goals, and we made them happen. We moved into the dream a day at a time, sometimes kicking, sometimes screaming, but all the while chasing tomorrow with our best effort.

2

Running a Corporate University Like a Business: A Financial Model

Jim Moore

For many internally focused corporate departments, the financial processes are administrative tasks that no one likes to handle. For SunU, the corporate university of Sun Microsystems, the organization's cost recovery model is an important part of its strategy. SunU's financial model calls for it to recover all of its costs from the internal clients who use its services. If the process is managed properly, at the end of the fiscal year, the internal revenues from clients are equal to the gross expenditures of the organization, and the net budget is zero. This sounds simple. To organizations that depend on external customer revenue to support the business, cost recovery is only common sense. However, among organizations that serve internal customers, a total, fee-based cost recovery system is not common.

Background

When I accepted the position of head of SunU in November 1994, one of my first tasks was to assess the client satisfaction with SunU. It was clear that the people who attended SunU classes found them very useful. The "smile sheets" were uniformly high. However, the support of senior executives was mixed and lukewarm at best. During a meeting I had with one business unit president, he pulled out his financial statements and pointed to a line on his spending report that was a $3 million allocation for SunU. He expressed concern that his organization had no voice in determining this expenditure, no control over the amount, and no knowledge of what, if anything, it was getting for its money.

In 1994, SunU's total spending was just over $12 million. Approximately $5 million of this amount represented the variable cost of delivering classroom education programs (primarily the vendor cost for instructors, since 99 percent of delivery was outsourced). This variable cost was charged back to the departments of the students in the classes through tuition. The remaining $7 million was for the fixed costs of SunU (employee-related costs, equipment depreciation, etc.) These costs were allocated to the various business units based on the number of employees in each business unit. The budget was negotiated as a part of the total human resource (HR) budget and was fixed annually.

The Financial Strategy

The reinvention of SunU in 1995 involved a number of strategies designed to better integrate the university with the business and to enable it to have more impact on Sun's performance. We decided that building a totally client-funded financial model would be one of these strategies. This decision was based on several assumptions:

1. Clients value what they pay for and tend not to value what is free. A nontraining example of this philosophy can be seen in the move on the part of corporations to charge employees for the use of fitness centers. The result in most cases was increased usage by participants because they had money invested.

2. Executives would be more satisfied if they had a choice of the training investments they made and control over their training budget.

3. By working only on those projects that line clients were willing to

pay for, we could ensure better alignment of our products and services with business needs.

4. The SunU staff would be more focused on satisfying the client, since the client was the source of the funding that paid the staff's salaries.

So, in 1995, we decided to reduce our net budget every year until we got to zero. We also told our internal clients that they were free to obtain their learning support anywhere. If they could find learning solutions from other suppliers that were better, faster, or cheaper than the learning solutions from SunU, they were free to go elsewhere.

Results

As Figure 2-1 indicates, SunU achieved its net zero budget in fiscal year 2000 and, in the process, grew its gross spending from $12.1 million to $42 million.

Implementation Factors

There were several keys to success in implementing this model:

1. *The will to do it.* First and foremost in importance was our determination to achieve a net zero budget. Each year we set a goal for reducing the budget and then found ways to make it happen. The fact that Sun's chairman and CEO told me in my first meeting with him that the SunU budget should be zero added to the motivation.

2. *Financial and information technology systems.* If implementing a sophisticated chargeback system had required manual data entries and processes or costly new data systems, we would not have attempted to use this methodology—the benefits would probably not have justified the costs. Sun is blessed with a highly integrated financial information technology (IT) system that allowed 40,000 students a year to click their mouse on the Web site to enroll in a class and allowed the corresponding financial accounting to happen without

Figure 2-1.

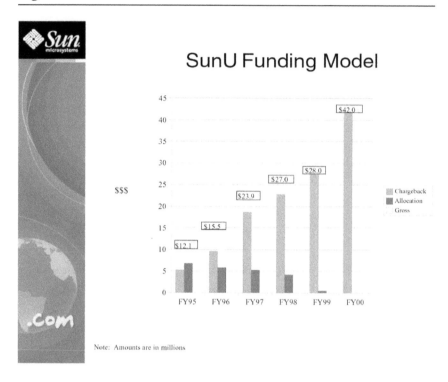

SunU Funding Model

Note: Amounts are in millions

human intervention. This meant that the user's department was charged for training and SunU was credited with "revenue." Of course, this is "funny money" and represents only internal cost allocations, but we treated it the way a stand-alone university would treat real money and used it to drive business decisions.

3. *Understanding of costs.* In order to properly price our products and services, we needed to know more than we knew at the time about all the costs that went into providing our learning products. In some cases the data we needed were available from existing reports, but in other cases we had to undertake detailed studies to identify the costs. This is normal stuff for training and consulting firms (and any firm that has to price its product), but it was a new requirement for an internal organization.

4. *Staff skills.* Preparing the SunU staff to fully implement a client-funded model was one of the biggest challenges. There was initial

resistance to the strategy. Some staff members felt that they were under too much pressure to "sell." In some cases, staff members' lack of ability to explain the model to internal clients created some confusion and concern on the part of those clients. The skills that were required were no different from those that are taken for granted at consulting firms—you've got to get the contract, deliver a product, *and* make a buck. But for an internal support organization, they were new. Therefore, we needed to work on our ability to sell consultatively.

5. *Training manager accountability.* The model I am describing is very entrepreneurial. Success required delegating net budgets as low in the organization as possible and allowing managers the freedom to meet those net budgets through any combination of revenue and costs they could achieve. No training manager had to say no to a client request because he lacked the budget (as long as the client was willing to pay). Net budgets were established for each manager within the university, and the managers were given the accountability, responsibility, and flexibility to meet them. Financial management was one component of the managers' performance appraisal and bonus calculation. Not every manager had a net zero budget. Some departments were "overhead" and had only cost budgets. Some departments were given budgets in which revenues exceeded costs (negative budgets) in order to subsidize other departments. Each manager had the freedom to set prices and control costs within her discipline.

6. *Outsourcing.* One of the benefits of this model is that it can respond to changing business needs. If a big, unanticipated need arose (a weekly occurrence in Sun's fast-paced, innovative environment), we did not have to go to the HR executive to get permission to overspend our budget (or have that permission denied). We just had to get the clients to agree to fund the training required. We rarely found a client with a critical need who was unwilling to fund the training. This client-driven, reactive model created a number of major spikes in the workload that had to be handled quickly. It also resulted in some valleys in the workload. We could not have responded and adjusted our spending to match client demand without our external partners. Almost 100 percent of classroom delivery and the majority of program development was outsourced

to external firms. These firms had long-term relationships with SunU, understood our culture and processes, and gave us great capability to ramp up (or down) quickly to meet widely varying challenges.

7. *Knowledge of "competitors'" costs.* We used a combination of cost-based pricing and market-based pricing. Some of the learning products we offered were comparable to learning products that were available in the open market. If our products were priced significantly higher than these products, it would reflect poorly on the corporate university. In addition, we told our clients that they were free to buy their education solutions from other organizations if they could get them better, faster, or cheaper. So, we monitored prices for similar products that were available in the public domain and attempted to be competitive (or dropped our higher-priced product).

8. *Flexibility in pricing methods.* When we identified an education opportunity with a client, we offered several options for cost recovery:

❏ The client pays development costs, and the delivery costs are charged back to the participants' departments through tuition.

❏ The client pays development and delivery costs, and tuition is "free" to participants.

❏ All development and delivery costs are recovered through tuition.

There was no universal formula for selecting a particular methodology. A case-by-case decision was made with the client.

9. *Judgment.* This was not a "turn-the-crank-and-the-right-numbers-come-out" kind of model. In some cases we did work for which we did not try to recover the cost, and in other cases we significantly overrecovered our costs. The reasons for adjusting prices were too numerous and complex to be covered by a formula or a policy, so we relied on judgment, a clear understanding of our philosophy, and open communication to make the model work. This was one of the biggest challenges for the SunU leadership team. Developing a common understanding of this strategy was

not a problem for my direct staff of twelve managers. Embedding this understanding among the almost one hundred SunU staff members was a bigger challenge. Perhaps it was due to their inexperience as business managers; perhaps it was their background as instructional designers, which led them to try to reduce behaviors to formula; perhaps it was my inability to clearly communicate the philosophy.

Other Options

I have led organizations in which there was a centrally provided budget (usually part of the human resources budget) in two other *Fortune* 100 companies. There was some comfort in knowing my organization's budget twelve months in advance, but there were problems also.

Setting the annual training budget at the corporate level was a contentious and painful process. In most cases, I was competing with my HR colleagues for very limited resources. Did we invest in human resource information systems (HRISs), compensation and benefits staff and programs, HR generalists, or leadership education, sales training, and IT skills training? Many of my HR colleagues saw the corporate university as a huge sinkhole of scarce budget resources. The corporate university budget became a target when other HR activities had to be funded. I found that line clients were always more willing to give resources to the corporate university than the HR budgeting process was.

In another company in which I performed the chief learning officer role, I managed a U.S.-based organization and a Canadian organization of equal size. In the United States, we had a client-funded model. In Canada, we had an HR-funded model, and training was "free" to line clients. Only a few months into the annual budget process, I found that we were telling our Canadian clients that we couldn't respond to their needs because we were out of budget; however, we never had that problem in the United States because if the client was willing to pay, we could meet the need. (And if the client didn't want to pay, she didn't have a very serious need.)

There are, in fact, many ways to fund a corporate university in addition to those presented here. In discussing training in Chapter 7, Linda Lewis explores several other methods.

Risks

Certainly, a client-funded model is not a panacea. Here are some of the most common challenges that caused us to question our approach:

1. *Putting profit over implementing strategic (but less profitable) initiatives.* The learning opportunities were limitless, but our ability to deliver learning products and our clients' ability to use learning products were not. So we had to make choices. Do we invest our time and energy in running an open-enrollment time management class that would generate large profits to subsidize our staff costs, or do we spend our time on a program that might have more strategic impact on the business but would generate less cost recovery for the corporate university? Of course, the answer is obvious (you do the right thing for the business), but the need to ensure that we recovered all of our costs could have created an inappropriate bias in our decision making. One of the roles of leadership in the corporate university is to ensure that the organization is continually focused on the initiatives that will have the most strategic impact.

2. *Being perceived as an uncooperative corporate citizen.* As a part of a large HR organization, we were asked to participate in and provide resources for a large number of special task forces and projects that did not relate to our educational offerings. Of course, we could not charge HR for the time we spent on these projects, and so the more of them we participated in, the more we had to raise prices on our educational products to recover our costs. Our HR colleagues who participated in these special projects did not have a similar problem. They had a fixed budget, and they could spend it on client-specific work or on special HR projects. So, sometimes, we said, "No thanks—we can't participate." This created the perception among some that we were not team players. However, in some cases, it kept us from wasting resources on non–value-added work.

3. *Managing in a downturn.* A flexible budget is good in growth conditions, but it can create challenges when rapid reductions are required. It is easier to add to a budget than to reduce it, and a fixed budget would prevent some of the tough challenges that result

when education demand goes away. However, in very tough times, even fixed budgets are susceptible to reduction.

4. *Cream skimming by clients.* As indicated previously, the corporate university contracted with external vendors for the development and delivery of most of our products. These vendor costs were passed along to internal clients with a markup to recover the overhead costs of the corporate university. In some cases, clients wanted to contract directly with the external vendor to avoid the markup. Our position was that clients were free to find their own education vendors, and if they could find the best vendors, negotiate contracts with them, schedule programs, communicate the availability of these programs, enroll employees, update training records, and perform quality control better, faster, and cheaper than the corporate university could, then they should do it themselves.

5. *Loss of control of the education budget.* When the education budget is put in the hands of thousands of line managers, as it is with this model, it is very difficult to apply top-down budget controls. The only organization that I observed to have a problem with this issue was the corporate finance organization.

6. *Responding to corporatewide mandates.* Occasionally, corporate initiatives were developed for which there was no clear client to fund the required education. Examples include diversity programs, new employee orientation, and high-potential leadership development programs. Finding someone to fund the development of these education programs was occasionally a challenge. Corporate staff often liked to generate ideas for new programs but less often wanted to do the hard work of obtaining the resources to fund all aspects of these initiatives. It is not realistic to expect the corporate university to have a pot big enough to fund the development of education programs to support all corporate mandates. Some people felt that the tuition for attending these classes should be free to avoid discouraging employees from attending. In my experience, I have never seen an employee fail to attend a critical program because the employee's manager could not afford the tuition. In addition, we expected the manager to fund the employee's labor costs, travel costs, and office equipment and supplies costs. It seems to me to be consistent to say that the manager should also fund an employee's development costs. They are part of running an organization.

7. *Funding e-learning.* E-learning products presented several challenges to this funding model:

   ❑ Development costs were high.

   ❑ Delivery costs were negligible.

   ❑ Users were willing to pay significant fees to attend classroom programs but expected learning delivered over the Internet to be free.

We used several approaches to recover the costs of e-learning:

   ❑ Our first choice was to embed Web-based learning as part of a total learning solution that included classroom activities for those skills that were best taught in a classroom and Web-based learning as pre- and postlearning activities. In those cases, there was a single fee for the program that covered both the Web and classroom components.

   ❑ If a stand-alone e-learning solution was the right answer, we attempted to find a client to fund the development costs and offered the program to participants at no charge.

   ❑ In some cases, we attempted to recover the development costs by charging enrollees a registration fee that gave them access to the learning product for a fixed period of time.

Conclusion

In my experience, the benefits of managing a corporate university with an entrepreneurial model far outweigh the disadvantages. It is probably not the most important component of an operating strategy for a corporate university, but it can help ensure linkage to the business. Success requires a combination of technology, systems, processes, skills, and art.

3

Corporate University Structures That Reflect Organizational Cultures

Karen Barley

Corporate universities emerged in the twentieth century as a continuation of the workforce education trend that began as early as 1914. Instead of coping with the perceived slowness and inapplicability of the theoretical learning found in traditional colleges and universities, business and industry turned inward and created training and development departments. These business units were designed to provide employees, both rookie and veteran, with the skills necessary to perform their duties with precision and efficiency. Training departments relied on their ability to teach employees routines, patterns, and tasks that would enable them to perform in a skill-based economy.

Around the midpoint of the century, as the United States moved from an industrial economy that was largely skill-based to an information economy that was largely knowledge-based, the effectiveness and timeliness of training and development departments became increasingly critical to organizational growth and prosperity. Learning became not a one-time instructional endeavor but a continuous process that required employees to learn quickly and regularly in order to keep pace with technological advancements and global competition.

The increased reliance on internal training and its shift from skill to knowledge cultivation led the human resource development industry to take a self-conscious look at its performance during the first half of the twentieth century. Plagued with the reputation for being expensive, extraneous, and inefficient, internal training units found themselves facing the very same issues that academia had battled in terms of the ability to deal with the specific learning needs of an organization and the employees who compose it.

To compensate for their tarnished reputation, training units looked to management models to revamp and revolutionize the way they designed and delivered learning in organizational settings. The training industry found that it had been neglecting critical elements of good business practice: strategy and value. Training had to develop clear connections to organizational missions and goals and had to prove that it contributed to the organization's ability to fulfill those missions and goals.

As discussed in the introduction, there has been no universally accepted definition of a corporate university, but in general, to varying degrees, a focus on strategy and value appears to be an element of a good corporate university. Whether their primary purpose is to build competence, drive organizational change, maintain corporate competitiveness, recruit and retain talent, or serve customers, most corporate universities are focused on strategic business practices and have a self-conscious awareness of their responsibility to contribute to organizational growth and/or effectiveness. Corporate universities are strategic in that they are planned and modeled to fulfill the organization's mission. They are results-oriented because they exist only as long as they can prove their value to the organization.

In bringing these critical elements of strategy and value into the foreground, corporate universities can take on a variety of shapes and organizational structures. Corporate culture, hierarchy, and leadership all affect the structure of a corporate university. In short, the best corporate university structures are those that harmonize with internal organizational influences and initiatives and mirror the current or projected corporate culture. This chapter explores various types of corporate university structures.

Corporate Alignment

The alignment of the corporate university within the corporate structure is one of the first things to consider in selecting a shape or model for any corporate university. There is a common misperception in the industry that a corporate university must report directly to a senior executive in order to be successful. All corporate universities need senior executive support; however, they do not necessarily need to report directly to a senior executive in order to have an impact on the organization. In fact, there are three main places where responsibility for corporate universities resides: a chief executive's office, a human resources office, and a business unit. The place within the overall structure of the company where a corporate university is incubated and from which it is launched has a direct impact on how quickly and comprehensively the university is accepted, adopted, and implemented.

In the Chief Executive's Office: The Top-Down Initiative

Corporate universities that originate in and emerge out of the executive boardroom are considered top-down corporate universities. They typically enjoy involved and engaged attention from senior executives, and their position in the organizational structure is often such that they report directly to a chief learning officer (CLO). That CLO also holds a seat on the executive council and plays a strategic role in determining how learning is driven and integrated throughout the organization.

Corporate universities with this structure are strategically positioned to have the quickest impact on an organization. This impact is fueled by the top-down approach. Directors and middle managers respond quickly to executive directives, and staff support and funds are speedily allocated when the executive who controls these resources is leading the corporate university imperative.

While top-down corporate universities have leverage and strategic position, some challenges can emerge. Top-down corporate universities may lack employee commitment. Like any executive directive, a corporate university that is led by senior executives may be perceived simply as another management trend that eventually will be replaced by a different fleeting initiative. Additionally, if the leadership within an organization is out of touch and is disassociated from the actual operations and employee opinions of the company, the top-down approach may not be the wisest choice.

This approach typically works best for companies in which employees respect executive initiatives and follow the leadership's vision. It demands impassioned leadership that is in tune with the corporate culture and employee attitudes. It is the wrong approach for an organization with wide gaps between the leadership and the workforce.

In Human Resources: The Lateral Approach

Perhaps the most common place for corporate universities to reside is in human resources. With this placement, the corporate university reports to a director or vice president of human resources who may be one or two tiers below the executive council. Unlike the situation with the top-down approach, where the corporate university sits in the highest levels within an organization, corporate universities that reside in human resources must gain executive commitment by pushing the idea and initiative up the chain of command and laterally throughout the rank and file.

Even though corporate universities housed in human resources must work harder to get executive support, they typically enjoy senior leadership commitment equivalent to that of the top-down corporate university. The achievement of commitment and direction from the executive council is sometimes delayed and/or filtered in the corporate communication chain. This can hinder progress and make the corporate university appear cumbersome and slow. Once it is achieved, however, that senior involvement can be leveraged for the lateral push of learning throughout the other business units and work groups.

Despite the most active and engaged involvement from senior leadership, however, the tactical team charged with implementing the programs is in a position equal to that of the business units. Achieving and maintaining cross-unit support for a corporate university that originates in human resources is critical. Establishing partnership councils and engaging subject matter experts in corporate university operations are ways in which some corporate universities housed in human resources respond to the lateral support challenges that they face.

One challenge to achieving this lateral support is the past reputation and credibility of human resources. Good or bad, the training department's service record will carry over to the corporate university. One way to counteract a poor reputation is to show immediately the value that the corporate university will add to each business unit. The ability to show this added value depends on the human resources practitioner's abilities. Trainers, instructional designers, and other human resources development practitioners are knowledgeable in the design and delivery of learning programs. This makes them good choices when the development and delivery of learning is being considered, but not necessarily the best employees to determine strategy and value considerations. To compensate for these deficiencies, the corporate university can provide learning opportunities to build those traditional business skills in its human resources development practitioners, or it can acquire business talent from other work groups throughout the organization.

Thus, the human resources lateral approach is best received and most effective in organizations in which the human resources development office has a proven track record and in which there is a consistent corporate perception of responsive service and successful learning solutions. It is also a good choice for organizations that cross-function and team regularly as they embrace the concept of internal partnership. It is not the right model for an organization in which business units operate like minicompanies within the larger organization.

In a Business Unit: The Grassroots Effort

A third place where a corporate university can emerge is within a business unit. These corporate universities report to a unit director or manager and provide learning opportunities exclusively for the employees of that business unit. Often, corporate universities emerge within business units either because senior management does not make employee development a top priority or, more commonly, because human resources has been unable to provide consistent and valuable learning opportunities that meet the targeted needs of the individual business units.

Like the corporate university within human resources, a corporate university within a business unit must work to achieve executive support for its endeavors. Unless the business unit is completely self-sufficient in terms of revenue and expenditures, it must show how its exclusive learning programs are helping it to perform better, stronger, and faster than in the past. A corporate university within a business unit, therefore, is at the mercy of the corporate budget process, just like the corporate university within human resources.

Strategically, unit managers and directors are arguably in the best position to determine the performance gaps and learning needs of their employees. They are closest to the employees and to the workflows. However, they may find it a challenge to show a maximization of corporate funds. Some business units are not large enough to fill all the physical or virtual seats in a classroom or on-line learning experience. In other words, the business unit may be paying for seats that it cannot fill. If there are no other employees outside that business unit who have similar learning needs, then the use of funds is perhaps efficient. However, if other business units in the company have similar learning needs and are not filling the available seats, then showing that the business unit corporate university is a wise use of corporate funds may be difficult. Business unit–to–business unit partnerships are a way to counteract this funding hurdle and to ensure that corporate training dollars are maximized.

While managers and directors of business units have the skills to manage their budgets and work out partnership solutions, they may not be the best individuals to design or select the most appropriate learning methodologies. Managers rarely are trained in learning style, instructional design, or facilitation. Business unit corporate universities work best when managers are committed to learning those competencies and making them part of their repertoire of skills, just as human resource practitioners in the lateral corporate university build their knowledge of traditional business skills.

A business unit corporate university requires a unit manager or director who is committed to employee development and is willing to add the role of employee development leader to the demands associated with his or her job. This type of corporate university works best in organizations in which business units retain autonomy and control of their own progression, and perhaps those in which they compete against other business units for performance standards. A business unit corporate university is best suited for an organization in which business units are allocated a healthy budget for employee development and have a strong commitment to continuous learning.

Content Structures

Developing a structure or visual image of how the content and functions of a corporate university should be organized is just as critical to the university's overall acceptance within the organization as the place where the idea of launching the corporate university originates and the unit assigned to manage it. The way content is organized should fit the culture and structure of the organization. An organization whose business units have great autonomy benefits from a content structure that replicates that individualism.

Such a structure would not be appropriate for a small organization that does not support an individual business unit structure.

Most visual structures have some common elements, such as a core curriculum, business unit or competency schools, and a leadership or executive development arm. A core curriculum is a program of learning that comprises competencies, skills, or knowledge areas that all employees, regardless of rank, need to know in order to maintain employment within the particular company. Topic areas in a core curriculum, in general, include things like corporate mission and culture, philosophy toward customer service, and specifics on product lines. Business unit or competency schools are more specialized areas of learning within the content model and typically house learning opportunities that are exclusive to one business unit in the organization.

Several different ways to organize content exist. Whether the organization is generic, academic, hierarchical, circular, or progressive, the visual depiction of that organization and the content arrangement guide the way in which employees understand the connection between curriculum and job performance. Moreover, the depictions of the different forms of organization are descriptive, and the form chosen should mesh with corporate culture and provide a quick understanding of the corporate university's role within the organization itself.

Organizational Chart

The Organizational Chart model of corporate university structure, shown in Figure 3-1, is a straightforward way to categorize the content of a corporate university. The core curriculum sits in a box located at the top of the chart. Other learning tracks stream from that core program. The learning tracks are typically modeled around business units, although they can also refer to schools for particular competencies. Visually, the Organizational Chart is an uncomplicated model that is appropriate for an organization with a flat organizational structure. The learning tracks should be designed and defined to fit particular business units or particular competency models; they become an overlay for the organizational chart found in the organization. From an employee perspective, this chart is user-friendly, as employees identify their school of learning based on its affiliation with their business unit.

In addition to being user-friendly, this model also shows a clear direction for progress. In each learning track, one program of learning is con-

Figure 3-1. Organizational Chart of corporate university content.

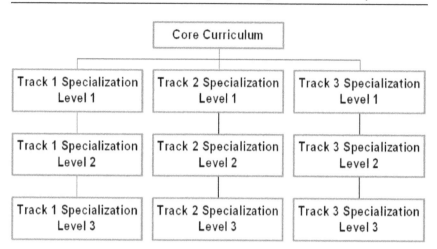

nected to a more advanced program of learning within the same track. In this structure, each program is both a unit within itself and one section of a larger learning enterprise. In other words, the various levels of learning within each specialization area are milestones in a long continuum of learning. The idea of progress is strong, and it could be strengthened even more by turning the model upside down so that the idea of upward movement is emphasized.

Because of its building-block structure, this model works well for organizations with academic partnerships. The tiered approach mirrors the certificate-to-degree pattern of learning that higher education is providing to business and industry. It places no emphasis on cross-functional competencies, which are in the foreground in the next several models. For this reason, the Organizational Chart is also a good model for a corporate university with little overlap in its learning tracks.

Temple

Widely known throughout the corporate university industry, the Temple model, shown in Figure 3-2, has a strong academic connection, as it is widely accepted as a depiction of higher education and the stability of traditional learning. The Temple provides a strong foundation for core learning programs. Based at the foot of the model, the core curriculum provides the basis for those competencies and knowledge areas that are

Figure 3-2.   The Temple model.

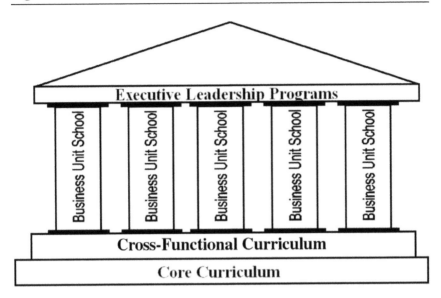

required of all employees, regardless of rank or tenure. The core step blends into a second step of cross-functional learning areas or skills and knowledge areas that are found in various business units and departments throughout the organization. These two steps are the foundation for additional, more advanced learning programs in business unit schools, depicted as pillars in the model. Specialized learning that is particular to individual business units is housed in the pillars. Executive or leadership development rests in the cornice and caps the core, cross-functional, and specialized learning areas.

Like the Organizational Chart model, the Temple model depicts a hierarchy or stepping-stones in learning. Core learning is the basis for cross-functional development, which then leads into specific business unit learning, capped by leadership learning. This hierarchy shows progress in learning, with a recognizable starting point in core learning and an end point in leadership development. This approach creates a linear learning process in which an individual moves from one stepping-stone to the next. While the feeling of advancement in learning is a positive result of using this model, it can have a detrimental effect if it sets up expectations that may not be fulfilled. If an employee moves through the model, will a promotion necessarily follow? If the answer is yes, then choosing a hierarchical model like this one makes sense. If the answer is no, the hierarchical approach may not match the company culture.

On the positive side, this model shows that the members of the senior leadership team have a role in learning. In fact, they are examples for learning. In some corporate universities, leadership development is an entirely separate program that exists outside the regular curriculum model. Separating leadership development programs from the corporate university creates a divide between leaders and workers, both visually and perceptually. The Temple model integrates leadership learning programs into the corporate university structure in an inclusive approach. Because leadership programs are positioned at the cornice, instead of as a foundational step or a specialized pillar, the model encourages employees to think of their leaders as drivers for learning and examples of the behavior expected of all employees in the company's quest for a learning culture.

The linear approach of this model, however, does not necessarily lead to a visual depiction of continuous learning. Unless the curriculum housed in the cross-functional step and the business unit schools is robust and plentiful, with constant refreshment and updating of content, employees may quickly exhaust its resources. At that point, formal learning stops. For this model to work in a culture that promotes continuous learning, all components of the model must be in a constant state of revision and addition. The linear approach makes employees feel that they can reach an end point in their learning cycle. To counteract that perception and generate continuous learning, the corporate university must engage and adopt new learning that keeps pace with organizational change.

For all of these reasons, the Temple is an appropriate choice for an organization with a strong commitment to learning in the business units. The pillars create a sense of autonomy and ownership that encourages participation in and endorsement of the corporate university. For an organization that is experiencing mergers and acquisitions, the Temple model is an adaptable approach. As each organization is merged into the parent company, a new business unit school or pillar can be added. The existence of the new pillar demonstrates to the newly acquired organization that it is assuming an immediate role in organizational learning and is fitting quickly into the learning culture.

Northern Orient Lines (NOL), a large shipping company based in Singapore, uses the Temple model in its corporate university. Launched in 2001, the NOL Global Campus selected the Temple model because of its strong foundation in core and cross-functional learning and because of the autonomy permitted in the business units. The NOL Global Campus model, shown in Figure 3-3, divides business unit learning into four pillars that represent the major divisions in the global organization: American President Lines (APL) Logistics, APL Liner, Corporate Functions, and NOL Chartering. Each of these pillars contains modularized learning programs that are connected to performance issues particular to the jobs that fall within that functional area in the company.

Pyramid

The next curriculum model, the Pyramid, shown in Figure 3-4, is similar to the Temple model in philosophy but different in organization. Like the Temple model, it includes the idea of hierarchy, as foundational programs lead into more specialized areas. Conceptually, the model shows learning as being broad at the base, or the core, and more specific as the diagram narrows to a pinnacle with the leadership programs. Unlike the Temple model, however, the Pyramid organizes its learning around job categories.

Figure 3-3. Northern Orient Lines Global Campus.

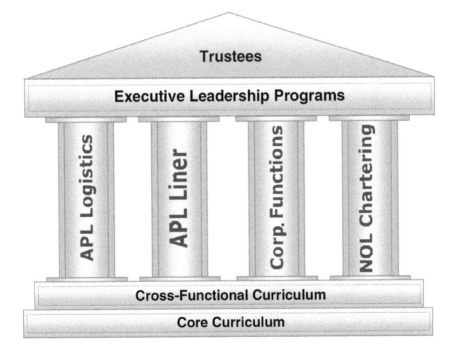

Figure 3-4.   The Pyramid model.

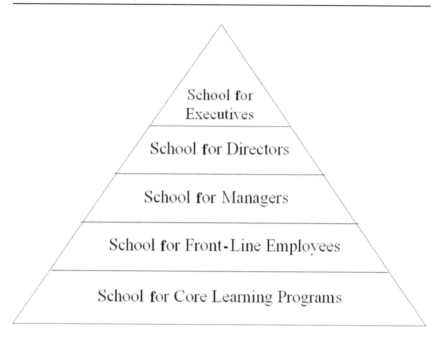

Instead of business unit schools, programs of learning that are specific to job series in categories such as front-line, managerial, and director level are developed in the Pyramid.

This pinnacle indicates a clear sense of upward movement and mobility and is not upside down like the Organizational Chart. Learning programs are connected sequentially, with each program building on the foundation of its predecessor in a linear pattern. This concept, much like the education models in American higher education, sends the message that an employee can move upward through learning. In other words, the model implies that learning and promotion are connected.

This model is appropriate for an organization that promotes employees based on the achievement of certain standards, one of which is learning. The military, for example, might use this model in connection with performance standards and testing in order to promote soldiers to the next rank. In fact, any organization could use this approach for promotion. The key is showing that learning is a part of the passage from one job to the next, along with managing employee expectations.

Sun Microsystems, Inc., based in Palo Alto, California, has developed a hybrid version of the Pyramid model. SunU stratifies learning around major job categories, as shown in the front face of the cube in Figure 3-5. In keeping with the concept of the Pyramid structure, notice that the SunU model moves from custom and new hire learning programs, which appear at the bottom of the list, to leadership and management development opportunities, which appear at the top. This approach mirrors the SunU hierarchy and provides a sense of movement in the curriculum structure. The SunU model takes the idea of stratification a step further, as it shows the variety of learning methods available both in each job category and in distinct regions throughout Sun Microsystems. The model is collective, contained, and comprehensive and is certainly an advanced and adapted version of the Pyramid.

Corporate Pie

A more insular approach, the Corporate Pie, seen in Figure 3-6, is a fluid way to group and format learning opportunities for employees. The core curriculum rests in the center and visually brings to the foreground the centralization and core significance of the core curriculum. Two major

Figure 3-5.   The SunU model.

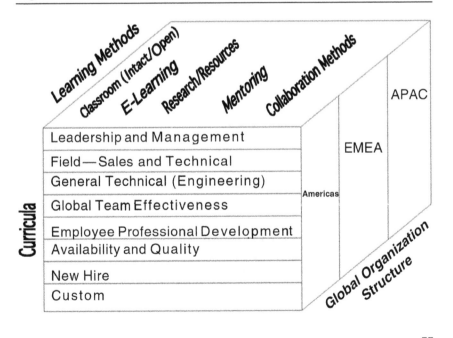

Figure 3-6.   The Corporate Pie model.

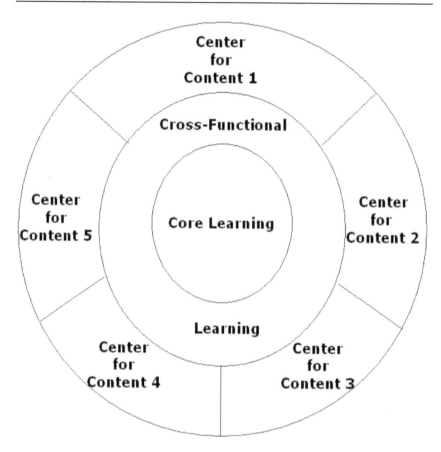

rings surround that core: a cross-functional school of learning and business unit or content schools. The cross-functional school of learning houses competency development programs that are necessary for a variety of business units. In other words, these competency areas are not exclusive to one particular business unit but are representative of a learning need that occurs throughout a variety of business units. The business unit schools or content centers offer learning opportunities that match competency areas that are specialized and exclusive to each business unit.

Visually, this model allows for quick integration of new business unit schools and new rings if necessary. For that reason, it is adaptable to an organization that is expanding through internal growth or mergers. New business unit schools or content centers can be included in the model without interrupting the existing schools or violating the overall integrity of the model.

This model considers leadership or executive development to be equivalent to other business units or content schools within the university. That is, a center for leadership development would appear as one slice of the external ring, not as a pinnacle or cornice program as in the Temple and Pyramid models. In this way, the Corporate Pie projects a different, more egalitarian attitude toward leadership. Organizations that encourage employees to work as partners with leaders within an organization or that use rotating management models might find the Corporate Pie appropriate for their corporate university content alignment.

At the Ritz-Carlton Leadership Center, housed in The Ritz-Carlton Hotel Company, L.L.C., corporate offices in Atlanta, Georgia, the Corporate Pie model serves as the foundation for the corporate university's curriculum. With learning at the core and surrounded by cross-functional and content area rings that match corporate objectives, the model, shown in Figure 3-7, truly captures the Ritz-Carlton mission and philosophy of excellence. An exterior ring that contains an advanced seminar series, partnerships with colleges and universities, and a special ambassadors program further exemplifies the concept of excellence.

Pinwheel

Of all the curriculum models described here, the Pinwheel, shown in Figure 3-8, is perhaps the most progressive. As in the Corporate Pie, the core curriculum rests at the center of the concentric circles and is surrounded by rings for cross-functional and business unit learning. What distinguishes this model from the Corporate Pie, however, are the arrows that project learning from each of the rings outside the insular, employee-only approach. This model emphasizes an outreach component in which learning programs are provided not only internally to employees but also externally to a variety of affiliates to the organization. Learning designed in each of the rings, including the core, is developed to be applicable to both internal employees and external affiliates based on the philosophy that both employees and affiliates contribute to organizational growth and effectiveness.

The outreach approach considers business partners, vendors, suppliers, clients, customers, sister and parent companies, families of employees, and the community at large as constituencies that are all affiliates of the core

Figure 3-7.   The Ritz-Carlton Leadership Center's model.

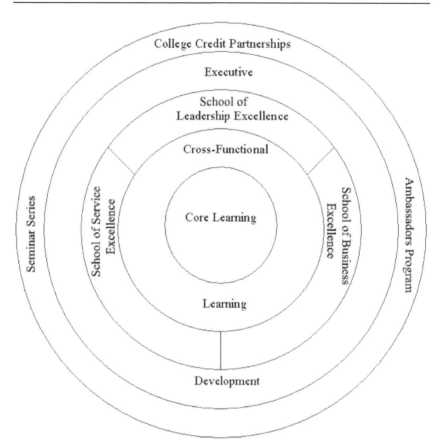

business of the organization. By providing learning opportunities to these affiliates, the Pinwheel model broadens its perspective from insular to more global. The outreach approach educates partners about the way in which the organization conducts business. Moreover, reaching out to affiliates outside the walls of the organization provides opportunities to bring in new ideas and perspectives that can benefit the organization. In other words, the corporate university taps a market outside the company that balances a completely insular approach and keeps the organization from becoming too intertwined around its own thought patterns about running a business.

Because of this consideration of outreach, the Pinwheel model is appropriate for organizations with a charter or mission to serve the commu-

Figure 3-8. The Pinwheel model.

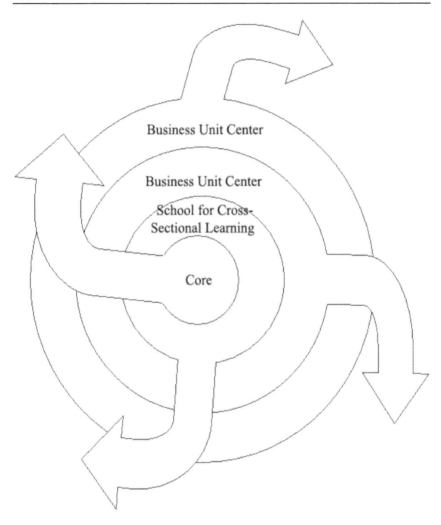

nity. Governments—especially on the local level—membership associations, and not-for-profit organizations are good examples of organizations that would find the Pinwheel approach suitable. These organizations are chartered to reach an audience outside their corporate walls, and that purpose is reflected in the Pinwheel's emphasis on outreach. As a result, the host organization gains strong ties with its constituency, membership, or community, respectively. Moreover, this outreach can be a valuable revenue source because of its stretch to a market outside the organization's walls.

In addition to governments, associations, and not-for-profits, the Pinwheel model fits companies that are made up of a variety of business partnerships. Business-to-business partnerships demand collaboration between and among the businesses. A Pinwheel corporate university can be used as a way to leverage and perpetuate the spirit of collaboration. Sister and partner organizations become stakeholders in the corporate university, and all players in the revenue stream share a constant and consistent learning message.

The City of Tucson, the local government entity in Tucson, Arizona, uses the Pinwheel model for its emerging corporate university. The charter of the city government provides for outreach of service and opportunity to the city's constituency. The Pinwheel model emphasizes that outreach concept, while still providing strategic, results-based learning for employees of the city. Depicted in Figure 3-9, the City of Tucson's model positions executive development learning in the center because city initiatives come from executive decisions. Other learning programs in cross-functional, job-specific, and core areas radiate from that executive center. This unique order of the learning rings exemplifies the structure of the City of Tucson. Each of those rings carries an arrow leading outside the contained model. These arrows show that the learning in each ring is likewise chosen and offered for its value to City of Tucson citizens. It is a progressive model for an innovative city.

Internal Structures

All of these models represent ways to organize content and curriculum. What they lack, however, is a representation of the internal structure of the corporate university as it provides service to its customers, or of tasks other than the design and delivery of content. Internal structures need to enhance both the strategy of the corporate university and its drive to achieve organizational effectiveness. Moreover, the corporate university should be arranged internally to support the collection of meaningful data that show the value of the corporate university.

There are two ways to organize the internal functions necessary to run a corporate university. In the comprehensive version, each practitioner engages all the competencies necessary to launch and support a new con-

Figure 3-9.   The City of Tucson University model.

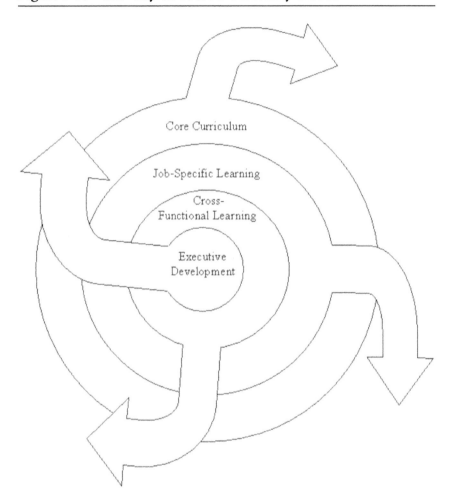

tent area. The specialized version requires practitioners to focus on one slice of the entire services package. Just as the content structures mirror corporate culture, the choice between the two internal organizational models should carefully consider the dynamics of the organization as a whole as it supports both strategy and value.

To determine internal structure, an understanding of the five major functions and the cornerstone philosophy required to run a corporate university is necessary. These functions are organizational assessment, strategic alignment, curriculum development, program implementation, and program evaluation; Figure 3-10 organizes these functions into a usable model. This corporate university design model acts as a guide in organizing the tasks associated with running a corporate university into departments or business units.

Specifically, partnership is the cornerstone of the model and the guiding force behind the design and management of a corporate university. The model relies on the idea that the entire organization shares in the ownership of the corporate university and contributes to its success or failure. Organizational assessment describes the practices engaged in to assess learning needs, target audiences, and value additions that should affect the content development and overall strategies of the corporate university. Assessment might also be understood as market analysis and business justification.

Strategic alignment is a check system that ensures the existence of an analytical and structured framework that informs content, management, policy, and evaluation. Strategic alignment ensures that all events and initiatives that fall under the corporate university strategic umbrella are consistent with the larger purpose of the program and contribute to the overall goals of the company. Curriculum development covers the processes and practices that are used to decide on and develop new content and to review existing content for currency.

Figure 3-10.   A corporate university design model.

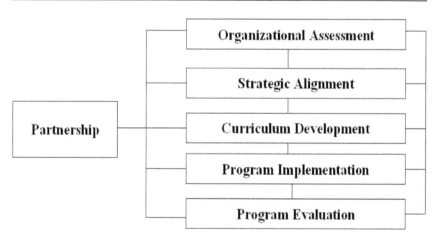

Program implementation involves the marketing of initiatives, the management of services, and the delivery of content. The selection of learning management systems and their maintenance, registration and billing functions, faculty support services, and participant support services fall into this category. Finally, program evaluation is the capstone of the model and is critical for the value and return on investment of a corporate university's content and services.

In the comprehensive version, each practitioner is charged with performing all these corporate university functions. From needs assessment to evaluation, one practitioner carries out the tasks necessary to identify, justify, develop, deliver, manage, and evaluate a particular content area. This approach lends itself to continuity in development and ownership of content. Practitioners take great pride in seeing a program of learning through the entire cycle of development, from management through evaluation. This approach allows seasoned practitioners the opportunity to take ownership of the programs they develop and the ability to expand their competence across the entire corporate university development and management continuum.

On the negative side, however, the comprehensive approach also lends itself to potential overlap of services, especially in the areas of needs assessment and implementation. While one practitioner is engaging in a new needs assessment to support the launch of a new curriculum area, another practitioner may be investigating a similar need. From an employee's perspective, the inundation of needs assessment requests, from surveys to focus groups, can appear disjointed and can have an overwhelming impact on time and resources. Moreover, the management of learning through electronic means and of facilities, students, instructors, and financial services—those tasks that fall into the category of implementation—can become cumbersome and confusing when each practitioner is responsible for handling these tasks in connection with individual programs or learning.

In short, this approach to internal structure demands a broader competency package from each practitioner. At times, practitioners in the comprehensive version will focus on the tasks where they have the greatest competence and neglect the competency areas that they are not adequately equipped to perform. For a mature corporate university with practitioners who demonstrate the broad array of competencies necessary, the comprehensive version is an appropriate choice. It allows for practitioner ownership and challenge as the practitioner moves one content area through the entire continuum. It is also an option for small corporate universities where human resources must be stretched to provide a holistic package of services.

For new corporate universities or those that are finding it a challenge to transform practitioners' skill and competency bases, the specialized version is a more viable option. In this approach, each component of the design model represents a service department within the corporate university, such as the program implementation department or the strategic alignment department. Practitioners perform tasks within their assigned department. The advantage to this approach is that the practitioners have the opportunity to focus on their most polished competency areas. It also avoids redundancy and provides a better system of checks and balances for value and strategy. This approach works best in corporate universities that have enough personnel to departmentalize and that demand a wide spectrum of competencies from their staff.

The challenge for the specialized version is maintaining interest among staff who have been in one competency area for a long time. Practitioners who feel that they have been, in fact, compartmentalized into one aspect of the corporate university cycle can experience boredom and believe that they do not have the opportunity to stretch their skills beyond the demands of their current job. A way to counteract that challenge is to provide a staff rotation in which practitioners move from one major task within the model to another on an annual or even semiannual timeline.

Another challenge with this approach is communication. Especially in small corporate university teams, the specialized version places great responsibility on practitioners to share their processes—and meet deadlines—seamlessly. The approach requires trust, solid teamwork, and shared responsibility for the end product, service, or program. If one practitioner who is responsible for performing one specialized task in the cycle falters, the remaining tasks and actions topple in a domino effect. Building redundancy, where each practitioner charged with a specific function has a partner or backup, is one way to ensure that the system keeps running. Overall, the team requires regular and consistent communication channels so that updates are provided and shared.

Thus, structuring a corporate university—organizationally, academically, and internally—requires an intuitive understanding of the corporate culture and framework. Companies, like snowflakes, are unique, and an organization's corporate university must respond to, adapt to, and celebrate that differentiation. While benchmarking and capitalizing on the lessons of other companies are great ways to capture new ideas, a solution that works smoothly for one company may encounter resistance and opposition if it is superimposed on another organization.

Likewise, as the company redefines itself or adopts new initiatives, the corporate university must keep pace with those changes. Whether it drives or supports new organizational movements, the corporate university must be flexible enough to clarify its focus or adapt to cultural influences to ensure that it is aligned with organizational strategies and values. To reinforce this point, remember that a corporate university is not a pot roast; it cannot be cooked in an oven and emerge a perfect finished product. As the structure and shape of a company change or shift, the corporate university must redesign and reinvent itself. There is no period when it can rest on its laurels if it is to be valuable to employees and a tool for keeping the organization on the cutting edge. Knowing the corporate culture should guide decisions regarding the structure and organization of any corporate university. Whether the program emerges as a top-down, lateral, or grassroots effort, selecting the corporate university model that best fits the attitudes, styles, leadership, and structure of the organization directly affects the program's longevity and acceptance.

CHAPTER 4

The Corporate University as a Strategic Lever

Integrating the Strategic Objectives of the Firm with the Desired Outcomes of the Corporate University

Tom McCarty

To those of us who have been in the training and education business for any length of time, it seems intuitively obvious that business managers invest in training and education because they believe that the training programs in which they are investing will help them achieve their business goals. And those of us who manage corporate universities accept this premise as one of the fundamental pillars of the corporate university—the corporate university must provide strategic leverage to the business executives that it serves. Strategic leverage is the ability to invest focused resources in ways that ensure or accelerate the achievement of specific strategic goals. We almost accept this at face value, and statements demonstrating strategic linkage appear within most corporate university mission statements, strategies, and goal statements.

In practice, however, the promise of strategic leverage often cannot be supported by an actual demonstration of strategic impact. A common complaint of business managers is that training initiatives and the training activities in which their employees are engaged are disconnected from their business priorities. Many corporate universities are experiencing reductions in their budgets at a time when well-aligned investments in human performance improvement could very well hold the keys to improved corporate performance.

The problem could be that while most training and education professionals conceptually understand the need to link training investments to corporate objectives in ways that ensure that the training investments will help to drive improved corporate outcomes, the models for acting on that understanding are not readily available and require discipline and insight to implement effectively. We know, however, that the opportunity exists to provide greater strategic impact from the corporate university's program implementation through a framework that has demonstrated practical effectiveness at Motorola University.

The framework has three key components:

1. *Achieve alignment* across the business leadership team.
2. *Mobilize* teams to take focused action.
3. *Accelerate* teams to accomplish the desired results.

Within that framework, an *action learning methodology* facilitates the integration of individual and project goals with training and coaching activities to ensure that predetermined, measurable business goals are achieved.

A methodology for conducting *performance gap analysis* is integrated into a *performance contracting process* to ensure that key stakeholders agree on the performance improvement desired and are aligned on the roles and responsibilities required of each stakeholder in the achievement of these performance targets.

The framework, as well as the supporting models, will be illustrated through various examples and two case studies, which will be used to demonstrate the practical application of this approach to achieving strategic leverage. As a result of applying this approach, corporate universities will move from viewing strategic leverage as a conceptual goal to achieving strategic leverage as a practical matter of solid execution.

Case Study #1—Sales Effectiveness

In the early 1990s, Motorola's Communications and Electronics business unit found itself facing a problem that was common to many organizations at that time. During the 1980s, in an effort to drive revenue growth and market share, the communications business unit had built a direct sales force of more than 3,500 sales representatives around the world. The strategy had been highly effective: The organization had achieved double-digit sales growth and was number one in market share in nearly every market in which it competed. Customers who could benefit from wireless two-way communications systems were happy to pay a premium for sales representation that could guide them toward an effective solution. Following a model that had helped IBM, DEC, Xerox, and Hewlett-Packard achieve success in the 1980s, Motorola leaders recognized that high-tech buyers required a high-touch approach. That approach required direct sales representation and total market coverage.

Unfortunately, the situation changed quickly as offshore competitors discovered the wireless communication market. They were able to offer competitive products at dramatically reduced prices through dealer channels with much lower sales costs. Many customers who had been educated and assisted in the purchase of their original system by a Motorola sales representative no longer felt the need for a high-touch relationship and moved their purchases to dealers who offered lower prices and immediate delivery on two-way wireless devices like walkie-talkies and mobile radios.

Motorola's Communications and Electronics executives realized that they had to act quickly if they were to continue to achieve their revenue and margin targets. A team was chartered by the business unit's general manager to make recommendations that would ensure continued growth and profitability in the face of new competition and changing customer requirements. The team completed a customer analysis, a competitive analysis, and a benchmarking analysis of companies in noncompeting industries that were facing similar problems. This effort yielded a plan that integrated recommendations regarding product strategy, recommendations regarding distribution channel strategy, and an approach to boosting the effectiveness of the direct sales force. For the purpose of this case, we will focus on the campaign to improve both customer satisfaction and direct sales force productivity through a "reskilling" of the direct sales force.

The Challenge

In order to boost sales coverage and market penetration, the business created a dealer channel and migrated 75 percent of the accounts to the dealers. The accounts that were still assigned to the direct sales force were those that had the promise of high growth through account penetration and the sale of full communications solutions across the account. The challenge, therefore, was to "reskill" the salespeople so that they would have the ability to penetrate their accounts at multiple levels, with emphasis on reaching the executive decision makers, and would have the ability to strategically position themselves as consultants who could offer real business solutions in the form of wireless communications systems. This meant that the sales force would need to possess capabilities in the areas of account management, consultative selling, and executive selling. Analysis showed that only 30 percent of the 1,500-member sales force had experience in these areas.

The Contract With Senior Management

It was recognized early in the process that asking a seasoned sales force to develop these three new capabilities would require a major investment of time in training, reading, and conducting account analysis and planning. Achieving the desired outcome would require a significant shift in culture. For that reason, it was imperative that senior leaders be actively engaged in the effort and be willing to contribute their time, thinking, and resources. To receive that level of support from senior leaders, it was critical to demonstrate a clear linkage between the effort required of them and the achievement of their business goals.

With all of that in mind, a four-hour session was facilitated in which the leaders agreed to revenue, profitability, and performance goals for the organization. Revenue margin and product mix goals were established at the account level, and specific behavior changes were defined at the sales rep level. Having established the goals, the senior leaders also agreed to provide $1,000,000 to fund development expenses, including salary and expenses for a team of ten instructor/coaches, and to provide sales managers to conduct formal account reviews. These agreements were documented in a performance agreement between the business unit leaders and the newly appointed training director.

The Action Learning Solution

With the performance contract in hand, the training director led the design and development of the learning solution and proceeded with its implementation. The solution strategy was that sales teams would be introduced to new behavior models and tools to support those behaviors through a series of four workshops: Account Planning, Consultative Selling, Advanced Account Management, and Executive-Level Selling. In order to ensure that the behaviors were directly applied to achieve the desired results, each workshop contained modules in which plans for specific accounts were developed. A specific schedule of account reviews was established to ensure that the plans were carried out and the desired results were occurring.

Further assurance of the direct application of these plans came as ten successful, experienced sales managers were placed in full-time instructor/coach positions for a two-year period. These instructor/coaches not only facilitated the delivery of the workshops but also worked directly with the sales teams to refine the account plans, develop executive proposals, and conduct coaching sessions. In addition, line sales managers were trained in a new model of strategic coaching to enable them to effectively assist in account planning and actively drive the account review process.

As the sales managers became more rigorous and thorough in the account review process and the instructor/coaches became more persistent in their follow-up, it became apparent to the sales representatives that this effort was not just another passing fad and that there was an organization-wide expectation that their capabilities would improve and the desired results would be achieved. As a result, participation in the workshops was universal and engaging; creative account plans were developed; and consultative approaches to executives within the target accounts began to bear fruit.

The Assessment Process

Throughout the implementation process, improvements were monitored using a number of planned assessment activities. Account plans were reviewed and rated against a best-practice model, and account managers were rated by their sales managers against a capabilities model. Customers rated their account manager's capabilities through a third-party survey. Finally, sales managers were rated on their ability and willingness to actively support this process as strategy coaches and review session leaders. The assessment process was effective in helping the implementation team know where to apply remedial efforts and when to communicate best practices that surfaced. It also aided the senior leaders in making changes in sales manager and account manager assignments. Most importantly, the constant feedback gave all stakeholders confidence that they were going to achieve the desired results and encouraged them to stay the course during the two-year effort.

The Results

The results were impressive: Sales productivity doubled, customer satisfaction improved by 30 percent, and share of wallet inside the targeted accounts improved significantly. No single group or single training intervention was responsible for these results. Rather, it was the integration of training, coaching, assessment, and focused leadership over a two-year period that enabled the results to be delivered as promised.

This story should serve as a best-practice case study in the use of training for strategic leverage. In the next section, we will examine the models that were applied to create this success story.

The Macro Framework: Align, Mobilize, Accelerate

This case study teaches a lesson in fundamentals that most training managers understand intuitively. That is, training is more effective when it is supported by visible leadership, delivered to intact work teams, and linked directly to a key work process or key business problem. However, while they understand those fundamentals, many training managers continue to offer training events on an open enrollment basis, without leadership support or a clear business imperative. Motorola has developed the framework illustrated in Figure 4-1 along with supporting tools to ensure that more of its training is deployed in a manner that is consistent with the fundamental assumptions.

Align

With this framework, full-scale training deployment begins with a process (depicted in Figure 4-2) that enables the organization and the requisite leadership team to understand their current performance gaps, agree on their improvement targets, and develop a scorecard if none exists. When a scorecard does exist, the preferred approach is to develop a deployment scorecard from the business unit's existing scorecard that establishes the outcome-based metrics that will guide the deployment and allow leaders to review deployment progress against their desired business results.

In the case study, alignment was achieved during a four-hour session with the general managers responsible for the targeted population. The managers were presented with a productivity analysis and benchmarking

Figure 4-1.

Sustainable Business Performance Improvement

data that demonstrated the performance gap. A facilitated activity led them to agree on sales productivity standards and customer satisfaction goals. They were then presented with an analysis that demonstrated a direct linkage between the key drivers of both productivity and customer satisfaction and the training implementation strategy that was being recommended. By facilitating the session with the leadership team, the training project team was successful in establishing results-based metrics that were linked directly to the sales strategy. The result was strong leadership support and a sustainable funding strategy.

Figure 4-2.

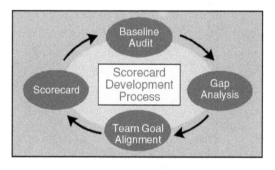

Insight 1, Align

Using the Performance Excellence Business Model as a framework, create relevant "line of sight" improvement targets, stretch goals, and appropriate measures by engaging in the scorecard development process.

Mobilize

Having achieved leadership alignment, the framework suggests that the surest path to effective implementation is to mobilize participants by deploying them in empowered teams.

The key to mobilizing teams is to follow the three central principles depicted in Figure 4-3. First, establish what the relevant team structure will be so that team members are able to make the necessary decisions and take the actions required to make the training being implemented operational. Once the teams are identified, their work must be recast wherever possible as customer-focused team efforts. (For example, what customer are we trying to serve and how will our training positively affect that customer?)

Second, organize the team efforts into projects with clear charters, agreed-upon success criteria, and an understood management review process. The charters are one-page documents that spell out the desired outcomes and the primary activities that will lead to those outcomes. Success criteria are used to establish time frames and to link the team efforts to the

Figure 4-3.

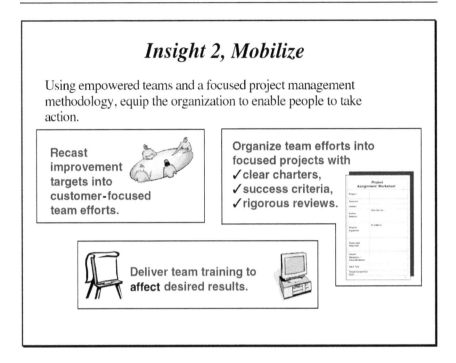

leadership scorecard. The leadership team communicates the process for reviewing team progress against the milestones and success criteria.

Finally, wherever possible, deliver team training on a just-in-time, as-needed basis rather than according to a preset schedule. To make this possible, training must be tools-based and constructed in modules and must not be dependent on live, expert instructors. By utilizing these principles, Motorola enables teams to become energized, focused, and motivated to rapidly apply the training that they are receiving.

In our case study, the teams formed were focused on specific accounts, and charters and performance goals for each account team were developed early in the process. Both the workshops and the review processes were facilitated to encourage teamwork within these account teams.

Accelerate

Once the leadership team is aligned and the teams are mobilized, the overall effort can be accelerated by applying action learning, campaign planning, and clock management (see Figure 4-4). Action learning is a methodology that ensures the integration of individual and project goals with training and coaching activities. This methodology is explained in the next section. Campaign planning is an approach that applies basic project management principles to the implementation plan. The campaign plan will detail, in a project management format, the teams that have been targeted, the nature of their charters, their expected results, and the timetable on which the members of each team are expected to complete their training and achieve their desired results. The clock management concept is based on an understanding of the fact that teams lose their motivation to change if their efforts fail to produce results within sixty days of the launch of those efforts. Clock management causes the "campaign manager" to group team projects into sixty-day deliverables and then drive the leadership team to rigorously review the teams against those deliverables at the appropriate milestones. Acceleration, therefore, is achieved through application of good project management and proactive, timely intervention of facilitators, coaches, and leaders.

Figure 4-4.

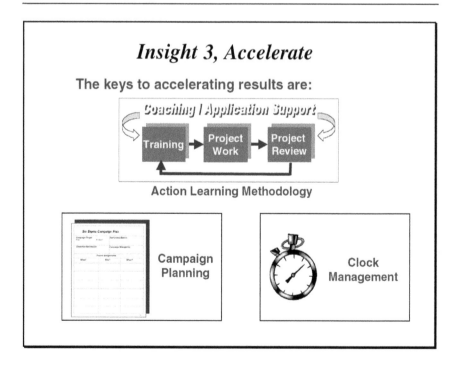

Within our case study, the acceleration principles were applied by holding the account teams to the action plans and detailed timelines that were developed and embedded in their account plans. Achievement of the timelines was ensured through rigorous account review sessions.

Action Learning as the Engine That Drives the Macro Model

As mentioned in the previous section, the action learning method is critical to effective implementation and to ensuring that results occur on an accelerated basis. Action learning is the method used to make sure that the individual is fully engaged in the implementation process and that the individual's learnings and resulting actions are directly linked to the desired strategic objectives. For example, if the strategic objective were increased revenue, then the action learning method would be a rigorous review process that would be integrated with sales training to ensure that the individual actually applied the training by writing improved account plans that drove increased sales to the account. There are five components to the action learning method (shown in Figure 4-5 and described in Figure 4-6): (1) feedback diagnostics, (2) individual preparation, (3) live team-based workshops, (4) structured on-the-job activities with application consulting support, and (5) ongoing executive sponsorship and follow-through.

Feedback Diagnostics

In the diagnostic step, the individuals who are targeted for the learning intervention receive performance feedback from peers, bosses, and customers. The purpose of the feedback is to allow the individuals to understand their current performance and to address the need for movement to the desired performance level. Therefore, the feedback is delivered in a structured way. It can be as simple as documented conversations or as sophisticated as the commercially available 360-degree feedback instruments. What is critical is that as a result of this step, individuals understand the performance goals, are aware of the gaps between their current performance and these goals, and are "ready" to engage in a personal learning and development process for the purpose of achieving the desired performance goals.

Figure 4–5.

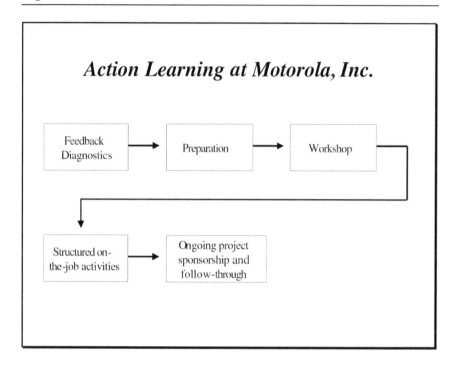

Individual Preparation

As a result of the insight achieved during the diagnostic step, the employees become aware of the learning gaps created by the difference between what is required of each individual given the new strategic objectives and each individual's current capabilities. These insights, along with coaching from a manager, motivate the employees to begin their preparation. This step could include individual self-study and background reading as well as meeting with their sponsor to establish the critical business issue driving the learning project. This step is important because it establishes a partnership between the learner and the sponsoring manager and ensures that the manager is actively engaged in the process. The step also allows the learner to gain management perspective on the desired business improvement targets.

Live Team-Based Workshops

As a result of the diagnostic and individual preparation steps, the individual has reached a state of readiness to learn and is positioned to attend a live

Figure 4-6.

Action Learning at Motorola, Inc.

Step	Activity
Diagnostic	• Feedback from peers, subordinates, bosses, and customers • Understand current situation from outside perspective
Preparation	• Meeting with sponsor to establish critical business issue • Build background on problem area being targeted
Workshop	• Create framework for learning • Build new knowledge and skills • Work on critical problem in small peer-to-peer work groups • Facilitator encourages discovery-based learning and serves as application consultant
On-the-Job Activities	• Application consulting continues • Preestablished action plans are carried out • Peer-to-peer coaching network builds • Sponsor follow-through to encourage and remove barriers
Follow-Through	• Second diagnostic measures improvement • Publish success stories • Students become new facilitators

workshop with other learners—preferably other team members with common performance objectives. During the live workshop, facilitators work with the team members to create an environment of shared performance goals as well as aggressive group learning goals. Team operating principles are established to encourage knowledge sharing and team collaboration. The individuals work on their critical problem area in small peer-to-peer work groups while the facilitator encourages discovery-based learning and serves as an application consultant to the work groups. In this environment, the individual learners build new knowledge and skills and prepare to apply the new knowledge to the work project to which they have been assigned.

Structured On-the-Job Activities

During the live workshop, the learners make specific plans for the immediate application of their learnings in their work process and are supplied with tools and templates to facilitate those activities. The on-the-job application of the learning occurs in the next stage, which is called *structured activities*. During this step, the facilitator of the live workshop is available to serve as an application consultant to the teams, either on-site in the work process or remotely via telephone or e-mail. The action plans that were developed during the workshop are executed, and team members build a peer-to-peer communication network to encourage collaboration, sharing of what is working and what is not working, and group problem solving. In this stage, the sponsor is responsible for reviewing each individual's progress to provide coaching and encouragement and to remove organizational and resource barriers that slow the individual's progress toward the achievement of the performance goals.

Sponsorship and Follow-Through

The result of successful completion of the structured on-the-job activities is that the learner applies the specific models and demonstrates a likelihood that the application of these models will lead to the desired business results. Application of these models allows the individual to enter the follow-through step. During this phase, a second diagnostic is used to verify that the desired behavioral changes have occurred and that application of the new knowledge and skills has indeed caused the desired business improvements to occur. Documentation of success allows the success stories to be shared and appropriate recognition, reward, and celebration to occur. As part of a virtual reinforcing cycle, the successful participants become the facilitators for the next wave of learners.

Application of Action Learning in the Case Study

One of the key success factors in the sales effectiveness case was the utilization of the action learning methodology. In the diagnostics phase, a survey instrument was mailed to key contacts within each sales rep's account so that the sales reps received direct feedback from their customers on their ability to collaborate and develop value-adding solutions for those customers. The preparation stage included reading two books (*Consultative Selling* by Mack Hanan, James J. Cribbin, and Herman C. Heiser, and *Successful Large Account Management* by Robert B. Miller, Tad Tuleja, and Stephen E. Heiman). In addition, the sales reps spent time with their managers establishing stretch revenue and product goals for each account, with clear linkage to the new strategic objectives. Armed with customer feedback and stretch sales targets, the reps participated in workshops facilitated by experienced sales managers and worked directly on developing focused account plans built from best-practice models advanced during the learning modules.

The structured on-the-job activities included building and presenting a solution storyline, identifying executive targets within each account, and then building an account plan to reach the executive and present the executive story. Since revenue and product mix targets had been established prior to the live workshop, the effectiveness of the training was measured in terms of individual and team performance relative to progress toward the agreed-on goals. Leading indicators such as number of quality account plans developed, number of high-impact storyline presentations completed, and number of proposals generated became the metrics that guided team-level application consulting. A formal process of monthly account reviews ensured that the sales managers were showing visible sponsorship and were actively engaged in the coaching process.

Over the twelve-month performance period, sales to the targeted accounts increased significantly. In a follow-up assessment with key customers, the customers indicated an improved perception of their account manager as a partner bringing value-adding solutions.

Gap Analysis and Performance Contracting

I have described an implementation framework that allows Motorola to align a leadership team on an agreed-on set of desired strategic outcomes, mobilize teams toward results-based targets, and then accelerate both the speed of the deployment and the speed of achieving results. I also described the action learning method, which uses a five-step process to ensure that the targeted teams and targeted individuals within those teams are clear on their objectives, are open to learning, have a supportive environment in place, and achieve the desired results.

Key to the success of both the implementation framework and the action-learning model is an active partnership with the business unit that is the target of the effort. Motorola builds the foundations of that partnership by jointly conducting a performance gap analysis and by documenting the nature of the partnership in a performance contract. A jointly conducted performance gap analysis will provide a common operating picture of the current reality, a common picture of the desired state, and a solution path for achieving that state. The performance contract clearly establishes roles and responsibilities by not only describing how the solution team will perform but also describing how the client team will contribute to the solution.

The Performance Gap Analysis

While a number of effective approaches to performance analysis have been documented in the literature, Motorola has found that a quick, straightforward, team-based approach usually nets as much useful data as some of the very detailed approaches. As a framework for conducting a gap analysis, we utilize the Performance Excellence Business System (depicted in Figure 4-7). The Performance Excellence framework uses seven categories (leadership, strategic planning, customer/market focus, information and analysis, human resources, process management, and business results) to create a business model that stresses managing any enterprise as a balanced business system.

The categories of leadership, strategic planning, and customer/market focus help to ensure that a business unit's strategic emphasis is aligned and

Figure 4-7.

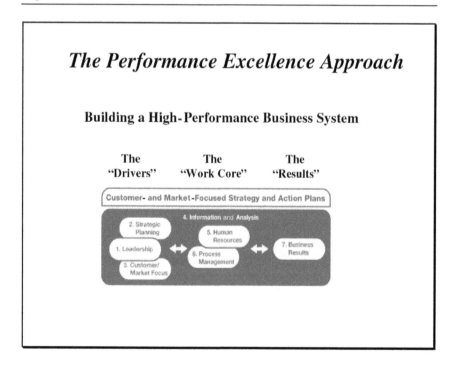

The Performance Excellence Approach

Building a High-Performance Business System

The "Drivers"	The "Work Core"	The "Results"

Customer- and Market-Focused Strategy and Action Plans

4. Information and Analysis

2. Strategic Planning

5. Human Resources

1. Leadership

7. Business Results

6. Process Management

3. Customer/Market Focus

that a focus on the right customers and markets drives all of the strategies. The categories of human resources and process management help a business focus its people capabilities and its work processes on execution of the defined strategies. The business unit stays on track as it measures its progress in terms of business results as defined in the business results category. The Performance Excellence framework defines criteria for excellence in each of the seven categories, and the target business unit's performance is compared to those criteria for excellence to establish the baseline assessment.

The Performance Excellence framework establishes objective criteria and provides standards for business performance that allow the assessment process to be conducted in a focused, objective manner. As a result of the gap analysis, a clear picture of the performance improvement targets can be established and the team can get enough background information to develop a solution strategy. It is assumed that because the analysis was performed in partnership with the targeted business unit, a collaborative agreement regarding the desired solution can be developed with relative ease. It is important to document that collaborative solution while all parties are in harmony.

Performance Contract

The means by which this collaborative solution is documented is called the *performance contract*. The performance contract represents a written consensus among all participants in the solution regarding the expected outcomes; resource requirements; a delineation of roles, responsibilities, and decision authorities; and key deliverables with milestones. A critical aspect of the performance contract is the recognition that achieving the desired performance outcomes is a responsibility of the solution provider, the sponsoring business unit, and the participants. The heart of the performance agreement, therefore, is the articulation of the roles and responsibilities of the various parties and a written consensus among all parties that they are committed to carrying out those roles and responsibilities for the purpose of achieving the agreed-on outcomes.

Key to understanding the performance contract is the recognition that it represents the result of a collaborative process in which the solution team and the client came to a shared understanding through mutual exploration of the problem and the potential solution. In the absence of that collaborative process, a performance contract is not likely to represent truly shared understanding. However, the goal of reaching a documented performance agreement can often drive the necessary process.

With that in mind, it should be noted that performance agreements do not need to be lengthy documents, loaded with legalese. Rather, the most effective performance agreements can be clearly articulated in one or two pages. As an example, the matrix illustrated in Figure 4-8 represents the performance agreement that guided a major effort to build the "value analysis" skills of a major account team. In a three-page matrix, the agreement articulates the key activities and desired outcomes and the critical roles and responsibilities of five key players in the solution (leadership, participants, support functions, the training team, and a key vendor). This particular agreement guided the activities of the five parties throughout the twelve-month performance period. The account managers developed the skills that would enable them to conduct value analysis within their accounts and thereby develop profit improvement proposals that would position them as consultants and allow them to secure incremental business within their accounts. The results could not have been achieved without sustained collaboration among all parties, and the performance contract was the platform for that sustained collaboration.

Case Study #2—Six Sigma Implementation

The intention of this chapter was to describe an approach in which training serves as a strategic lever for accelerating business results for our key clients. I have described the align-mobilize-accelerate framework, the action learning methodology, and the role that performance contracting plays in integrating these activities with our business partners. While the first case study I provided involved sales acceleration, the area in which this model has been best applied is the implementation of the Six Sigma quality management methodology to transform businesses for the purpose of dramatically improving customer satisfaction and achieving breakthrough business results.

This story is important because when Motorola introduced the Six Sigma quality management methodology in the late 1980s, the implementation strategy was primarily a wide-scale, global training initiative. While Motorola experienced significant returns on its training investments during the first few years, it soon became clear that a training-focused strategy was not going to achieve results that were either breakthrough in nature or

Figure 4-8.

Example of a Performance Contract

Activities and Desired Outcomes	USCG Special Markets				Aarthun Training Group, Ltd.
	Mgt.	Sales force	Sales Support	Worldwide Learning Services	
1. Design and develop 3-day Value Analysis Workshop	☑ Provide SMEs	☑ Provide SMEs	☑ Provide SMEs	☑ Provide SMEs and Project Manager	☑ Conduct data collection ☑ Develop first draft
	☑ Review/revise first draft	☑ Review/revise first draft	☑ Review/revise first draft	☑ Review/revise first draft	☑ Make revisions on first draft ☑ Produce revised materials
	☑ Review revised draft	☑ Review revised draft	☑ Review revised draft	☑ Review revised draft	☑ Make final revisions ☑ Produce pilot materials
	☑ Management representation and participation in pilot equals feedback for improvement	☑ Individuals selected for representation and participation = feedback for improvement		☑ Participation in session as conduct feedback session	☑ Conduct initial pilot ☑ Make revisions from pilot ☑ Produce final materials for implementation
2. Implement workshop Deliver initial training	☑ All management will attend training and receive specific training on how to support/ reinforce the Value Analysi^8 Process	☑ All salespeople will attend training	☑ All support people will attend training	☑ All Worldwide Learning Services people will attend training to provide support and reinforcement to participants	☑ Ongoing— continually updating and improving materials from implementation feedback

Example of a Performance Contract

Activities and Desired Outcomes	USCG Special Markets				Aarthun Training Group, Ltd.
	Mgt.	Salesforce	Sales Support	Worldwide Learning Services	
3. Initiate Reinforce the Value-Added Process with customers	☑ Require 3 PIP within 30 days ☑ Monthly project reviews	☑ Complete 3 PIP of top customers and prospects ☑ Review with management	☑ Support sales force in completing the PIPs ☑ Review with management	☑ Ride-alongs ☑ Telephone consulting ☑ Project review with sales and management	☑ Telephone consulting ☑ Spot checks ☑ Compile and start to build data bank of VAP projects ☑ Ride-alongs
4. Achieve bottom-line results for Motorola, USCG markets	☑ Monthly reviews with sales force	☑ Monthy reviews and continue to complete VAP for all new customers	☑ Monthly reviews and continued support to sales force	☑ Monthly updates as to VAP progress	☑ Continually update VAP data bank (make available to all who participate in ongoing monthly process) ☑ Ride-alongs as requested ☑ Telephone consulting ☑ Spot checks as requested

Figure 4-8. (continued)

Example of a Performance Contract

Activities and Desired Outcomes	USCG Special Markets				Aarthun Training Group, Ltd.
	Mgt.	Salesforce	Sales Support	Worldwide Learning Services	
5. Tracking and measuring the bottom-line results	☑ Provide data from monthly reviews	☑ Compile data	☑ Provide support to the compilation of data	☑ Partner for ROI analysis publish ☑ USCG Special Markets bottom-line results	
6. Scorecard	Goal 1. Business opportunity identification 2. Business based proposal generation 3. Sales revenue from new proposals	Measurement 10 per account manager 10 per account manager $10,000,000 in incremental revenue		Goal 1. Reduce budgeted program costs 2. Achieve implementation timelines 3. Participant satisfaction 4. Participant performance	Measurement % budget expanded Variance to timelines Level one evaluations See participant scorecard

sustainable over time. Faced with that reality, Motorola University tapped into its experience with action learning, change acceleration, and performance contracting to develop an implementation strategy that delivered results for Motorola business units and their suppliers and customers. When viewed in its entirety, the Six Sigma implementation model serves as a useful example of the integration of action learning, change acceleration, and performance contracting to achieve sustainable, breakthrough, business results.

Six Sigma Implementation Phase One: Align the Leadership Team and Prepare the Individual Learner

A key tenet of a Six Sigma business improvement campaign is achieving bottom-line business results in an accelerated time frame. Success is not measured in terms of hours of courseware completed, but rather in terms of achievement of results relative to preestablished goals in the areas of process improvement, financial gains, customer satisfaction, and innovation and growth. Establishing the goals in these categories requires an understanding of current performance levels in these areas as well as desired performance.

During phase one of the Six Sigma implementation, our activities map directly into the alignment stage of the broad implementation framework and the preparation step of the action learning model. The performance gap analysis is completed, and the performance contract is negotiated.

The preferred approach to a performance gap analysis within the Six Sigma implementation is to conduct a full Performance Excellence audit, as described earlier in this chapter. That audit yields data in all four results categories and generates targets for improvement opportunities. The audit itself can be performed as a wide-scale extensive audit or with a focused, cross-functional team that generates a "minibaseline" assessment.

Upon completion of the baseline audit, the implementation moves to the leadership alignment workshop. During this two-day workshop, the members of the business leadership team work together to develop a consensus picture of the current reality and the desired improvements. The team learns the Six Sigma business improvement approach and then works through a series of activities that generate the following: a prioritized set of customer expectations, a strengths/weaknesses/opportunities/threats analysis, a situation analysis, and a prioritized set of strategic objectives. While the audit results feed these activities, the team members add their perspective on the current state of the business.

Having reached consensus on the current reality, the leadership team then moves to an activity that allows it to establish metrics in each of the four categories (process improvement, financial gains, customer satisfaction, and innovation and growth) and also to establish stretch goals in each category for the Six Sigma business improvement campaign. After establishing the goals, the members of the leadership team work together to determine what the key performance drivers are within each category. Those performance drivers point directly to specific opportunities for improvement. These specific opportunities become the basis for launching cross-functional teams that are chartered to achieve specific improvements within a four- to six-month time frame.

The performance goals and team charters that were established during this two-day leadership alignment workshop become the basis for the performance contract with this business team. In addition to agreeing to the performance goals and project charters as part of the performance contract, the business unit leaders also agree to provide the resources required to support the projects (people, time, and money) and to actively engage in an ongoing project review process that allows them to show visible support and provide critical business guidance on a periodic basis throughout the campaign. With agreement on these critical elements, the implementation campaign moves to phase two: Mobilize the teams and conduct training workshops.

Six Sigma Implementation Phase Two: Mobilize the Teams and Conduct Training Workshops

With clear charters, clear outcome-based goals in hand, and enthusiastic sponsorship from their leaders, the teams are prepared for success. Real success in an accelerated time frame requires that team members receive training in processes and tools that will enable them to develop new insights and breakthrough ideas concerning these performance improvement opportunities.

The key activity during phase two, therefore, is the delivery of focused training workshops that build team understanding of the Six Sigma continuous improvement methodology. At the same time, individuals with critical roles in the implementation receive focused leadership training and intensive technical training. For example, the managers (called Champions) who are directly responsible for the teams' results receive leadership skills training that is focused on empowering the team to make decisions and execute those decisions quickly and on understanding the Six Sigma methodology in enough detail to provide management coaching to the team.

The team leaders (called Black Belts) receive more than 150 hours of training, delivered in four week-long segments spread over four months. During these intensive technical workshops, the Black Belts learn the define-measure-analyze-improve control methodology and the statistical tools available to add precision and deep analysis to the problem-solving process. Throughout this training, the Black Belt candidates also develop their team leadership and project management skills.

In keeping with the action learning methodology, these Black Belts are working on their specific projects during these workshops and are receiving expert (Master Black Belt) coaching on the job during the weeks in between the monthly workshops. This application of the action learning method allows the instructors to review project data during the workshops and allows coaches to keep the projects on track during the intervening weeks. As a result, the Black Belt candidates develop quickly, and the projects deliver their results, on time, as promised.

The final target population for training is the team members (called Green Belts). During forty hours of workshop-based training, team members learn the problem-solving model, the key tools available to support the model, and the roles and responsibilities of a team member in a project team environment. The goal of the Green Belt training is to provide the team members with the skills they need in order to support their team leader in delivering the results of the project to which they have been assigned.

Six Sigma Implementation Phase Three: Accelerate Results Through Coaching and Management Review

Phase three of the Six Sigma implementation parallels the structured on-the-job activities step in the action learning model. As mentioned earlier, a key on-the-job activity in Six Sigma implementation is the expert coaching that the Black Belts and teams receive at set intervals across the life of their projects. The most important activity in this stage is the systematic, rigorous review of the projects that is built into the performance contract and implementation plan.

There are two levels of review for the projects. Champions (the operational managers closest to the projects) receive weekly feedback from the Black Belts on the projects' progress, and a project does not move to the next stage of completion until the Champion for that project has signed off on the project review. A more strategic review of the projects occurs on a monthly basis. During these formal reviews, the Black Belts present their projects to the Champions and to a senior leader steering committee. In these reviews, the Black Belts demonstrate their progress relative to the results commitments that they have made, test potential solutions with senior leaders, and make their case for additional resources or changes in project scope where necessary. It is through these review processes that the teams and the projects stay tightly linked to the desired business results and leaders stay actively engaged in the process. The result is a tightly managed business improvement campaign that achieves the predicted business results in the time frame expected.

Ongoing Monitoring of Results

As the final element of the Six Sigma implementation, an ongoing process of monitoring the performance of the business process in which the solution was implemented ensures that the solution that was installed delivers its promised performance improvements on a sustainable basis. Black Belt candidates are certified as skilled Black Belts only after these performance data are accumulated and audited by a financial analyst.

Conclusion

The Six Sigma business improvement campaign delivers desired business results in accelerated time frames because the implementation plan integrates the align-mobilize-accelerate framework with a full action learning methodology, enabled by a clearly articulated gap analysis and performance contract. Successful corporations like Motorola, GE, and Allied Signal have achieved millions of dollars in annual savings and have demonstrated that training and development can play a strategic role in a corporation's results when they are tightly integrated with the business goals of that corporation.

Combining the align-mobilize-accelerate framework with the action learning methodology provides a practical approach to delivering strategic business results through integrated learning solutions. The case studies document the fact that corporate universities can use this approach to deliver bottom-line results in areas like sales effectiveness and Six Sigma business improvement. The documented success of this approach should challenge all of us to refine and improve it through wider and more consistent application. Leaders of corporate universities should insist on a level of partnership with business units that will enable the type of collaboration necessary to achieve the strategic leverage that is illustrated in the case studies. Business unit funding of learning solutions should be viewed as investments, and the corporate university should be held accountable for the promised return on those investments.

This chapter has outlined an approach that makes the promise of strategic leverage a practical reality. The corporate university serves as a strategic lever to the organization when this approach is applied.

Strategic Partnerships for Corporate Universities

Mark Allen

Corporate university directors and deans, I've got bad news for you: You've got a big job to do. Depending on the size and scope of your corporate university, in order to do a good job of aligning your workforce with your organization's strategy, your task list looks something like this:

- ❏ Conduct needs assessments
- ❏ Design educational programs
- ❏ Deliver educational programs
- ❏ Hire vendors to deliver educational programs
- ❏ Assess technology options
- ❏ Develop executives and managers
- ❏ Manage vendor relationships
- ❏ Market programs internally and possibly externally
- ❏ Evaluate programs

For many corporate universities, this to-do list is representative, but not exhaustive.

Do you have expertise in all of these areas? (Don't despair—few people do.) Is your staff large enough and expert enough to perform all of these functions—and perform them well? For most corporate universities, the answer is no, yet you still have the responsibility for performing all of these functions.

Here's the good news: You need not do it alone. There are numerous companies, universities, and individuals that have the expertise you lack and that are willing to work with you to accomplish your goals.

In this chapter, when I discuss partnerships, I am not talking about a simple buyer/vendor relationship in which expertise is purchased. Some relationships are entered into to meet an immediate need. True strategic alliances address needs that extend beyond the current issues into a longer time horizon. These alliances are related to the strategy of the corporate university and its parent and are not merely a tactical response to a current need.

A true partnership is one that is long term, has strategic intent, and is mutually beneficial. Those who provide the services may also receive benefits from the corporate university in the form of expertise or education, but even if the quid pro quo is simply monetary, it is the long-term time frame and strategic nature of the relationship that defines it as a partnership. So if you purchase a program from a vendor, that is not a partnership, it is a purchase and the solution to an immediate need. It may grow into a partnership over time if it addresses the strategic goals of the corporate university, but merely providing a product or service does not qualify as a partnership. If the relationship is entered into with the goal of being long term, with an eye toward expanding, and with the long-range goals (as opposed to an immediate need) of the corporate university in mind, then it is a partnership.

There are many potential partners for a corporate university, including traditional universities, nontraditional or for-profit universities, consultants, technology/distance learning providers, and even other corporate universities. For many corporate universities, the best solution might be partnerships with some combination of these options. This chapter discusses the potential providers and the advantages and possible disadvantages of each.

Traditional Universities

The growth of corporate universities was originally driven by the executive development function. For decades, many companies have used university-based executive education programs for management and executive development. University programs range from a few days to three or more weeks in duration. Although university programs were a popular option a decade or more ago, companies today are demanding shorter, more focused courses.[1] This shift in demand led companies to bring university professors in-house to deliver company-specific programs. Companies then began to form hybrid programs that combined university faculty with in-house experts. As companies learned that in-house experts provided more value and were more efficient, corporate universities expanded while university executive programs declined.[2]

One reason for the migration of managerial development programs to corporate universities is dissatisfaction with the performance of business schools. There is abundant research showing that employers are not satisfied with the skills of graduates of business school programs.[3] Although these studies generally agree that business school graduates are competent in technical areas (such as finance), they lack skills such as communication, team building, and the ability to work in groups. It is because of this dissatisfaction with traditional business schools that corporations moved so much of the education function in-house. The inefficiency of business schools in providing education that their customers found relevant opened up the field of executive education to a market economy and has spurred the expansion of corporate universities.[4]

However, the pendulum may be swinging back. In 2001, *Business Week* reported that traditional business schools' share of the executive development market was $800 million.[5] Corporations from both the United States and the rest of the world are coming to American business schools for corporate education programs. "Once viewed as a cushy perk for the newly promoted, these programs have become an integral part of corporate strategy—and serious work for participating executives."[6]

What do these schools have to offer corporate universities? The first thing is cutting-edge research into business and management principles. Chances are, if you want to teach Accounting 101 to your marketing department, you've got someone in-house who has the expertise. But if you want the latest, most up-to-date information, it is generally better to go outside, and universities are still the place for cutting-edge research.

Of course, universities are also the best and usually the only option if degrees are important to your workforce. If you have a number of employees who want to complete their bachelor's degrees, it is far easier to work with your local university than to develop an in-house degree program at a corporate university and deal with accreditation hassles. And despite the literature showing some corporate dissatisfaction with MBAs, there is still much demand in the marketplace for that degree. When The Boeing Company's Military Aircraft & Missile Systems Group recently wanted to give its people the opportunity to earn an MBA specializing in organization development, it worked out a collaboration with Pepperdine University. The university's MBA program is now offered on-site at Boeing's Long Beach, California, facility. It is a Pepperdine MBA, but it is delivered at Boeing, exclusively for Boeing employees.

An article in the *International Herald Tribune* endorsed this approach. "The linking of business school/corporate U seems ideal, since it gives corporate universities the academic stamp of approval they lack, while furnishing real-world situations where the schools can hone practical skills they can't acquire on an insulated campus."[7] In addition, the universities and professors gain research opportunities and real-world business examples to enrich their teaching.

Such partnerships between corporations and universities are likely to proliferate in this country (just as has happened in Australia, as Ian Dickson reports in Chapter 12.) As a matter of fact, the on-site program at Boeing grew out of an entity that Pepperdine has developed called Corporate University Partners. The idea is that the university works with corporate partners on a long-term basis. Not only will the university provide classroom education, but as the professors get to know the company issues, the relationship can expand to include everything from short, nondegree courses to longer-term executive development programs, to degree programs, and even to consulting. The old model of university executive education programs was to sell seats in programs; the new model is to develop relationships.

There are potential downsides to working with universities. Traditional open-enrollment programs have been criticized as being too general. Considering the amount of money they spend on these programs, corporations prefer education that is focused on their industries and their issues. Even custom programs are criticized—the curriculum may be designed around company needs, but the professors are often unfamiliar with industry specifics and company issues.

Of course, the partnership is designed to overcome these obstacles. As universities and their professors work with their corporate counterparts over a period of time, they become familiar with the company and its industry. Remember, these are long-term strategic alliances, not one or two customized programs. The corporate partner benefits from having a faculty that teach about company-specific issues (and may bring their expertise to the company through consulting engagements, as well), while the faculty benefit from being able to incorporate greater industry knowledge into their teaching and research.

The idea of partnerships between corporate and traditional universities was endorsed in an article in *The New Yorker* that suggested that "a new kind of institution would come into being as the result of an alliance between a state-university system, a 'content provider,' like Disney, and a technology firm, like Motorola."[8] While collaborations that result in new institutions have not yet appeared on the landscape, these types of relationships are emerging as strategic partnerships. *Business Week* agreed: "More companies seem to be choosing an individual brew of B-schools, outside consultants, and inside projects."[9]

Nontraditional/For-Profit Universities

Of the more than 3,400 colleges and universities offering accredited degree programs in the United States, the vast majority are not-for-profit. The entire public higher education system of course is not-for-profit, but so are most of the private colleges and universities. Over the past two or three decades, however, there has been a growing movement toward a new breed of university—one that is operated for a profit but is still fully accredited and provides a wide range of degree programs.

The largest of these is the Apollo Group's University of Phoenix. Publicly traded and definitely in business to make a buck, Apollo Group runs the University of Phoenix (and several affiliated companies) to serve the large and growing number of adult students who want to complete a bachelor's degree or earn a master's degree. Since its start in 1976, the university has experienced extraordinary growth; it is currently the largest private university in the United States. The university has more than 100 campuses in 20 states and Canada and enrolls more than 100,000 students in degree programs in business, nursing, education, and other disciplines. As a natural extension of its degree programs for adults, the University of Phoenix has started working with corporations to provide certificate programs and on-site education.

Phoenix is not the only large for-profit educator. DeVry Institutes are located throughout the United States and offer degree programs in technology and business at the associate, bachelor's, and master's level. The Keller Graduate School of Management is owned by DeVry and offers master's degrees and graduate certificate programs. In addition, Keller has a Center for Corporate Education that is designed to provide nondegree courses to the corporate world.

Another nontraditional university is Jones International University. Jones is the first accredited university that is 100 percent online. Although it offers bachelor's and master's degree programs in a variety of disciplines, Jones has no classrooms. The University of Phoenix's Online "campus" enrolls more than 28,000 students, making it the largest provider of degree programs over the Internet, but the vast majority of Phoenix's enrollment is still in classroom-based programs. Naturally, Jones International University has offerings in professional and executive education designed to offer nondegree education to corporate customers in an on-line format.

A negative to these nontraditional universities is the fact that they lack the reputation of a traditional university. Lacking in tradition and often dismissed as diploma mills (despite their accreditation and their growing acceptance in the marketplace), these schools do not carry the name-brand cachet of their older, more established, nonprofit counterparts.

So why are corporations choosing to enter into partnerships with these nontraditional universities? First of all, they offer speed and flexibility. Traditional universities have a well-earned reputation for moving slowly. The pace of the academic world is often glacial compared to the speed with which corporations like to move. *Flexibility* is also not a term that is often associated with traditional universities. The nontraditional universities, being for-profit corporations themselves, are often able to move more quickly and be more flexible than traditional universities.

Please note that while I have characterized traditional universities as being slow and inflexible, this does not apply to all institutions. As the higher education marketplace becomes more competitive (and some institutions fight for their very survival), we will see more and more universities become faster and more flexible. I believe that some institutions will consciously adopt a strategy of flexibility and will distinguish themselves in the marketplace and thrive because of it, while others that remain inflexible will wither.

Another badge of honor for the for-profits is a customer focus. Because they recognize that students (and corporations) are customers, the nontraditional universities have designed their offerings for convenience and ease of use. Many traditional universities have stuck with a "here are our offerings—line up and take them" mentality that will not serve them well in the corporate education marketplace. Education that is customer-focused (as opposed to generic) is what many corporations are demanding.

Another advantage to partnerships with nontraditional universities is technology. Some traditional universities have excellent distance education technology, but most have little or no expertise in this area. The nontraditional universities (the University of Phoenix and Jones International are just two of many examples) often have extensive technology platforms that can easily be adapted for corporate education initiatives. Of course, universities are not the only source of distance learning technology. The next section describes the many hardware and software vendors that are potential partners for corporate universities.

Technology/Distance Learning Providers

There are countless companies that are entering the distance learning field. Some provide software, some provide hardware, some provide courseware, and some provide complete turnkey solutions. If your corporate university is contemplating offering programs using distance learning technology, your biggest problem will be selecting from among the wide array of vendors.

Partnerships in this arena can get very murky. Some traditional universities offer distance learning programs and even complete corporate training solutions. You can certainly turn to the nontraditional universities for distance learning solutions. Some companies, such as Quisic and UNext, have invested heavily to develop university-quality business courses using state-of-the-art technology. Other companies offer hardware and/or software that will let you develop your own courses.

The first question here is whether you want a partner or a vendor. As discussed earlier, there are differences. The stakes in learning technology are high because the investment in infrastructure is steep and does not allow for mistakes. Once you invest in a platform, you are pretty much committed to using it for a long time to come. Therefore, you want to select a partner that you believe will still be around in a few years (this landscape changes so rapidly that it is hard to keep track of the players) and one that not only offers the technology you need, but also has people that you can rely on to have a good working relationship with you even after you have made the initial investment.

One example of a partnership between a corporation and a distance education company is the alliance announced in 2001 between General Motors and UNext. The partnership was announced as a four-year alliance, so both organizations are obviously thinking of this as a long-term relationship, not merely the provision of a service. This partnership is designed to provide General Motors' employees with access to nondegree management and executive development courses and an online MBA program through UNext's Cardean University. Cardean University is itself the result of a strategic alliance between UNext and five prestigious universities: Columbia (University) Business School, Stanford University, the University of Chicago Graduate School of Business, Carnegie Mellon University, and the London School of Economics. I think the upcoming years will bring more announcements of partnerships of this type involving leading corporations, distance learning companies, and top universities.

The companies in the distance learning industry have many potential benefits. Obviously, they have the technology. More important, they may offer a one-stop solution to all of your corporate distance learning needs. While this is a high-risk strategy, if you find an appropriate partner and no longer have to seek vendors for each new project, the payoff can be large.

Another potential benefit is distance learning expertise. Here I am not referring to hardware and software; I am talking about expertise in how people learn using technology. Beware of vendors who extol the technical capabilities of their offerings—instead, look for people who know what they are doing with regard to helping people learn, as opposed to merely distributing courseware. A distance learning partner that understands how technology can be used to actually assist people in learning can provide value to a corporate university that extends far beyond the distribution and communication advantages of computer technology.

Training recently described three different types of partnerships that corporate universities may enter into for distance education: classic, portal, and tailored training.[10] In the classic approach, individual employees take on-line courses offered by traditional or nontraditional universities, with the employer paying the bill. The employer's involvement is generally either entering into an agreement with the university to provide these courses, making information about options available to the student, or possibly simply writing a check (only in the first case would this truly be considered a partnership). The advantage to this approach is that employees usually have numerous options and are able to select the program that best meets their individual needs.

In the portal approach, the company works with a university—or, more usually, with several universities and possibly some private training companies—to create a catalog of on-line courses that are available to employees through the company's portal. The technology for the portal is provided by a distance learning company, so corporate universities that use a portal approach are typically in partnership with a technology company and several universities and content providers. This approach definitely lends itself well to partnership arrangements as opposed to mere vendor relationships.

The third type of partnership is the tailored training approach. In this case, the corporate university works closely with one or more traditional universities, nontraditional universities, or private content providers to develop courses that are specifically designed to meet the organization's learning goals. These types of arrangements can range from working with suppliers to develop a course or two to full-fledged partnerships with content providers that supply courses on an ongoing basis.

Consultants

Partnerships do not have to be with an organization—they can be with an individual. And there is no shortage of individual consultants who are willing to work with your corporate university.

These consultants are of many types. Some have content area expertise and are brought in to teach in their functional specialty. Others are process experts—experts in corporate university structure and organization, instructional design, executive education, or program evaluation. A third category of consultants is those who are brought in for their expertise in learning technologies.

Again, you can bring in a consultant to teach your workforce marketing or strategy, but that is not a partnership—the consultant is a hired gun. When the consultant works with the corporate university over a long period of time and is used for a specific strategic purpose, then there is a partnership.

Sometimes the lines get a little murky. Many consultants who are subject matter experts are also business school professors. You can purchase their expertise by working through their universities, or you can contract with them directly. The latter route is usually cheaper, but it does not come with the additional services—facilities, registration, course materials—that working with the executive education department of a business school provides. Of course, when you work with a university, you are typically limited to its faculty. If you hire individual faculty members directly, you can pick and choose the best professors from various universities.

An individual consultant with expertise in the corporate university process or learning technologies is a potentially powerful partner. Such a person can work with you in setting up and designing your corporate university and can be a truly strategic partner in helping you execute your corporate university strategy.

Of course, consultants are not always individuals. Consulting companies range from firms with only a few partners to huge firms with thousands of employees. The huge organizations offer tremendous expertise in a wide range of areas, but this expertise comes at a price. The first price is monetary—the big firms charge big fees for their services. The other price is in continuity. While you can hire a big consulting company for a period of time, it is usually not feasible to enter into a long-term partnership with such a company. These companies can come in and do a job for you, but it is generally not cost effective to work with them on an ongoing basis.

Smaller consulting companies are a different story. As with individuals, you can enter into long-term, strategic partnerships with them. As the relationship develops, these consultants not only bring expertise, but also add knowledge of your company and its issues, making them even more valuable to you. And their experience working with you makes the consultants more valuable as they market their services in the corporate university community.

Other Corporate Universities

A potentially rich source of partnership help is the corporate university community. This book is designed to bring together corporate university professionals to share their expertise with other practitioners facing the same issues. This exchange does not need to be restricted to the printed page.

Corporate universities can band together to form consortia. If the corporations sponsoring these universities are in the same industry, the consortium can be focused on industry-specific issues. The companies can join forces to develop programs that can benefit the industry as a whole. It can be costly to hire a university to develop an industry-specific executive education program. However, if that cost is spread out over several companies, a high-quality program can be developed at a reasonable cost to each organization.

Consortia among corporate universities in different industries can also be formed. In this case, the organizations are either working together to develop general-interest programs or collaborating on corporate university process issues. In the first case, once again the costs of developing programs are borne by several organizations instead of one. The downside is that the program lacks an industry- and company-specific focus, but the upside is cost saving.

In other cases, corporate universities can collaborate by sharing best practices. Benchmarking has been a popular way to learn in the corporate university world. Robert Fulmer describes the results of some benchmarking studies in Chapter 6, while Motorola University is inundated with requests for benchmarking visits from up-and-coming corporate universities. But learning can be shared through means other than benchmarking. While benchmarking typically takes place over a fixed period of time, a consortium of corporate universities can work together on an ongoing basis to share best practices. I often hear corporate university deans trying to decide on the best approach to a problem, and I know that they are not the first to wrestle with that issue. I would guess that whatever issues are facing your corporate university are not new to the world. A consortium of corporate universities designed to share best practices can be beneficial to all parties—and can exist for a relatively small cost.

Multiple Partnerships

The options discussed here are not presented as a menu of possibilities out of which one must be chosen. For many corporate universities, the best solution is two or three partnerships. For example, you can partner with a university for classroom learning and with a technology provider for distance education.

Another possibility is a partnership that involves multiple parties. Perhaps you can form a three-way partnership in which the university provides content for a distance learning program and a technology provider contributes the learning platform. Because of sticky issues like intellectual property rights and confidential information, the nature of the partnership needs to be spelled out explicitly in advance, but such an arrangement can be the best solution for addressing all of your needs.

Partnerships can even be formed with several entities of the same type. When the Los Angeles Police Department sought to develop leadership training for its senior officers, it formed a partnership with four different universities in the Los Angeles area: Pepperdine University; the University of Southern California; the University of California, Los Angeles; and The Claremont Colleges. Rather than being limited by the expertise of one university or faculty, the LAPD has taken advantage of the resources available from a variety of local universities and is able to capitalize on the strengths of each.

From Pepperdine, the LAPD has called upon the Graziadio School of Business and Management to provide sessions on management and organizational issues. At USC, the School of Policy, Planning, and Development has offered modules through its Center for the Administration of Justice. UCLA's contribution has been through its School of Public Policy and Social Research. From Claremont, the Claremont Graduate University has offered sessions in a variety of disciplines.

By utilizing the four universities in this manner, the Los Angeles Police Department has been able to give its senior officers advanced instruction across a range of areas that no single university could have provided. The universities each gain revenue from providing these courses and help to fulfill their missions by serving an important sector of their community. The faculty gain expertise from working with one of the largest law enforcement organizations in the nation. The Police Department gets high-level training for its senior officers, and the officers get an education that helps them to run the department more effectively and efficiently. This partnership has been beneficial to all parties in the three years of its existence and is likely to continue.

Of course, working with multiple universities is not without its potential perils. As an article in *The Chronicle of Higher Education* exploring the growing trend of universities partnering with each other to satisfy the needs of corporate clients pointed out, "Sustaining a partnership among business schools with different cultures and goals can frustrate even the most diplomatic of potential allies."[11] The potential benefits are large, and therefore the participants have an incentive to try to work well together. After all, if they fail to collaborate in a way that meets the corporate customer's needs, they may "lose out on a lucrative deal to a for-profit school or a corporate university."[12] Just like the competitive corporate world, the world of higher education is discovering that competition is an incentive for adaptability and that it is often better to work with other organizations than to compete with them. The old maxim of "if you can't beat 'em, join 'em" certainly applies to the world of corporate education.

Conclusion

There are very few corporate universities that can perform all of their functions in-house and do them well. Most choose to specialize in a few areas and employ outside vendors to provide the rest of the services. Jim Moore described in Chapter 2 how Sun Microsystems' SunU outsourced 99 percent of its instruction. Rather than providing expertise in teaching, the core competency of SunU is vendor selection and management.

Other corporate universities have chosen to go a different route. By entering into long-term strategic alliances—with traditional universities, nontraditional universities, distance learning providers, consultants, other corporate universities, or some combination of these—they have succeeded in advancing their mission while securing expertise that was lacking within their organization. So while much of the world may be a lonely place, corporate university management need not be a solitary pursuit—there are plenty of people and organizations out there that are willing not only to sell you their products and services, but also to work with you to help you achieve your goals.

Managing a Corporate University

CHAPTER

6

Best Practices in Corporate Universities

Robert M. Fulmer

Corporations are coming to realize that their most important assets are not equipment, technology, or machines, but rather human capital and the know-how that resides in the minds of their employees. It is not enough to recognize that "people are our most important asset." The "right people at the right place with the right skills" are required if the company is to have a real competitive advantage. Corporate universities are linking employee learning to overall company strategy, and as a result corporate universities are becoming the connective tissue of organizations. At some organizations, corporate learning programs are even beginning to drive the business.

This chapter highlights some organizations that use management and executive development programs to drive their businesses. After an overview of different types of corporate universities, I will present the findings from several research studies I have conducted that focused on management and executive development in a number of best-practice corporate universities.

For years, wise companies have gladly paid for their employees to attend continuing education classes at nearby colleges and universities. Today, while that practice continues to have a place in the corporate university movement, it is even more likely that you will find college-sized educational organizations existing within corporate domains for the purpose of making the organization into a "learning organization."

As Saturn executive Peggy Berger phrased it, "People really are the last true competitive advantage. Everyone knows about fast-to-market, quality, and re-engineering. They no longer provide a competitive advantage, merely entry onto the playing field. Innovation and people are the only edge, and companies that recognize that fact and organize their systems and structures around it will enjoy [success]."[1]

In 1994, Jeanne C. Meister, the publisher of *Corporate University Xchange*, identified thirty companies that shared the common goal of seeing "training as a process of life-long learning rather than a place to get trained."[2] Just two years later, she updated the research and found that almost a thousand firms were involved in the process, and she estimates that today there are over two thousand groups that call themselves "corporate universities." These firms recognize that the prominent players in the twenty-first century will be those who turn a smarter workforce into a dollars-and-cents competitive advantage. They also recognize that investments in education will not provide the desired payback if they are limited to casual and accidental educational programs at nearby colleges and universities. In their commitment to smarter workers as a bottom-line advantage to the company, these companies have organized themselves as learning systems. They have integrated aspects of hiring, training, recognition, and advancement into an educational system that is widely publicized and promoted, and in which participation is high. The resulting individual and collective learning has reinforced the original hypothesis and led to even more extensive financial investment and leadership commitment.

Leading business organizations value their people highly and conceive of corporate education as an investment in human capital that makes their businesses more competitive. In the same way, several of the partners participating in the global best-practices study sponsored by the American Productivity and Quality Center (APQC) and the American Society of Training and Development (ASTD) (1998) indicated that they actively seek to promote from within, thus capitalizing on the depth of experience that already exists within the organization. For example, at Arthur Andersen, the companywide use of an existing knowledge-management system has affected the design and delivery of training, because knowledge and expertise are readily available on its intranet.

The Growth of Corporate Universities

A 1998 benchmarking study conducted by the ASTD found that although the average operating budget for corporate universities had grown to $12.4 million by the mid-1990s, 60 percent of the groups reported budgets of $5 million or less. Of course, the budgets of giants like Motorola, General Electric (GE), and Arthur Andersen significantly increased the average figure. Perhaps more significantly, organizations with corporate universities reportedly spent 2.5 percent of their payroll on learning. This figure is almost twice the national average.[3] One of the first studies of leading corporate universities (those at Motorola, GE, Arthur Andersen, and Apple Computer) discovered that these companies shared similar strategic orientations for their corporate universities. Their common focus was on aggressive growth and continuous innovation.[4]

The differences among these trailblazers of industrial-strength corporate education seemed to be those of emphasis—some emphasized the career development of their employees, whereas others emphasized the addressing of key business issues through corporate education. For example, Arthur Andersen has a carefully designed career ladder, and specified courses are required at each stage in an employee's career. The company's career tracking system maintains an up-to-date record of the educational progress of each of its employees throughout the world. At the other extreme, GE has organized its famous Crotonville educational facility around the assumption that certain educational "moments of opportunity" carry valuable paybacks for individual leadership and organizational performance.

One writer has ventured to define the corporate university as "a function or department that is strategically oriented toward integrating the development of people as individuals with their performance as teams, and ultimately, as an entire organization by linking with suppliers, by conducting wide-ranging research, by facilitating the delivery of content, and by leading the effort to build a superior leadership team."[5]

Corporate Universities' Reasons for Being

The corporate university is a powerful tool for the creation and management of knowledge capital within the organization. When asked to indicate the reasons for the creation of the corporate university, 77 percent of the respondents to the APQC-ASTD screening survey indicated that either knowledge management or the creation of knowledge was a driver.[6] They reported that the creation and management of knowledge drove the development of the corporate university, and that their corporate universities were responsible for knowledge management within the organization to a great extent.

The corporate university is the logical and most effective tool for grounding new hires in the corporate culture. Accountants and consultants at Andersen go to St. Charles to be immersed in the culture of the organization as well as to learn new tools for the next stage of their career. GE's Crotonville is reserved for "A players," those key managers who have high potential and performance and who seem likely to benefit most from this exposure at key "teachable moments." Saturn uses its corporate university to develop leadership at all levels. Saturn people think of their training visits to Spring Hill as pilgrimages to the "Holy Land," taken to become more enlightened about the company. Every new Saturn employee begins his or her indoctrination with a full week at "Saturn ground zero" (in Spring Hill, Tennessee), learning skills and company values. The same is true for car builders, retailers, and suppliers. The result is that Saturn's learning organization gets the first shot at shaping those who will shape the company. Dana University was founded in 1969 to reinforce "the Dana style." Eddie Bauer University teaches the corporate culture in every course it offers to associates in the field. In sum, whether courses are offered at dedicated learning facilities or over the Internet, the corporate university plays a pivotal role in teaching and reinforcing the culture of the company.

Lynn E. Densford[7] has described another critical value of the corporate university. Besides improving business results and spreading the corporate legend, corporate universities help their companies attract and retain top-flight employees. In-house training is one of the biggest carrots in corporate America. *Fortune* magazine's annual listing of the "100 Best Companies to Work for in America" always places a high value on the educational opportunities available through these companies. According to *Fortune*, "extensive and ongoing training and development" is second only to stock options as a primary means of attracting and keeping talented workers.

"The 100 best are making major investments in employee education at multi-million-dollar facilities and through generous reimbursement programs," *Fortune* states. "On average, the 100 best lavished 43 hours of training on each employee in 1998—almost a full day more than last year.

Some companies have begun to advertise these learning labs in their recruitment materials."[8]

Of course, the ability to attract and keep good workers has always been a mark of strength in determining companies' financial standing. Institutional investors naturally gravitate toward companies with stable, skilled workforces.

Approaches to the Corporate University

As corporate universities have evolved, they have taken a variety of forms. Some are far more "corporate" than they are "university." Others are only warmed-over training departments with college course numbers tacked onto the old courses.

For some companies, the *in-name-only formula* works fine. A training department in sheep's clothing can make everybody feel more up-to-date and innovative, without bringing about an undue disturbance of comfortable corporate traditions. The added attention might even result in some new equipment, improved presentation skills, and more interesting classes. But unless the studies are generated by and connected to the corporation's goals and objectives, it is unlikely that dramatic contributions to profitability, strategy, innovation, or competitive advantage are going to accrue.

A far more appropriate and excellent model could be called the *initiative-driven educational program*. This type of corporate university exists to facilitate the accomplishment of a corporatewide initiative, business plan, or project. Motorola University successfully drove the quality initiative throughout Motorola. It was even involved in Motorola's strategic planning and entry into various global markets. Emerging functions of corporate universities now include advances in thinking about globalization, productivity, process improvement, and empowerment.

The *change-management corporate university* concentrates on facilitating major changes and transformations within a company. However, a university with this goal must be prepared to reinvent itself once the desired change has been accomplished. There will always be new idea worlds to conquer and new changes to be managed, but the change-management university must expect to go through a metamorphosis each time the corporate goals or leaders change. As an example, National Semiconductor

University drove a change-leadership program through its company in the mid-1990s and then shifted to a skill-development program.

The *leadership-development corporate university* is best exemplified by GE's Management Development Institute at Crotonville, New York. This institute, which had historically focused on developing managers and leaders for GE, took on new life when CEO Jack Welch made it his tool for orienting and assimilating new managers. Crotonville has driven programs such as Work-Out and the Change Acceleration Process (CAP) and illustrates the principle that the most successful corporate universities have been those with (1) CEO support and (2) a single, clear focus.

A *business-development corporate university* is chartered to help the company develop opportunities and explore possibilities. If an organization is opening international offices, its corporate university can prepare employees; educate them about the new country; do research, recruiting, and development; and generally support the process. Interestingly, these kinds of activities require quite different skills and capabilities from those required by the normal training department.

The *customer/supplier relationship management corporate university* is similar to the business-development university. It focuses on educating and managing employees, leaders, and suppliers about customer and supplier relationships. This is a practice common among manufacturing companies such as Ford and Motorola.

The *competency-based career development corporate university* focuses on individual skill development and the process of career development. This may include developing a performance management system or engaging in career development activities.

Most corporations require the corporate university to provide evaluative metrics to senior managers or to the board of directors. The metrics required are usually different from those used for the evaluation of other business units. Examples of metrics required include percent of payroll, student days, tuition fees, courses delivered, programs conducted, reduction in turnover for those receiving training, increased productivity (pre- and postbehavior assessment), increased skill in managing savings, instructor payroll cost savings, increased sales due to training targeted toward key selling programs, expectation versus proficiency, expectation versus performance, expectation versus importance, and profits versus performance.

The traditional role of corporate training has been a function of the human resource department. The success of corporate universities has demonstrated that the learning experience needs to be kept separate from traditional human resource processes. Many human resource functions focus on credits and annual reviews. In a corporate university, it is important for learning to be the primary focus. The employee should be taking courses to learn and to improve his or her job performance, not simply because of a requirement. The relationship with human resources should not override the corporate university's day-to-day operations.

Most of the learning organizations in the APQC study are funded by their corporations and operate as cost centers. They usually exist either as line items in the corporate budget or are supported through chargebacks to the business units for training services. There are good reasons for each approach. The line-item approach is preferable when business units are likely to decide to spend their money on other things. On the other hand, the chargeback system clearly demonstrates that the business units consider the university's products worth paying for. Saturn University maintains its own budget and funds corporate training. There is no system of charge-backs to the business units. For Saturn, delivery of corporate training is funded centrally.

Benchmarking Management and Executive Development at the Corporate University

Since 1997, the APQC has conducted a series of "best-practice studies" to explore various aspects of the organizational challenge of management and executive development. It was my privilege to serve as the subject matter expert (SME) or study adviser for three of these projects. Much of the material in this chapter is based on these studies. The purpose of APQC's original multiorganization benchmarking study of corporate universities was to identify and examine innovations, best practices, and key trends in the area of corporate learning initiatives and to document the processes involved. The goal was for participants in the study to be able to direct their own training processes more effectively and identify any performance gaps. Saturn was benchmarked again in 1999 as a leader in developing leaders at all levels.

Twenty-nine businesses participated in the APQC study. They coop-erated in the planning, completed surveys, and hosted on-site interviews. Of those twenty-nine organizations, five were identified during the consortium as having strong, innovative corporate universities: Arthur Andersen, Dana, Digital Equipment, Eddie Bauer, and Saturn.

To evaluate the design of each corporate university's learning process, the project team looked for (1) alignment of the curriculum with business needs, (2) application to international audiences, and (3) clear definition of boundaries, degrees, and credits.

Measures of actual delivery of the universities' promised products included whether they were (1) using traditional or nontraditional methods, (2) using technology to reach their audiences, and (3) partnering with local resource providers.

We viewed corporate universities as having lasting organizational structures if they were systematically developing (1) their university infrastructures and (2) their relationships with their corporations.

Some of the principal findings of the research are as follows:

1. *The corporate university's influence on the corporation.* Best-practice corporate learning systems should extend beyond the narrow concept of the corporate university and dovetail smoothly with the mission, values, and culture of the organization. They consciously and constantly involve business units in all aspects of the learning process. A critical component of this involvement must come from above—there must be a strong commitment on the part of senior management to the development and education of the workforce. A core philosophy of learning is a theory of knowledge acquisition that drives course design and delivery, as well as interaction with business units. The core philosophy of learning is usually synonymous with, or closely aligned to, the mission of the corporate university.

2. *The corporate university's structure and organization.* Obviously, the entire corporate structure cannot and does not adjust itself to the ideal scenario for the corporate university. The university must fit within the corporate chart and still be able to reach its highest potential. The organization's business strategy not only drives the structure of the leading corporate universities, but also is the reason that those universities exist. On the other hand, most of the outstanding corporate universities were freed long ago from the restrictive domain of human resources and were given the authority, responsibility, and respect of functioning as separate and productive cost centers.

3. *The corporate university's learning processes.* Outstanding corporate universities do not follow a universal process map when they design their systems and the approaches to their learning interventions. More often, they determine their training goals and the related requirements only after identifying and focusing on expected outcomes. In short, they make the teaching technique fit the learning challenge. They rarely make blind rushes toward the latest educational technologies. While they are not uninformed about or opposed to technology, they utilize automated training devices only when those devices uniquely facilitate the training process. Saturn's People Development mission is simply stated: to provide world-class programs and tools that support development of the skills people need to successfully achieve Saturn's mission and business strategies, and also support the realization of individual career fulfillment and personal growth.

4. *The corporate university's management of information.* If any truism perfectly characterizes the corporate university, it is "knowledge is power." The corporate university is a powerful tool for the creation and management of knowledge capital within the organization. Benchmarking frequently rises to the top in searches for techniques for managing knowledge and information.

When asked how his organization defines a corporate university, an Arthur Andersen representative replied, "We don't." This statement represents the wisdom of the corporate university's ignoring existing corporate university models and creating a one-of-a-kind organization that reflects and reinforces the culture, mission, and values of its company. Leadership corporate universities define themselves clearly and go as directly to the achievement of their goals as possible.

Support From the Top

One of the most important keys to the success of a corporate university is the strong commitment of senior management. In some of the more successful universities, the education effort has been driven by senior managers who understand the long-term value of shaping an organization by constant communication and education. In others, management has supplied strong

115

financial support. The fact that the financial support has continued even during economic downturns is further proof that these managers recognize that the corporate university is no budget frill.

The organization's business strategy almost always determines the structure of that organization's corporate university. The corporation, not the university, establishes the organizational hierarchy. This enables the company to perform educational needs analyses and facilitate the implementation of the strategy. The corporate university can then ensure that the workforce has the necessary skills and knowledge to accomplish the identified tasks. It is clear that what drives the continued support of corporate learning is a corporate-culture commitment to the development of people.

How They Develop Their Training

One of the most interesting observations that have been made by people who have studied the corporate university movement is that corporate universities must take care not to become too much like regular universities! Unfortunately, some companies do nothing more than create neat logos and sweatshirts for their reengineered training departments and label all their training courses as "101s." But the bottom line is that they make no fundamental changes in their approaches to the training and development of their employees.

Everyone who has ever attended a traditional university is aware of the ivory-tower syndrome and the tendency toward territorial protectiveness through entrenched tradition. Colleges have not typically been viewed as the most flexible, progressive, or change-oriented of institutions. This is illustrated by the claim that, in the time of Orville and Wilbur Wright, there were college courses being taught in aeronautical engineering that concentrated primarily on explaining why a heavier-than-air machine could never fly. The innovation of flight had to come from two bicycle mechanics who had not taken such courses.

While colleges and universities continue their struggle to break their tradition-kills-innovation reputation, corporate universities know that their activities must continually prove themselves in view of their companies' bottom-line objectives. A corporate university must be monitored, flexible, and focused on the strategic imperatives of its sponsoring organization. To add real value, a corporate university must become a generator of learning and innovation; it must never be a stodgy, academic repository of dead information to be parroted.

There appears to be no standard approach or process for designing learning interventions. Corporate universities have to maintain the flexibility to adapt to the changing demands of their business environments. Every university has its own methodology. The design process, whether what is being designed is discrete courses or entire learning programs, is thought by many to be the scientific part of the learning process within the corporate university. From needs analysis, to course design and development, to the eventual delivery, each corporate university remains distinct.

Benchmarking is a key driver in the creation and innovation of the corporate university. Benchmarking has become a widely used practice within most corporations, especially in the creation or re-creation of new products or processes. Learning best practices from others has not been lost in the corporate university world, either. Following the Motorola credo of "stealing shamelessly," leading corporate universities use benchmarking as an initial step before implementing their own practices. Whether it be for designing courses or for designing the corporate university itself, benchmarking has proved to be a valuable tool for beginning the change process. The corporate learning community even welcomes other corporations to benchmark, realizing that it has the potential to learn from them as well.

Executives Teaching Managers?

Since corporate universities do not offer tenure, many keep their full-time staffs to a minimum and gain double value by using part-time or short-term teachers from throughout the company. By recruiting from within the organization or using executives as facilitators or teachers, they (1) capitalize on these employees' unmatched experience to upgrade the educational offerings and (2) build increased commitment to the corporate university itself as former teachers return to work in all parts of the company.

Using Educational Technology

Saturn offers 800 courses and delivers more than 10,000 classes, for a total of more than a million training hours a year. The company utilizes several training facilities for the delivery of training. The Northfield facility has sixteen classrooms, four computer labs, two computer-ready technical labs, a conference center and theater, a distance-learning facility, a robotics lab, a video editing suite, and a workplace development center. In addition, the manufacturing facility at Spring Hill has twenty-four classrooms for car-building classes and 180 "team centers" where teams of car builders can meet. Saturn also has several other facilities for specific training needs and in addition utilizes space at General Motors and rents space when necessary.

In most corporate universities, the use of technological teaching devices begins only after a close examination of the business process itself. It is rare to see a thoughtless, automatic rush to use the latest forms of media for training. For example, Saturn stores all individual training plans in a huge database. This database, which was designed by Electronic Data Systems (EDS) and Saturn, keeps track of all 8,200 team members' annual requirement of 92 hours of training. Saturn uses the database to follow how many hours and what kind of training each team member has received and how close each team member is to his or her goal. The database also shows whether there are enough teachers, classroom space, and registration for each class.

In 2001, Dow reported a externally developed online learning and training program through which more than 600 courses were offered online. In one week, Dow employees completed 14,000 courses. Examples of training courses that were available on-site include safety training, an executive-required course on respect and responsibility training, and compensation planning tools. Dow currently has sixty tools and classes available online in its internal development program.

One effect of technology has been the rapid pace with which it enables change in business today. The changes affect not only the products or services provided by a corporation, but also the way in which the corporation is organized. As this is recognized throughout the corporation, it is mirrored in the infrastructure and delivery of the learning within the corporate university.

Much has been said about on-line registration for courses and the cost savings associated with distance learning. Most corporate universities realize the need to implement new applications, but, so far, they have resisted the urge to simply replicate the current way of doing business and automate it. Instead, leading corporate universities have opted to closely examine the learning process itself and make use of new technologies only when they make sense. These corporate universities have discovered that (1) using an intranet and new software applications will increase the visibility of the corporate university's offerings, and (2) distance learning forces a reevaluation of the learning process and can change not only the delivery of the learning intervention, but the design as well.

Using an intranet for course catalogs and employee registration holds a great deal of interest and value for all corporate universities, especially as virtual offices and telecommuting become more popular. Most corporate universities have moved to on-line course catalogs and will be making the shift to allowing on-line registration in the near future. With the implementation of new technology, trail-blazing organizations have been able to better market their programs and meet the needs of their employees.

While the movement to implement new technology within the corporate university infrastructure has taken off, the implementation on the delivery side has been much slower. The most popular method of delivery remains the classroom.

Many corporate university leaders admit that some form of distance learning will eventually dominate their delivery of learning experiences. However, initial resistance to this new technology remains strong. Employees feel more comfortable in a classroom setting. To overcome this resistance and to add more social interaction to distance-learning approaches, some corporate universities are busy improving the interaction of their distance-learning offerings.

Measuring Results

Staying in touch with customers is essential for any business. Many corporate universities are able to provide educational activities that help business units better understand their customers and bring those customers innovative and targeted service. The universities involve the company's business units in tailored learning experiences related to design, delivery, and other critical processes. The benefits of this specially designed training accrue in two directions: The business units discover the answers and new strategies that they need, and the corporate university staff becomes more conversant with the overall business and more meaningfully centered on the customer-first philosophy that needs to be a part of all of its courses.

If a corporate university cannot be justified in terms of the business and cannot forecast an improvement in the bottom line of the business (over the status quo), there probably should not be a corporate university.

Summary

The corporate university represents business leadership's growing commitment to continuous learning as a source of competitive advantage. Corporate universities are linking employee learning to overall company strategy, and as a result corporate universities are becoming the connective tissue of organizations. Corporate learning programs are even beginning to drive businesses.

While some corporate universities are little more than old-time training departments with new stationery, the establishment of a corporate university often does indicate an increased commitment to developing managers and executives. Organizations with corporate universities reported spending 2.5 percent of their payroll on learning. This figure is almost twice the national average.

The corporate university is the logical and most effective tool for grounding new hires in the corporate culture. It is also a natural for the regular reminding and re-energizing needed by other employees. Most important, graduates of these universities should be uniquely qualified to assume key roles in the ranks of managers and executives in their alma mater's corporation. The ability to attract and keep leaders has always been a mark of strength in determining companies' financial standing. Institutional investors naturally gravitate toward companies with stable, skilled workforces. Corporate universities are helping firms win the war for talent.

CHAPTER

7

The Corporate University Training Function

Linda H. Lewis

Traditional, more parochial notions of training are often reflected in metaphors that fail to recognize the strategic and competitive advantages of training and the complexity of development. One of these metaphors is "sheep dipping"; the implication is that, after being bathed in the same training curriculum, all employees will emerge replete with the skills, knowledge, and abilities that they require for success. Another metaphor, likening the training experience to a car wash, is an even more simplistic view of the training process: Just run those who need spit and polish through the line, and they'll come out bright and shiny on the other end!

Fortunately, a more sophisticated understanding of training and development has developed over time. Companies and their workforces have become acutely aware that training is neither a one-time event nor a one-size-fits-all approach, but rather a continual process of stimulating, reinforcing, and leveraging learning. Those who lead and manage others are partners with training professionals in the training process, assessing employee needs and collaborating to identify relevant learning opportunities for individuals and work groups.

Why Training?

Today's learners are discriminating consumers and are not just learning for the sake of learning. Employees engage in training because they need to enhance their skill sets, obtain certifications, learn something new to keep pace with changing times, or fill competency gaps. If they fail to do so, their promotions or bonuses may be in jeopardy. In corporate America's fast-paced business environment, employees must not only focus on critical priorities, but also engage in ongoing professional development to ensure their currency, competence, effectiveness and, ultimately, their success.

Corporate universities play a pivotal role in assuring workforce readiness by offering a wide range of learning opportunities. However, training is only one aspect of a complex educational process. Training facilitates the development of specific skills; education improves individuals' ability to think and challenges them intellectually. While training is the catch-all term that is most commonly associated with corporate universities, both training and education should coexist in every learning venue. In order to maximize outcomes and promote the transfer of learning, individuals must not only acquire new skills, but also be able to make critical judgments about how to apply and modify their newfound knowledge and integrate it into their day-to-day work.

Strategic Value of Corporate Universities

Dynamic corporate training strategies that assist the workforce in anticipating and proactively managing change, maintaining equilibrium, and adjusting and readjusting to ever-increasing demands are essential. As organizations continue to evolve and reinvent themselves through mergers, acquisitions, divestitures, and new products, there is a concomitant need to realign individuals' capabilities with the organization at large. The value-added of quality training and the potential losses that can occur as a consequence of inadequate training cannot be ignored. Research suggests that when training is well aligned with business needs, it becomes a strategic advantage for the company. Data from the American Society for Training & Development (ASTD) indicate that U.S. companies that spend more on training per employee outperform the market.[1] Specifically, firms that invest $1,595 per employee on training experienced 24 percent higher gross profit margins, a 218 percent higher income per employee, and a 26 percent higher price-to-book ratio.[2]

While companies that fund corporate universities may have different mental models guiding their willingness to invest in employee development, they can no longer afford to view training an as entitlement. Employers expect that there will be a return on investing in individuals' growth and that the company's sponsorship of workplace learning will not only enhance productivity and competence, but also contribute to increased employee satisfaction and commitment.[3] The attributes of companies that employees value most lead to the highest levels of employee satisfaction. Research by the Corporate Leadership Council indicates that development reputation, or the extent to which managers or companies invest in the development of employees, bears a significant relationship to employee satisfaction.[4] In addition, employee satisfaction with the company's opportunity for development has the strongest negative correlation with intention to leave an organization.[5] These data highlight the contribution of corporate training and development to increasing employee satisfaction, commitment, and retention, all of which are critical to high performance and organization success.

One way to determine the relevance or potential value of training is to question whether the corporate business strategy requires it. Although corporate strategy by itself doesn't identify the need for training, it does translate into business plans. Such plans help training professionals determine what strengths and competencies employees need (and by when), so that their staff can develop appropriate training to enhance the ability of the workforce to achieve business goals. To be effective in their roles, corporate university training staff must be not only technically proficient in their functional area, but also savvy partners who are well versed in the business. They must be able to demonstrate measurable results to management and accept responsibility for improving human performance on the job.

Training environments are invaluable communication venues, helping employees understand the company's direction, strategic imperatives, and vision. Once employees "get it," they are better able to align their individual objectives with corporate goals, prioritize their work appropriately, and focus on the critical few things that provide the highest value.

What employees need to learn, above and beyond their current assignments, depends in large part on what companies want them to contribute. Most top-tier firms expect the workforce to innovate, to make recommendations, and to execute on approaches that contribute to organizational success. Companies that understand the strategic advantage of training are often firms whose CEO has a personal commitment to workplace learning and is a champion of the corporate university. A CEO's leadership can provide great leverage for integrating training into the company's strategic goals. When training has a true sponsor at the top, support cascades more readily throughout the organization, enabling training leadership to have a seat at the business roundtable and to be a partner in decision making. Although having CEO sponsorship is the ideal scenario, it is not uncommon for training support to erode if the senior-most champion leaves. Thus, in order to realize a sustained commitment, training must be institutionalized—built into the very fabric of the organization through an infrastructure. A necessary first step to making the function integral to an organization's long-term success is thinking of training as a strategic lever rather than nice-to-have—as an investment in the future rather than a cost.

Leveraging Training

The conventional wisdom is that the training experience itself is the most critical element in developing individuals' skills, knowledge, or abilities. In point of fact, the training event makes only a minor contribution to overall training results. What occurs *before* and *after* the actual training is key to realizing the total value of any learning opportunity. In order to train for impact and reap value-added training outcomes, significant attention must be focused on interactions between manager and employee pre- and post-training. In addition, there are critical roles for training professionals in this same before-and-after period in order to maximize the value of training. Figure 7-1 illustrates the critical leverage points for attaining optimal training results.

Think back to your own training experiences to test the assumption reflected in the graphic. As an employee, were you ever told that you were to attend a class, but you had no idea what the program was about or how it would benefit you? Have you encountered colleagues in training sessions who could neither tell you the purpose of the training nor articulate what they hoped to learn when queried by the facilitator? When such scenarios occur, it is unlikely that pretraining development discussions took place

Figure 7–1. Leveraging the value of training.

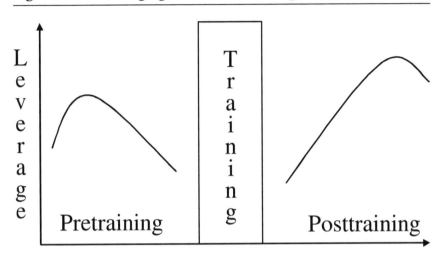

between manager and employee, and equally unlikely that the two collaborated in selecting a particular development option.

Pretraining Partnership Between Manager and Employee

Prior to determining if a training solution is appropriate, managers should actively engage with employees to assess their current competencies and determine competency gaps. Such discussions may be part of a performance management and development planning process or simply an observation that changing business requirements will require new skills. Whatever the impetus, the joint understanding of the development need, complemented by an agreed-on approach for closing the competency gaps, is a critical initial step in the training and development process. After this, the next step is to identify the most appropriate learning opportunities to meet individual needs.

Using the term *learning opportunity* as opposed to *training* can expand the way managers and employees think about alternative approaches to closing skill gaps. On-the-job training, classroom-based programs, rotational assignments, shadowing, desktop learning, mentoring, and coaching are just a few possibilities to explore before opting for a particular training approach. A far cry from "sheep-dipping" notions, the optimal scenario occurs when manager and employee explore an array of opportunities together, while always keeping the learning objective at the forefront. For example, depending on the competency gap, training for an aspiring human resources generalist might include shadowing a highly skilled senior generalist on the job, followed by individual coaching. However, for an experienced generalist, immersion in new employment law guidelines may be just the right targeted approach. In either case, the potential efficacy of training is predicated in large part on the initial discussions between manager and employee to explore alternatives and select the best one(s) to meet identified needs.

To reinforce the importance of pretraining discussions, companies often implement protocols to spark joint participation in development decisions. For example, in some companies, employees can't sign up for training without manager approval or sign-off. In my current organization, Charles Schwab & Co., Inc., once there is agreement that training is appropriate, managers receive e-mails from Schwab University letting them know when their employees are enrolled in a specific course or program. The communiqué, which is also sent to the employee, includes a description of the upcoming training as well as the proposed goals and objectives. Receiving this message helps to ensure that both manager and employee are clear about the purpose of the training and the hoped-for outcomes.

Posttraining Engagement with Direct Reports

Equally as important as pretraining assessment and planning are the follow-up conversations between manager and employee posttraining. Once again, e-mails automatically generated from a corporate university mailbox can be a great vehicle for stimulating discussions. For example, following the training, managers may receive an on-line synopsis of what transpired in the program, along with a list of recommended questions they can ask their employees when debriefing the experience. This posttraining juncture is a teachable moment, when manager and direct report discuss the application of newly acquired skills in the workplace.

Although in corporate universities the spotlight is often on trainers and learning facilitators, the pivotal role played by managers in the training process cannot be underestimated. Managers are in a unique position to reinforce, recognize, and reward accomplishments and successes that are a result of successful learning experiences. As coaches, mentors, feedback givers, and motivators, managers are invaluable business partners who collaborate with training professionals to enhance learning outcomes.

Pre- and Posttraining Roles for Training Professionals

Many people think of corporate trainers as individuals who are skilled in the art of "standing up and delivering" training. However, today's training professionals possess much broader skill sets. Before delivering training, they conduct root cause analyses and needs assessments. Rather than developing and delivering a standardized curriculum, they frequently collaborate with line managers and HR professionals to create just-in-time training venues, tailor offerings to business-specific needs, and design hands-on experiences.

Following training, the facilitators provide feedback to both manager and employee and explore additional ways to embed the learning into the way they do the job. For example, a corporate university facilitator who conducted a training program for new managers may subsequently collaborate with a well-respected line manager to design follow-up brown-bag sessions. How did the theories and models presented in core management training play out in actual practice? What land mines have you discovered, and how are you responding? As a new manager, what are the issues you're grappling with and want to talk through? Such a just-in-time approach in the posttraining stage not only taps the creativity and competence of training professionals and their management colleagues but, even more important, helps learning to take hold. When this happens, the training is truly leveraged and value realized!

Corporate University Training Venues

There are many different training venues common to both large corporations and small companies. Historically, corporate universities offered the workforce a cafeteria menu of training programs. This approach still exists in many organizations today, although printed course catalogs have been replaced by disk and Internet access. Training curricula, often defined as offerings appropriate to one's role, title, or level in the organization, are targeted to specific constituencies. While some courses are available to the entire employee base, most are tied to the core competencies associated with particular positions or levels of experience (e.g., team leader, first-time manager, or experienced manager). Although the training curriculum in best-practice corporate universities is becoming increasingly smaller and more focused on business issues, several generic categories of training prevail. The most common are:

- ❏ Executive education
- ❏ Management development
- ❏ Personal and professional development
- ❏ Technical training
- ❏ Special initiatives

By purveying training opportunities across different companies, one can develop an intuition as to where the emphasis is being placed (who's being trained), where training dollars are being directed (internally/externally), and what kind of training is a priority. Each of the following categories of training fulfills a need and reflects the unique aspects of the company's culture and training philosophy.

Executive Education

Executive development is a strategic tool for bettering business. Those individuals who have achieved executive status in corporations have already benefited from a variety of learning experiences throughout the course of their careers, including mentors who served as guides along the way. While many participated in external executive programs at top-tier schools as they moved through the managerial ranks, companies are increasingly customizing executive education through consultants, universities, online tools, and internal programs.[6]

Although the use of external programs is still a common approach to executive development, the trend in those corporations with the most highly lauded executive development programs is to build those programs internally.[7] Companies typically have a highly experienced executive education professional or team dedicated to developing senior leaders (the top 300). Common internal arrangements include specialized programs that are tailored to executives' needs. These customized sessions run the gamut from roundtable dialogues with world-class consultants to programs that deepen leaders' understanding of leadership.

Corporate universities striving for "best in class" performance of this type must address the challenge of executive education on three levels:

development of individual leaders, socialization to the company's vision and values, and integration of strategic leadership initiatives into learning experiences. At Charles Schwab and Co., Inc., the corporate university plays a key role in managing executive leadership development. By translating *Clicks & Mortar: Passion Driven Growth in an Internet Driven World* (a book co-authored by the company's co-CEO) into a three-day development experience for intact senior executive teams, Schwab's corporate university addresses all three levels of executive leadership development. Individual leaders receive real-time feedback on their strengths and development needs within the context of Schwab's culture; executive teams understand how they are doing individually and collectively at growing and enhancing the culture; and both individual executives and the senior team explore how they can better align business processes and systems with the firm's culture.

Schwab's Passion Driven Leadership program seeks to expand and grow the effectiveness of individual leaders at the same time that it enhances the effectiveness and performance of the firm. This example illustrates how partnerships between corporate university staff and senior leaders can be leveraged to create a strong foundation for growing and aligning the company's talent "portfolio."[8]

Depending on the issues the business is facing, educational opportunities may focus on business strategy, building shareholder value, motivating and inspiring the workforce, communicating during difficult times, and team leadership. In addition, the internationalization of the business community has increased the focus on globalization. As a consequence, executive education often has a global focus, equipping individuals with the tools they need to realize business results. Although almost all executive development occurs in response to specific, individual needs, there are sometimes corporatewide educational opportunities in which all top-level executives engage. The intent in leveraging joint learning opportunities is to create a shared mindset, develop a common language, and ensure a certain level of expertise at the executive level.

Whether internal or external, the success of executive programs has a lot to do with the ability of participants to network, commiserate with colleagues in similar roles, and talk about issues to which only those at the top are privy. Because of its unique nature, executive learning is most often measured subjectively rather than in terms of transference of skills to the workplace.

Management Development

Managerial training is prevalent across corporate America. As individuals move beyond their technical expertise and assume managerial roles, they need training in decision making, team building, strategic planning, business ethics, and managerial leadership. Many companies have an established corporate university curriculum designed to support individuals at different stages in their management careers. However, in recent years, there has been a move away from a required curriculum to a focus on competency gaps. Exceptions to this trend are first-time or entry-level managers, for whom a core set of offerings is usually recommended.

One of the more challenging aspects of management development is helping managers become more facile at managing the "harder softer" stuff! Most recently, corporate university staff in my organization launched a massive companywide education and training effort to equip managers to lead and manage change more effectively. Having experienced economic downturns, precipitous stock market declines, terrorist attacks, and downsizing in a short, six-month span, managers realized the need to develop additional expertise and competence to lead their teams through change. What could they do to help employees gain focus, reduce stress, and remain productive while navigating in white water? In partnership with HR professionals, organization effectiveness and organization development staff from Schwab University designed and deployed tools, developed job aids, and facilitated customized interventions and "Adapting to Change" programs. As a result, managers with little previous experience in change and transition developed significant bench strength and new competencies, closing skill gaps in areas not previously explored.

Corporate universities frequently utilize internal staff to facilitate management development programs and learning opportunities. Although many programs are developed in-house, companies also purchase vendor-developed curricula and tailor their content to the company's core management competencies.

Based on a manager's level of experience or current skill levels, additional training may be appropriate in such areas as interpersonal skills, organizational development, conflict resolution, and the like. Training is enhanced by the use of role-plays, simulations, and case studies, all of which facilitate applied learning. Virtual technologies also exist, enabling managers to obtain degrees and certifications online or at a distance. Yet despite the plethora of available technologies, ASTD's State of the Industry Report indicates that the majority of companies use classroom-based training.[9] The excitement about e-learning has not increased the utilization of new technologies as rapidly as was projected, mainly because of difficulties with and obstacles to implementation.[10]

One of the most exciting innovations in both management and leadership education is action learning—a form of on-the-job learning that enables individuals to develop strategies to address business problems. The process is designed to directly transfer learning to the work environment and enables participants to spend less time in training and more time performing their jobs.

Action learning programs most frequently focus on "high potentials" and are sponsored by senior line management. Learning is reality based, involving actual data and real work as teams collaborate to solve actual business challenges. In an action learning environment, trainers don't design programs—participants do. Training professionals serve as coaches and facilitators, providing just-in-time learning opportunities to support problem solving, team building, communications, decision making, etc. Learning experiences encourage involvement, inquiry, critical thinking, experimentation, and practice as part of a discovery approach. The methodology allows team members to experiment with new ideas in their workplaces through a process that provides support, resources, and networking. Acquired knowledge and skills are put to work both during the program and back on the job. Vastly different from classroom-based offerings, action learning has come to be viewed by leading companies as a proven technology for organization learning and change.

Personal and Professional Development

In contrast to a core curriculum that is recommended for everyone, professional development opportunities are specific to individual needs. Personal and professional skills training is a way to close individual skill gaps, maintain currency, or enhance individual capabilities, enabling employees to continue to grow and learn. Those who are interested in career growth often expand their repertoire by participating in continuing professional education programs in such areas as time management, project management, and presentation and communication skills to increase their competence.

This category of training is often outsourced, and vendor delivery is commonplace. Master agreements, rights-to-print, and group pricing enable companies to respond quickly to the more generic, transferable needs commonly associated with personal or professional development. The utilization of external consultants and vendors allows corporate university staff to focus on facilitating the critical few professional development programs that incorporate unique aspects of the firm's culture or require a comprehensive understanding of the organization. Additional offerings that are identified as needs across the entire organization may also be taught by internal staff, especially if business-specific knowledge is necessary or if vendor costs are excessive.

Technical Training

For the most part, technical knowledge is a requirement for technical professionals to qualify for their positions. While four-year colleges and universities and trade, technical, and vocational schools provide baseline skills for entry into corporate roles, in order to keep pace with technological advances, individuals must continue to upgrade their skills, maintain their certifications, and obtain additional credentials. Except in situations where upskilling requires a protracted commitment to training before an employee is able to achieve the required level of competence, it is not only economical but good business to upgrade and enhance employees' technical skills.

Each year companies invest a significant portion of their training dollars in technical/functional training that is specific to the unique needs of line organizations, strategic business units, and individual enterprises. More frequently than not, technical training rests outside the purview of the corporate university, remaining a line, business, or enterprise-specific accountability. For example, many companies offer extensive training to information technology (IT) professionals, who must perform faster and with higher quality and greater precision than ever before. According to ASTD benchmark data reflecting U.S. training expenditures, training investment leaders spend a significantly higher percentage of their training budgets on technical processes and procedures and on information technology. In 1999, companies spent a lower percentage of their training dollars on almost all other types of training.[11]

As workplace technologies continue to evolve, and as U.S. businesses compete on the international stage, companies are becoming more aggressive in linking their technical requirements with corporate strategic goals. Managers in areas such as information technology must carefully evaluate organization requirements so that technical training can be structured to meet companywide needs as well as the needs of specific target populations within the organization.

Special Initiatives

As business priorities shift, so does the training agenda. Senior leadership decisions, regulatory requirements, and performance metrics are examples of what can precipitate the launch of a special initiative. On the other hand, a firm may simply want to make its commitment to a particular issue, value, or constituency highly visible, capitalizing on the capabilities resident within the corporate university to do so. For example, my firm, committed to enhancing work force development, implemented a corporatewide mentoring program to help accelerate career growth. As part of a mentoring initiative, the corporate university holds mentoring information sessions to describe the program and eligibility criteria, ultimately identifying and making meaningful matches between more experienced senior professionals (mentors) and individuals seeking specific guidance and coaching (mentees). In addition, an internal mentoring Web site that includes tools, articles, and suggestions for developing mentoring relationships broadens the corporate university's reach to stimulate interest beyond the formal program to informal and group mentoring opportunities. Given the significant numbers of program participants, mentoring is quickly evolving from an initiative to a practice that's institutionalized throughout the company.

Clearly, some company initiatives are short lived ("flavors of the month"), whereas others are sustained over long periods of time. Performance management is one that frequently emerges strongly before or after a downsizing, often because the existing performance ratings were seen as not being consistently valid for use as a basis for making layoff decisions. As a consequence, training on how to set goals and objectives, give feedback, provide coaching, and evaluate performance becomes a priority; however, momentum may fade once the workforce becomes more proficient and performance management processes are evident in day-to-day practice.

Special initiatives are often accompanied by the need to ramp up quickly in response to an urgent need. In some instances, there is a window of opportunity to plan and prepare, while at other times, the need is immediate. Teamwork and collaboration are essential on high-priority initiatives, making cross-functional, cross-organization participation imperative.

The most concentrated example of the use of teamwork to carry off an almost impossible challenge that I've experienced was VisionQuest—the simultaneous engagement of an entire workforce at Charles Schwab.[12] What started out as a team-building and strategy design activity with senior management grew into a day-long event requiring 1,421 certified facilitators, trained and guided by a twenty-member core team. On a single Saturday, 13,000 employees in ten locations worldwide came together, both in person and through a live satellite network, and aligned around the firm's vision, values, and strategy. This multimillion-dollar event, facilitated by the firm's co-CEOs, remains one of the proudest moments in the company's history and helped to mobilize an entire corporation. Although the corporate university spearheaded the undertaking, its successful execution required the combined talent and energy of managers, HR staff, and senior leaders. The event not only re-enrolled thousands of current employees, but also served as a powerful vehicle for orienting more than five thousand new employees to the culture. What better example of leveraging the training function could there be than this!

Supplemental Tools and Technology

No matter who the target audience is or what the category of training may be, learning is supplemented, supported, and reinforced by a wide variety of tools, technologies, and job aids. On-line computer-based training, Web sites, cable and interactive TV, CD-ROMs, company intranets, and e-books are all examples of multichannel vehicles. Iterative messages, reinforced through such multiple delivery mechanisms, make it possible for "anywhere-anytime" learning to occur. In 2000, on average, benchmark firms delivered 8.5 percent of training via learning technology, and subsequent estimates projected that more than 19 percent of training would be leveraged through this medium.[13]

While many organizations are exploring the notion of e-universities, experience suggests that exclusive reliance on any one learning modality is unwise. The key to successful corporate universities rests in the ability to offer a multiplicity of venues and approaches, making it possible for individuals to capitalize on their preferred learning style as well as stretch beyond their comfort zones and experiment with alternative delivery channels.

Training Considerations

The way in which training is organized, funded, and delivered through a corporate university varies from company to company. While successful training outcomes can be achieved through very different approaches, it is important to understand the potential upsides and downsides of various alternatives.

The following is an overview of the critical choices that organizations make when they create a training function within a corporate university and decide how to organize, deliver, and fund that training.

Training Delivery

In the days when corporations had the luxury of discretionary spending and believed that functional training specialists were best equipped to deliver training, large, in-house training organizations thrived. Consisting primarily of individuals with backgrounds in adult learning, education, training, and organization development, many corporate universities hired skilled training professionals to design and deliver programs. This approach contrasts with the very early days of corporate universities, when it was common to find line managers doing the training because the pipeline for producing skilled training professionals was still being built. Today, training delivery mechanisms reflect an eclectic mix of each.

Who should do the training? In point of fact, many managers are well suited to the role because they have real-world experience. When they teach management development courses, they are credible and are able to use their own stories and experiences to motivate others and to bring the models they are discussing to life. Training professionals who are skilled in andragogy (the art and science of helping adults to learn) bring a different type of expertise to the table. Trainers may have to work to establish their credibility if they have never managed; however, managers who are re-cruited to train may be weak in content or lack presentation and facilitation skills.

In the final analysis, anyone who facilitates others' learning is both a teacher and a learner at the same time. For managers, conducting training is a time to learn and grow. As they refine content, describe best practices, and share lessons learned, they have a rare opportunity to refine their own practice. Experience suggests that, when they learn by doing, managers can become good facilitators rather quickly. They develop proficiency by observing exemplary trainers who serve as role models and coaches. In the same way, trainers also grow, develop business acumen, and add invaluable case examples to their repertoire as a result of co-facilitating with managers. Thus, pairing the two can produce dramatic results.

Time is the biggest factor constraining managers, as well as line and

135

HR staff, from taking on training assignments. Even volunteers who are anxious to contribute to the training agenda may be able to train only intermittently because of the demands of their full-time roles. Since corporate universities are seen as centers of excellence, it is important to have a sufficient number of experienced training professionals. Additional training capacity and bench strength can be increased by developing a cadre of adjunct faculty. Using a train-the-trainer approach (commonly referred to as T3), individuals can become proficient with the content and deliver a variety of training programs according to an agreed-on schedule.

Most T3 programs put would-be trainers through a rigorous certification process. Aspiring adjunct trainers must learn the curriculum and demonstrate their ability to deliver the material in a manner consistent with the intent of the program. However, a common shortcoming of T3 programs is that corporate universities sometimes fail to reevaluate trainers after a period of time. Quality control and ongoing adjunct faculty assessments are important to ensure that the strategic intent of the offering is preserved and that curriculum content and delivery methods haven't shifted to reflect individual agendas.

Internal staff, external vendors, training firms, and consultants can conduct T3 certifications as well as serve as adjunct members of the training function. Decisions as to when, how, or whom to tap depend largely on answers to the following:

❑ Are unique skills sets and special expertise required to train on a particular topic? If so, are such skills and experience currently resident in the organization?

❑ Does the time required for internal staff to design the training argue for another approach?

❑ Will time-to-market take so long that the lost opportunity costs are too great to rely solely on internal staff?

❑ Is the training especially complex or unique to the company (e.g., does it require the utmost understanding of the organization and its culture and requirements), so that tapping external resources is inappropriate?

❑ Does the topic or material require the credibility of a seasoned professional, experienced in consulting with other leading-edge firms, who can bring an external perspective to bear?

❑ Is it more appropriate to utilize internal staff or external resources as facilitators if the content is sensitive or confidential?

Ultimately, whoever delivers training is a partner in the training process. Whether the providers are internal or external, they must collaborate to design, position, deliver, and evaluate training.

Training Structure

In training circles folks talk about the upsides and downsides of an organization's training structure, be it centralized, decentralized, or a combined approach. After many years leading corporate universities, I have seen the pendulum shift from one extreme to the other depending on the corporate culture, the current business climate, the seated CEO, and the sway of consultants recommending organization redesign. The following descriptions highlight the pros and cons of various organization designs and their unique characteristics.

Centralized Training. Centralized training, most frequently located in company headquarters, brings all the critical pieces of a training organization together, usually under a corporate university umbrella. The rationale for creating a centralized corporate university is grounded in the company's desire to facilitate a standardized approach to learning across the entire organization, promoting consistency of content and ensuring that similar learning experiences are available to everyone regardless of enterprise or business unit. Be it orientation for new employees, core skills for managers, or communication of the firm's strategic priorities, centralized structures facilitate the development of a common language and shared experiences companywide. In turn, individuals develop competencies that are transferable across all lines of business.

One of the primary benefits of centralization is cost-efficiency, which is achieved by negotiating volume discounts, avoiding duplication of effort, and eliminating redundancies. Master agreements with vendors make it possible to realize cost savings and to obtain special add-ons, including rights-to-print and permission to tailor vendor-developed materials.

While cost-efficiency and economies of scale are prime considerations, the biggest advantage to having a corporate university is that it fosters the transfer of best practices and facilitates organizationwide sharing of lessons learned. It also enables the training entity to function more like a consulting firm (i.e., to use knowledge management systems to leverage previous work and existing curricula so as to avoid reinventing wheels). In addition, a centralized structure allows the entire organization to share common systems that support training, such as enrollment and scheduling programs, employee training histories, course completion reports, development plans, etc. Rather than making multiple investments in technology solutions in different business units, common platforms and backroom functions can be leveraged to advantage. Repetitive, volume-driven processes, such as shipping materials, distributing prework, and collating evaluative data, can all be managed through a central source. Whether the organization decides to outsource administrative components or to utilize internal staff to provide support services, centralized training functions are most frequently responsible for training design, delivery, vendor contracts, training metrics, technology enhancements, and quality controls.

Another advantage of centralization is the ability to make better use of time—one of the most precious commodities in corporate America. For example, appearances by corporate executives in classes or on videos are important vehicles for engaging, aligning, and motivating the workforce. Being able to garner leaders' time is a feat in and of itself, but it is more easily accomplished when there is a centralized point of coordination that can tap multiple delivery channels.

Lest it appear that centralization is nirvana, for many organizations the downside often outweighs the benefits. Quite simply, a company's overall corporate structure, philosophy, or culture may preclude its centralizing training—or any other decentralized function, for that matter. In many corporations the company's strategy and profitability are predicated on having separate lines of business or enterprises (i.e., each stands on its own as a profit/loss center). Such an organizational structure affords each line of business maximum autonomy, giving it discretion and control over what to do and how to do it in order to achieve the best possible business outcomes. While this philosophy is most prevalent among holding companies, it is also alive and well in entrepreneurial corporate cultures that favor local control and rail at anything that is mandatory or that is perceived as constraining the leaders' free will to act locally in the name of unique business requirements.

Decentralized Training. Although not the antithesis of centralization, decentralized training brings its own challenges at the same time it facilitates the delivery of training that is tied directly to individual enterprise or line priorities. Some companies view centralization as cumbersome and bureaucratic and instead create separate, decentralized training organizations. Decentralization supports strategic business units, their specific needs, and their unique minicultures. The belief is that trainers who are on the line payroll have the deepest understanding of the enterprise they support and can provide highly relevant learning opportunities because they are closest to the customer.

Decentralized structures tend to work well when organizations have a diverse array of products or are founded on a holding company model. Despite the increased costs associated with this structure, many believe that the benefits far outweigh the duplication of effort and limited economies of scale. The downside of decentralization is that a silo mentality can easily develop, restricting the movement of individuals across different businesses and undermining opportunities for teamwork and collaboration. Because decentralized structures are more susceptible to the influence of local management and are more difficult to control or monitor, some question whether the training that is offered supports the firm's overall strategies and corporate priorities. Although line-specific training organizations have the best interests of their strategic business units at heart, they may be inadvertently curtailing the implementation of learning opportunities that would be of benefit to the entire organization.

Vendors frequently benefit monetarily when companies implement a decentralized training model. Fee structures can vary among line organizations, depending on the negotiating skill of each organization's training professionals. Increased costs also accrue as a consequence of developing duplicate programs. Decentralized training groups may either purchase or develop what they perceive to be the best choice for their business. The oft-quoted phrase "not invented here" epitomizes the reluctance of decentralized units to introduce training they didn't design or have a hand in selecting. Depending on the number of business lines, the net result may be the coexistence of dozens of classes on the same topic with only minor variations among them.

Organizations most frequently make the transition from decentralization to centralization during a time of organization transition, when all aspects of the business are under scrutiny. Another impetus for restructuring occurs when there is a change of leadership at the top; however, whatever the drivers for implementing a new training structure, decisions are sometimes made in the absence of hard data. In fact, the very nature of decentralized training can inhibit tracking actual training-related costs and quantifying potential structure-related savings. This dilemma can occur if individual enterprises track and code training-related costs in different ways. The consequence, in the absence of accurate information, is that it is difficult to make a compelling business case for one approach or the other.

It is not unusual for individuals to underreport or overreport spending. When money becomes tight, managers may use one budget line to support another, making it difficult to determine whether expenditures were directed toward training and development or used to support another business need. For example, there may be no way to distinguish a consultant who was hired to deliver training from a consultant who assisted with business strategy. Unless a rigorous reporting, coding, and accounting discipline is in place, rolling up the total cost of training can be problematic. In turn, without an accurate baseline of training costs, comparisons between the costs associated with centralization and those associated with decentralization are spurious.

To complicate matters, in gathering hard data, budgets, or metrics to inform structural decisions, the very nature of budget analyses or organizationwide audits creates anxiety, especially among individuals affiliated with the functional entities being surveyed. Are we not viewed as adding value? Are our jobs in jeopardy? Such concerns may cause further rifts among already siloed organizations, each of which may work even harder to defend the merits of its contribution. In the long run, using the total cost of training and specific case examples to demonstrate inefficiencies or missed opportunities may be so difficult that anecdotal information, organization power and influence, or gut reactions can ultimately drive structural decisions.

Combined Approach. Combining elements of centralization and decentralization can be a way to capture the best of both worlds. With a combined approach, training on particular types of subject matter or for particular target audiences is coordinated from a single point, and the remainder is decentralized. A commonly utilized framework assigns responsibility for technical training to the lines of business and responsibility for the softer stuff (management development, personal and professional skills, leadership education) to a corporate university or centralized entity.

Many companies bifurcate training-related accountabilities in yet another way: by centralizing design and development and decentralizing delivery and execution. This strategy allows field-based organizations and separate business units to tailor core curricula to meet local needs. Still other companies may opt to centralize all technical training, believing that it involves universal, theoretical content that can be easily customized on the job through individual application in the workplace.

Companies with a combination of centralized and decentralized training must work diligently to define the roles and responsibilities of the various staffs. Without a clear delineation of accountabilities and function, "scope creep" blurs distinctions between the centralized and decentralized organizations, and the benefits of a combined approach cannot be fully realized.

In the final analysis, the success of decentralized training depends on the ability of training professionals to collaborate and act as partners regardless of which part of the firm pays their salary. In each of the companies where I've led corporate education (The Travelers, Kaiser Permanente, and Charles Schwab & Co., Inc.), the corporation supported both a centralized corporate university as well as decentralized training groups. However, the structure played out differently in each company as a result of the overlay of additional guidelines that defined the company's approach to doing business. For example, at The Travelers, the corporate entity was funded differently from the line training organizations. A large part of the corporate university curriculum was supported through chargebacks to line customers. This approach created inequities between line and corporate functions. The corporate university continually needed to prove its value-added based on the willingness of clients to dedicate budget dollars and pay for services, whereas line training groups received funding allocations from each business line. As part of a profit center, line training groups had greater ability to define and fund the requisite needs. Corporate education, on the other hand, was viewed by many as a cost center and was dependent on others for funding, making it difficult to project a consistent baseline budget and manage staffing levels.

Funding

As discussed by Jim Moore in Chapter 2, the age-old question of who foots the bills is revisited regularly in training organizations. This is especially true during economic downturns, when training dollars are scarce and companies scrutinize all line item expenditures. Although corporations realize that knowledge acquisition is central to the competitive advantage of individuals and organizations, "accepted financial accounting and reporting structures treat training as a cost—and a hidden one at that."[14] No matter how training is funded, it is often the area that is most likely to be affected when finances are tight.

Some corporations view training as the price of doing business and establish funding levels that allow corporate universities to maintain the stability of their services and offerings. To ensure that allocation projections are accurate and reflective of actual business needs, many firms employ a zero-based budgeting system and build new budgets from the ground up each year. Based on business results, additional funds may be allocated to support special initiatives or meet unanticipated requirements.

More complex funding models are predicated on the idea that people are willing to pay for things that they value. If a line organization or a manager believes that a particular learning opportunity is appropriate, that organization or manager pays for the program or service. In turn, the training organization bills back the charges to the client, thus initiating a charge-back model.

Chargebacks are anchored in supply and demand. Such a system tends to stimulate training staff to maintain quality, for if they do not, clients will go elsewhere for services and training. Another positive characteristic is that chargebacks make costs transparent to customers and are favored by those who are striving to control costs and make thoughtful budgetary decisions. The implication for the training organization is that with charge-backs, a portion of the function needs to be self-supporting. This percentage will vary depending on the organization and the extent to which both staff and clients are experienced with such a model.

Such an arrangement is similar to the way consulting firms operate in most corporate universities. Baseline funding is usually available, and this ensures that there is sufficient funding to maintain a core staff; thereafter, the training organization expands or contracts based on demand, relying in some measure on external resources or adjuncts. This presents a challenge when there is increased demand in the marketplace for high-caliber consultants for whom everyone is competing. Additionally, continued use of external resources makes it hard to maintain consistency and continuity as different training professionals enter and exit on an ongoing basis. Schwab University charges clients/participants for venues that reside outside the recommended core curriculum and that require the use of an external consultant. This approach ensures that core learning opportunities are always available as part of the corporatewide offering, while discretionary or vendor-driven courses are available on an "as needed" or "by request" basis and charged back directly to business unit cost centers.

While chargeback systems help to control burgeoning growth within a training function, associated systems and personnel costs for record keeping, billing, and tracking can be significant. The greater the number of categories of service and variations in associated fees, the more difficult it is to sustain the approach. Frequently, tracking systems and staff cost more time and money than the benefits or the perceived value-added. Thus, because of the intricacies of managing small transactions, many companies are unwilling to implement chargeback systems unless the amounts total more than $1 million. The downside is that charging back has the potential to turn training professionals into marketers and advertisers, distracting them from higher value-added work.

Another caveat about chargebacks is that buyers of internal training are not always sophisticated decision makers. Some may be disinclined to accept a recommended approach, anticipating instead that they can save money by reducing services or scaling back a program to no more than a sound bite. For example, conducting a needs assessment may be critical to ascertaining whether a training solution is appropriate. However, some managers have a tendency to say, "This is what I need," and nix an assessment if it carries a price tag. To them, needs assessment may be a luxury, whereas for training professionals, it's a necessity. Therefore, corporate universities must take care in deciding what should or shouldn't be charged back in order to ensure the quality and integrity of the training process. Since it is not the "event" alone that adds value, but rather the pre- and posttraining experiences, those services or training that are deemed requisite should be available to all clients.

Figure 7-2 highlights the pros and cons of the allocation and chargeback models. In order for a particular training funding model to work, it must be compatible with the organization culture and congruent with the training philosophy that the company espouses.

A final consideration with respect to training expenditures relates to how training organizations spend their money. Make-or-buy decisions—choosing to develop a program internally or to buy it from the outside—can dramatically affect the available dollars. Figure 7-3 outlines questions to consider when balancing make-or-buy decisions.

Institutionalizing Training

Although the various ideas outlined in this chapter are fairly straightforward, the challenge for corporate universities is to link training to strategic goals. In order to remain viable, training organizations must contribute to

Figure 7.2 Pros and cons of funding models.

	Chargebacks	Allocation
Upsides	• Requires more careful monitoring of costs and spending. • Encourages greater attention to quality and client satisfaction. • Reduces fixed expenses, while increasing variable costs. • Encourages communication and better planning with line businesses/clients. • Ensures fair approach for areas that don't use services. • Secures ability to pay for what you value, want, and need.	• Easy to administer. • Able to scrutinize costs. • Consistent with a commitment to training as a core business strategy. • Guarantees a baseline of training and services. • Encourages cooperation and buy-in. • Engages clients in budget planning to establish appropriate funding levels.
Downsides	• Other functions or groups may not be on a chargeback system. • There is an absence of valid benchmarks and evaluative criteria. • Those with discretionary budgets may see training as a luxury and avoid spending during economic downturns. • Chargebacks may diminish commitment to core education and development programs. • A significant ramp-up period may be required before being ready to compete in the marketplace with external providers. • Costs to administer, maintain, and track chargebacks can be significant. Opportunity costs may be higher than benefits received. • May require staff to market services/programs. • Inconsistent access to educational opportunities may result. • There are no comparative protocols for deciding when to use external versus internal resources. • Market-driven approaches may lead to inconsistent chargeback rates. • Internal specialists may choose between cheating themselves or their clients, balancing value-added service and cost accountability. • Self-supporting functions may still be held accountable for recoverables, even if departments decide not to spend budgeted training dollars.	• Inconsistent with trends to monitor costs. • Spending not subject to day-to-day scrutiny. • Clients view the services as "free." • Customers have less control over decision making and service levels.

Figure 7-3. Make/buy decision making.

Time
- How quickly do you need to deliver?
- Is it faster to buy what you need or to create it yourself?
- Can you tailor an off-the-shelf product?
- Is using an internal resource more time efficient if company-specific knowledge is required?
- Are internal resources available, or are they tied up with other commitments?
- What's the geographical proximity of the potential provider?

Expertise
- What level of subject matter expertise is necessary?
- Is industry-specific knowledge important?
- Who will have the greatest credibility with the audience?
- What are the critical success factors that need to be considered (e.g., presentation skills, business acumen, international experience, company knowledge)?
- Does the company have internal resources of the right caliber?
- Is the national or international reputation of the provider important?
- Is it necessary to import fresh ideas and out-of-the-box thinking?
- Is the training to be delivered unique or specialized?

Quality
- Who can ensure the highest-caliber content and delivery?
- What are the client's expectations—the Cadillac version or the Chevy?
- Are bells and whistles important?
- What level of quality is needed to meet your training objective?

Content
- Are off-the-shelf products adequate?
- Do appropriate prepackaged materials exist?
- Can existing content be customized?
- Is an entirely new design necessary?

Audience
- What are the needs and standards of the client?
- How big is the group?
- Is the audience high-level, requiring outsider credibility?
- Is the subject matter sensitive?

Cost
- Is cost-effectiveness a prime consideration?
- Are there incentives to use a particular provider (e.g., grants, discounts, pilots, PR)?
- Are group rates, volume discounts, or special incentives available?
- Will there be a transfer of technology by the provider to the organization?
- Are there attendant costs beyond staff or consultant time (licensing fees, train-the-trainer, maintenance agreements, tailoring charges, production)?
- Are there cost-sharing alternatives?

the objectives of the individuals, departments, strategic business units, and enterprises that they support. They must be able to show how training furthers the attainment of corporate goals. If they are able to do so, corporate universities and their training functions should be able to garner support and commitment from the bottom of the organization to the very top and continue to develop the lifeblood of the organization—its people.

8

Using Technology to Enhance Learning in Corporate Universities

Brandon Hall

When we think about corporate universities and technology, it is important to think in terms of learning environments. The technology of the Internet not only has made more learning available to more people, but also has changed the way we learn. Now, as very young children access the Internet and link their way across the world, their brains themselves are being rewired; as they grow older, they will take for granted the ability to link to more information in an almost limitless fashion.

We are still in our infancy, too. Learning via linking, e-mail, self-paced courses, simulations, chat rooms, etc., is still a new frontier for us. While we may have come to accept these changes emotionally, our intellects are still catching up. And the ways in which our brains work can enable our learning, or they can interfere with it. The trick is knowing which methods of technology will smooth the way to learning and which will create speed bumps that dislodge learning.

This chapter describes the technologies that have proved themselves as learning enhancers. Some are simple, some are complex, and some are somewhere in between. But because learning itself is at the same time ephemeral and ubiquitous, these technologies have all created learning and environments for learning. Let's start with the simple stuff first.

Small Steps First

While you might want to dive into self-paced Web-based training courses right away, there are smaller steps that you can take. You probably use e-mail every day, so it is easy to overlook its instructional capabilities. Even something as simple as a reminder six months after a course can prompt employees to use the skills they learned but that may have fallen into disuse.

Thiagi (Sivasailam Thiagarajan) is a consultant who teaches trainers how to make the move into technology-delivered instruction. He says that too often we are obsessed with very costly technology—with long learning curves—when we think about using technology to teach. "My thought is there are many simple ideas which don't require you to become a millionaire or to become a Java programmer," says Thiagi.

He asserts that a few e-mail–based games (there are many free ones at his Web site, *http://www.thiagi.com*) can provide a high-touch, low-tech way for trainers to get online quickly. For example, in his game Half Life (not the radioactive shoot-'em-up game), a group of trainees is assigned the task of writing a thirty-two-word mission statement for the department. All of the trainees' e-mails and working mission statements are shared with everyone. Later, the trainees are encouraged to send a final mission statement—based on what they've read—that is only sixteen words long. Then, in three days, they are supposed to come up with an eight-word mission statement.

Want to do a review of material you've already taught a group? Why not try an interactive crossword puzzle? Thiagi has his trainees send him the clues and the answers, and he assembles a crossword that they can fill out online. You can try out the same kind of exercise at *http://www.web gamestogo.com/crosswrd/* without buying any software.

Thiagi will even create a bare bones simulation in the form of a simple spreadsheet that he e-mails to learners. The spreadsheet contains a company's financials, and employees can tweak different numbers to see how they affect productivity and/or profitability.

The next step might be hosting and moderating a threaded discussion group. With a little help from your Webmaster, this should be a snap. If you can't get the necessary cooperation, you can start a discussion group using an external Web site like Topica (*http://www.topica.com*) or eGroups (*http://groups.yahoo.com/local/news.html*). Discussion groups can generate a lot of learning, but it won't be the kind of top-down learning that has taken place in the past. In a threaded discussion, everyone is equal and everyone usually has something to contribute. The instructor becomes a discussion moderator, not someone who imparts knowledge as the participants patiently wait for it to rain down on them.

Good learning has always been about getting lots of minds involved—both instructors and students. A threaded discussion group does just that. The moderator can keep the discussion on subject and can put out the fires if a flame war (angry, personal e-mail attacks among participants) erupts.

The element most often cited as a negative in e-learning is the loss of human interaction, as that interaction is a very powerful factor in helping people learn. Using e-mail and discussion groups is a great and simple way to keep the human interaction, albeit asynchronously, in the loop.

Live E-Learning

The next obvious step in using technology to create learning is to create the classroom environment—with all its interactions and sharing—without the actual physical classroom. This is called *live e-learning* precisely because everyone gathers at the same time but not in the same place.

Live e-learning is the use of Internet technology to allow an instructor to provide live (also called synchronous) instruction to a group of learners. Instructors and learners can be separated geographically, yet still share an interactive learning experience. Using available features, instructors and learners can participate in discussions, view documents and visual aids simultaneously, and break out into virtual rooms for team processing. In addition, many products include record and playback functions for learners who want to refresh their understanding of the material or for new learners who were unable to attend a live session. Live e-learning takes experiences from the classroom to the Internet to extend channels of learning.

Again, in terms of creating a learning environment, live e-learning keeps the human element in the system. Instructors and students can interact in real time; the only thing that is missing is the face-to-face connection (although students can often see the instructor's face). What you as an instructor might lose in this environment is the clear knowledge that your students are awake and paying attention. Therefore, most live e-learning trainers ask a lot more questions and elicit more conversations with the students, just to keep them engaged. This push toward more interaction is certainly a step in the right direction for catalyzing learning.

If your corporate university wants to pursue live e-learning, there are some terms you will need to know before you sit down and talk to a supplier:

Live E-Learning Terms

Audio bridge: The use of telephones to transmit instructor/participant dialogue in a live e-learning session.

Bandwidth: The broadcast ability of a communications network or computer bus or channel. This is given in bits per second, bytes per second, or cycles per second (hertz). With hertz, the rate of vibration may be more than the actual bytes per second, since the bandwidth is the variance between the lowest and highest.

Browser: A program that enables you to access on-line data.

Collaboration: A situation in which all participants have equal ability to drive and share materials.

Connection speed: The time that it takes for the client computer to connect with the server.

Firewall: A method for keeping a network secure, filtering unwanted packets of information, and separating a company's public Web server from its internal network.

Half-duplex: A situation in which only one participant at a time can speak and be heard (similar to a walkie-talkie).

Full-duplex: A situation in which all participants can speak and be heard simultaneously (as in a normal telephone conversation).

IP (Internet protocol): The channel used to communicate with a different network or subnetwork.

Quizzing/polling: A feature of live e-learning that allows instructors to assess participants' progress through responses to formal and informal quizzes/polls.

Plug-ins: Audio, video, multimedia, and animation software applications that increase the features of your browser.

Record and playback: A feature that enables live audio and video instruction to be recorded and accessed at a later time.

Scalability: The extent to which a system can be expanded.

Voice-over IP: The two-way transference of audio over an IP network as used in a private intranet or WAN.

Whiteboard: A feature that allows participants to concurrently view one or more users drawing on an on-screen "sketch pad." Only one user at a time has access to the whiteboard.

How Can We Use Live E-Learning?

Many companies consider live e-learning to be an occasional alternative to the traditional classroom. In addition to using live e-learning as a training channel, you can expand your reach to customers, improve the team dynamics of a cross-country sales force, and work collaboratively with a manager or colleague regardless of location.

Here are some of the conveniences that live e-learning users have realized:

- ❏ An international pizza company uses live e-learning's real-time tools for delivering fast information from corporate headquarters to franchises, including new product information, new procedures and policies, and developments in minimum wage legislation.

- ❏ A live e-learning virtual classroom gave 8,100 pharmaceutical employees the ability to use a live instructor to lead a highly interactive class among its distributed workforce using audioconferencing, PowerPoint slides, Web-based material, shared whiteboard, shared software applications, and a host of student feedback options—all over the corporate intranet.

- ❏ An international car rental agency is leading the way to a new level of customer service by using a distance learning system, allowing the company to train 95 to 99 percent (versus the industry average of 60 percent) of all new counter staff to ensure superior customer satisfaction.

- ❏ Live e-learning enabled a large health-care organization to deliver orientation seminars to desktops at more than two hundred company locations, enabling all new hires to attend simultaneously and eliminating the need for travel.

- ❏ An international software company helps customers from around the world participate in live, interactive courses on software upgrades.

- ❏ A major telecommunications company estimates that it saves about $1,500 per trainee when it uses live e-learning instead of classroom training. The total estimated savings in travel, facility, and labor costs in 1998 came to $5.6 million.

If you are ready to go beyond thinking about live e-learning and really go out and do it, you need to answer a couple of questions:

1. Who will facilitate your organization's live e-learning classes?
2. Do you plan to hire experienced live e-learning instructors, or will current classroom trainers make the move to the virtual classroom?

It is important to gauge trainers' readiness for this new learning environment. Here are some points to explore before you throw your instructors in the deep end of the live e-learning pool:

❑ *Do instructors have experience using PowerPoint slides for instructional purposes?* Most live e-learning trainers and instructional designers choose to use PowerPoint slides to introduce information online. If your trainers are accustomed to using PowerPoint, this will be an easy and familiar method of instruction. If they are not familiar with PowerPoint, they may wish to develop these skills.

❑ *Can your instructors use other applications, such as word processing and spreadsheet documents, to demonstrate learning concepts online?* Live e-learning is very versatile and allows trainers to shift from one application to another with ease. Familiarity with applications such as Microsoft Word and Excel will be a plus for the live e-learning environment.

❑ *Will instructors be comfortable navigating the Web during a live class?* Again, trainers will have instant access to many resources on the Internet during their classroom session. Using these can enhance classroom learning, and not using them may raise questions about the techno-literacy of the instructor. If instructors won't surf the Net, their students may be doing it anyway.

❑ *Can instructors build a collaborative learning environment without face-to-face contact?* Trainers will immediately recognize there are many features of live e-learning that the traditional classroom cannot offer. One of the frequently cited advantages is the geographic freedom offered with this mode of e-learning. However, to accommodate the dispersed participant locations, trainers need to apply techniques to create a productive group learning environment. Most vendors offer training to prepare instructors for their virtual classrooms.

❏ *Are instructors interested in features such as "raise hand," polling, and whiteboard?* Live e-learning is a relatively new mode of instruction. If instructors are willing to learn how to use this powerful tool, training is available to prepare them. Because the virtual classroom is live and interactive, they will find that most of their previous training techniques can be applied to this environment. In addition, they will discover many new resources and techniques to extend their impact on participants' learning experience.

❏ *Is it possible to supply your instructors with assistants?* In most live e-learning events, there is a lot to be said for having an assistant, someone who will field typed-in questions, channeling some to the instructor and answering others while the class is proceeding. This assistant can also do a lot of troubleshooting and tech support as the class begins—e.g., helping when people can't log in, get stuck in the virtual lobby, or end up (somehow) inside the copy machine.

❏ *How can you better prepare your instructors for this new style of teaching?* Allison Rossett, professor of educational technology at San Diego State University and coauthor of the new book *Beyond the Podium: Delivering Training and Performance to a Digital World,* says that she prepares for live events by creating her own FAQs (frequently asked questions), so that she can respond to learners' questions that she knows will come up by cutting and pasting answers. "I anticipated what their questions were going to be. I'm a needs assessment person; I can do this. So can a good instructor," she says.

Figure 8-1 presents ten ways in which you can use live e-learning in your corporate university.

Authoring Tools

Clark Aldrich, GartnerGroup's former chief e-learning analyst, suggests that the best first step toward e-learning in a corporate university is to use

Figure 8-1. Ten ways to use live e-learning.

1. Live classes
2. Tutorials
3. Long-distance team building
4. Annual meetings
5. Project/study groups
6. New hire orientations
7. On-line selling
8. Help desk
9. Executive briefings
10. New product roll-outs

live virtual classrooms to do sales training. The next big win can come if you develop asynchronous training for high-turnover areas of the company. That means you'll need to develop training that will either be burned onto a CD or loaded onto the corporate intranet or extranet. This gives your staff a chance to stretch their instructional design muscles, but they will need to learn how to use authoring tools.

The terms *authoring tool, authoring program,* and *authoring system* are used synonymously in e-learning to describe a wide range of content development applications. When we attempt to define authoring tools, we come across applications that provide exceptions to almost every criterion. Attempting to compare two different authoring tools to find what they have in common can be much more difficult than listing their differences.

Authoring tools are often described as software programs that let you create content without the need to write programming code. For a large number of products on the market, this is true. Many of the most popular tools, however, including Macromedia Director, Macromedia Dreamweaver, and Click2learn's Toolbook Instructor, also include their own sophisticated scripting languages or use programming languages such as JavaScript to allow developers to create powerful e-learning content by writing functions line by line.

You can produce excellent content *without* writing a line of code with applications such the ones listed in the previous paragraph, but the scripting or programming language is available if you do need to create a function or calculation that isn't built into the system.

Authoring tools are often believed to be the realm of WYSIWYG (What You See Is What You Get) environments, where objects such as graphics and audio and video clips are simply imported and dropped into position on a page. In reality, many authoring tools lack a WYSIWYG environment. Many popular programs use a form-based interface. To create content, users enter content into fields, make selections using checkboxes and drop-down lists, and then preview or publish their work.

Some authoring tools use a timeline metaphor. You can drag objects and actions onto the timeline, and they will appear or disappear at a specific point in time. Other authoring tools use a flowchart metaphor instead of a timeline. You can add icons representing images, sounds, decisions, etc., to the flow line of a flowchart and then preview your application to see what your flowchart has generated.

Still other authoring tools, such as some popular products used to create software simulations, use a recorder metaphor. You turn the recorder on and click through a procedure. Then you stop recording and edit the result, adding text, audio, interactions, etc.

Very rarely, a new product appears on the market that uses an entirely different authoring metaphor. To author content using Digital Lava Publisher, for example, you work within a spreadsheet interface and synchronize events using the time stamp of a video clip.

E-Learning Content

When one looks at the richness and variety of available e-learning content, it shouldn't be surprising that authoring tools are so different from one another. E-learning content includes courses, assessments, simulations, demos, Web pages, and presentations. Also, e-learning content often includes Adobe Acrobat and Microsoft Office files, further blurring the line between authoring tools and other software applications such as conversion software and business application suites.

Authoring tools produce e-learning content that is as varied in format as it is in function and appearance. E-learning authoring tools publish content in HTML (hypertext markup language), DHTML (dynamic hypertext markup language), XML (extensible markup language), and Java applets, as well as in a large number of proprietary file formats that require a browser plug-in. In addition, individual authoring tools can publish content in different formats for specific situations. This permits authors to create content for an environment that allows the use of browser plug-ins or as generic HTML and JavaScript using the same tool.

Not only can modern authoring tools often publish content in many different formats, but increasingly, they are able to publish to entirely new platforms. As wireless information devices such as Palm and Windows CE hand-helds, pagers, and smart phones (among others) continue to find their way into our daily lives, training content is moving to these platforms. More and more vendors are either including the ability to publish to these devices in their existing authoring tools or, as is the case with Trivantis's Lectora Pocket Publisher, producing authoring tools specifically aimed at that fast-growing sector.

Authoring Tools and Standards

As e-learning becomes an increasingly popular training solution, learning management systems (LMSs) are being installed and implemented in growing numbers.

Although some LMSs contain limited built-in authoring capabilities, none offer the ability to create as wide a range of content as is possible with a suite of third-party tools. No single LMS, for instance, can provide the ability to create Flash animations, Java applets, animated .gif files, instructional games, etc. Authoring tools built into an LMS are often aimed at importing media elements such as images, audio and video clips, animations, and simulations, and then assembling the pages using this content. So, although your LMS may contain authoring capabilities, you may still find yourself turning to third-party authoring tools for the development of specific components.

Integration of authoring tool content with learning management systems raises the issue of interoperability. For an LMS to be able to track a course or assessment created with a third-party authoring tool, the LMS and the authoring tool must be able to communicate. The course, for instance, may contain assessment questions. The LMS must be able to track whether the student successfully answers these questions, as well as whether the course was completed or abandoned. For the LMS to be able to track the course and make assessments, communication standards need to be in place.

The e-learning world subscribes to a number of standards, including AICC (Aviation Industry CBT Committee), SCORM (Sharable Courseware Object Reference Model), IMS (IMS Global Learning Consortium, Inc.), and DCMI (Dublin Core Metadata Initiative). By far the most popular standards are AICC and SCORM. Of these two, SCORM is presently receiving more attention, even though the SCORM specification is still evolving, and no SCORM certification is presently available.

Authoring tool vendors such as Click2learn and Trivantis have made compliance with standards a priority. Click2learn's Toolbook Instructor and Toolbook Assistant and Trivantis's Lectora Publisher are all AICC-certified authoring tools. This means that the AICC has tested these products and attests that they conform to the committee's specifications. Other authoring tools on the market may state that they *conform* to SCORM or are *compliant* with AICC. It's important to remember, however, that terms such as *compliance* and *conformance* mean that the vendor feels that the product adheres to these standards. No objective third-party testing and certification have taken place.

Also, some vendors may claim that their product is "AICC-compliant" if they feel that they comply with *any* of the AICC's nine AICC Guidelines and Recommendations (AGRs). This can be quite confusing. When talking to vendors of "AICC-compliant" products, be sure to ask vendors which specific AGRs they comply with.

This may paint a poor picture of the state of authoring tool compliance with standards. In reality, standards compliance holds great promise for the future. Using compliant authoring tools, you will be able to create e-learning content and publish it to your learning management system and be assured of the interoperability of content and presentation.

Product Choices

Developers of e-learning content now have a greater choice of authoring tools than ever before. Not only are specialized tools available to create specific types of content, but many products are presently available that create traditional on-line courses. This means that content developers now have the ability to select the tools that are best suited to their preferred method of authoring or level of technical ability.

Ease of use has become an important criterion for many content developers. Some authoring tools on the market allow you to publish e-learning content to the Web after spending only minutes learning the tool. Many of these tools come with attractive graphical templates. With these tools, there's no need to design an interface (make the interface buttons operational, manually manage hyperlinks, etc.). The authoring tool does all that for you. You simply select your preferred graphical template, type in your content, and publish.

While ease of use may be an important requirement for some content developers, others may prefer a tool that provides powerful extensibility and flexibility. These authoring tools may take much longer to learn but give you complete control over the functionality and presentation of your content. Some of these products, such as Macromedia UltraDev, are so powerful that they even provide programmers and developers with the functions needed to write complex, database-driven Web applications.

Whatever your needs and preferences, you have a greater chance of finding the right authoring tool for your organization today than ever before. Products exist to fit all levels of technical expertise. Products exist to fit any budget. Products exist to deliver e-learning content to a wide range of platforms in many different formats. Finally, more and more product vendors provide fully functional trial versions of their authoring tools, allowing developers the luxury of working with an application before buying it. With so much choice, the golden age of authoring e-learning content is now!

Learning Management Systems

It might not be obvious at first glance how LMSs can actually help people learn. They are clearly good at registering and tracking students, keeping data on their performance, and generally automating a lot of the administration, but that doesn't necessarily help people learn. Or does it?

Let's start off by defining what an LMS is. An LMS is software that automates the administration of training events, registers users, tracks courses in a catalog, records data from learners, and provides appropriate reports to management. The database capabilities of an LMS extend to additional functions, such as company management, on-line assessments, personalization, and other resources. These systems administer and track on-line and classroom-based learning events, as well as other training processes.

LMSs are typically designed for multiple publishers and content providers. They usually do not include their own content authoring capabilities. Instead, they focus on managing courses created from a variety of other sources. Most recently, LMSs have begun to expand into broader areas, such as content management, e-commerce, and content delivery.

Most important, says Dave Egan of THINQ, an LMS supplier, the system helps organizations think seriously about the learning they want to deliver. "[It's] a way to think about how to codify the learning needs and the learning offerings and learning solutions inside your company," says Egan.

As a result, his company recommends that an organization carry out a couple of exercises before installing an LMS to make sure the system facilitates a learning environment. First, he parachutes learning strategists into companies that are considering an LMS. These consultants force the players to go through the process of analyzing their learning needs, learning objectives, business objectives, etc. This, he admits, is a painful process, but it's a necessary one. Then his group does a configuration workshop, which is a way of working through the technology. At this meeting, the switches and routers and navigation and assessments and reports are all worked out. At that point, says Egan, you have a pretty good road map for implementing your LMS.

As they evolve, LMSs can begin to actually affect the kind of learning occurring in a corporate university by:

❏ Customizing content, so that the right information and knowledge is delivered to the right people at the right time

❏ Mapping knowledge and competencies to specific business objectives

❏ Tracking users' learning progress, so that managers can make decisions about how to deploy resources and can spot trouble areas before they become critical problems

❏ Making both employees and managers accountable for specific learning and performance results

At a macro level, an LMS can improve both the speed of change within an organization and the quality and consistency of the performance resulting from that change. Moreover, LMSs can provide employees with ready access to resources and guidance, and that can minimize their discomfort with the constant pace of change. So how do these systems work, exactly?

An LMS is a software application that automates all facets of an organization's training programs. It is especially useful for large organizations with thousands of employees because it can track very detailed information about individual learners.

The benefits of an LMS aren't limited to the automation of specific training-related tasks, however. These systems are also valuable because they can map learning events to business objectives and then deliver those events to the appropriate learners. So, in addition to helping to establish a learning environment, an LMS can support organizationwide performance improvement through its automated tools. And that can really make a corporate university a valuable tool when budget cutters are wondering what, exactly, your system is doing for the company. Specifically, a typical LMS can do the following things:

- ❏ Register users/learners and assign them job roles
- ❏ Match business goals to job roles, certifications, and/or learning events
- ❏ Allocate specific job skills and certifications to specific job roles
- ❏ Assess learners' skill and certification gaps
- ❏ Plan learning paths and deliver learning events that address skill and certification gaps
- ❏ Measure individual learners' progress and organizationwide progress against business goals

Let's look at a brief scenario of one of the many ways in which an LMS can be employed to support an organization's business goals:

Profile

Women At Work Inc. (WAW), a maker of women's conservative career clothing, has traditionally sold its clothing only in department stores. Now, WAW is updating its image. The company recently created an on-line catalog for direct business-to-consumer commerce. The site launch coincided with the unveiling of its new "Funky Business" line of clothing for young career women. The executive team at WAW loves the new look of the business and the excitement it has created among the employees. So, WAW has decided to continue moving ahead technologically and has purchased and implemented an LMS. It hopes to use this LMS to align employee development programs with the company's stated business goals.

As one of its main goals, WAW wanted to improve the computer literacy and skills of its entire employee base. It decided to focus its efforts on the job roles that typically use computers the least or not at all.

Therefore, WAW created a job role database based on the existing job role definitions and categories in the human resources database. It also identified the job roles that were associated with the lowest levels of computer literacy. Then, it entered employee information for all employees in those job roles. Finally, the company purchased third-party off-the-shelf computer training.

The WAW training director then created a schedule for assessing the existing computer literacy and skill levels of all employees in the targeted learning group. The results of these assessments would become individualized learning paths for each employee. The company then set a time frame during which all employees within the targeted learning group should complete the computer skills assessment. Each targeted employee would take the computer skills assessment, and individual performances would be mapped to the set of required computer skills to identify skills gaps for each employee.

The LMS would then map out an individualized learning path for each employee that focused on closing that employee's skills gap. Then the employee would take the courses or individual learning events offered in the off-the-shelf courseware. Each employee's progress through the prescribed learning path would be tracked by the LMS, and at appropriate stages in the learning path, employees would take an assessment to identify any remaining skills gaps.

The WAW training director was able to use the LMS to generate a report on the progress of the targeted learning group. The director could then see how the group as a whole was progressing, as well as how individual employees were progressing through their learning paths. If necessary, the training director could offer remediation to learners who were having difficulty.

Finally, the training director presented an LMS-generated status report to upper management at the end of the second fiscal quarter. At that point, learner progress had been excellent, and WAW management was focusing on developing skill set goals for the company's more experienced computer users.

One thing to remember about LMS products is they often take time to set up and can be costly to purchase. If you're not ready to jump into that kind of commitment, many LMS vendors will allow you to set up your system on an external computer. This is called an "application service provider" model, and it bears some explanation.

An application service provider (ASP) is a company that offers individuals or enterprises access—over the Internet—to software applications and related services that otherwise would have to be located on an enterprise's own PCs. Using an ASP frees a company from the cost and effort of software installation and upgrades, since the application resides on the ASP's servers. With this model, you generally pay for the LMS services on a monthly or annual basis rather than paying up front for the software license (although there are as many different pricing models as there are LMSs).

Dudley Molina is the president and CEO of ePath Learning, a company that is primarily an ASP that sets up corporate universities. He encourages companies large and small to sign up on the ePath Web site, create a few courses, and get their campus started. This is particularly helpful for smaller companies, he says, because they can try their hand at e-learning without all of the investment in infrastructure and software programs. And if a company needs some help, ePath has instructional designers on staff who can guide it through the process of developing courses online. "Some take advantage of it and others don't," says Molina, "and others should."

Learning Content Management Systems

A new player on the scene bodes well for corporate universities in a variety of ways. This new software system is called a learning content management system (LCMS). It is a multideveloper environment in which developers can create, store, reuse, manage, and deliver learning content from a central object repository. THINQ's Egan says, "The process by which you can manage content itself becomes very important. There's a loose connection at the moment—that I am going to suggest will start tightening up—between content development, or content re-purposing, and managing that content."

Whereas the primary objective of a LMS is to manage *learners*, keeping track of their progress and performance across all types of training activities, an LCMS manages *content* or *learning objects* that are served up to the right learner at the right time. Understanding the difference can be very confusing because many LCMS systems also have built-in LMS functionality. The primary differentiator to determine if a product is an LCMS is that an LCMS offers *reusability* of learning content and is generally constructed using a learning object model.

Characteristics of an LCMS

An LCMS will generally have a majority of the following characteristics:

- ❏ It is based on a learning object model.
- ❏ Content is reusable across courses, across curricula, or across the entire enterprise.
- ❏ Content is not tightly bound to a specific template and can be redeployed in a variety of formats, such as e-learning, CD-ROM, print-based learning, Palm, EPSS, etc.
- ❏ Navigational controls are not hard coded at the content (or page) level.
- ❏ There is a complete separation of content and presentation logic.
- ❏ Content is stored in a central database repository.
- ❏ Content can be represented as XML or is stored as XML.
- ❏ Content can be tagged for advanced searchability (at both the media and the topic level).
- ❏ Pretests and posttests can be automatically aggregated from test questions written for the primary instruction. In addition, the system can deliver the test and prescribe learning based on performance.
- ❏ The system manages the development process by providing some level of workflow tools to manage a multideveloper, team environment.
- ❏ The system has version controls and archiving capabilities to store previous versions of content.
- ❏ The system provides advanced searching capabilities across all objects in the repository.
- ❏ The system is interoperable with third-party LMSs.
- ❏ The system includes a delivery engine for serving up content, auto-

matically, adding navigation controls, collaboration tools, utilities, and look and feel (skins).

LCMS: Looking Forward

LCMSs represent a big leap forward for e-learning and knowledge management. As LCMS developers increase their adoption of industry standards and move toward using XML to tag and organize data (which leads to easier sharing of media and information for everyone), they are providing the foundation technology for creating, managing, and reusing learning content. The growth of LCMSs will ultimately lead to more effective and efficient learning environments.

Egan's company not only provides an LMS, but also has a huge catalog of courses and content. However, Egan says that having abundant content has its drawbacks: "It sounds like a wonderful thing. Until, of course, you're inside Sears Roebuck and you don't want your employees to have 3,000 choices. You want them to have two." He adds, "Creating more noise faster doesn't help me." The LCMS movement promises to help separate the signal from the noise and should be a big step forward for those setting up corporate universities.

9

Measurement in Corporate University Learning Environments: Is It Gonna Show? Do We Wanna Know?

Laree Kiely

Corporate universities and employee development in general make up a multibillion-dollar industry. We tend to think of ourselves as the critical link between today and tomorrow in terms of employee skills and productivity. This noble scenario certainly dignifies our role and makes it vitally necessary. But something is wrong with this picture; something is missing, almost like a version of the children's "Where's Waldo?" cartoon, except that as you look more closely, you come to the eerie realization that Waldo actually isn't in there. I will argue that at the same time that our industry believes itself to be vital and important, it has failed to measure and demonstrate any significant effects of its work. Since this is a sweeping indictment, controversial, and liable to exceptions, the analysis of this chapter will show that the problem itself is sweeping, and that it threatens to sweep us all away with it. An industry that fails to confirm its necessity and its effects is a fragile and threatened industry. At the same time, as big as the problem is, it is one that can be significantly fixed, provided that we are willing to think differently about the strategies we mount and the tools we employ.

In *The Monster Under The Bed*, Stan Davis and Jim Botkin argue that business is taking over the business of education, even leaving academia behind:

> Behind it all looms a gargantuan government-run education system incapable of handling a doubling of knowledge about every seven years. The knowledge revolution will power the new global economy, reshape many of our institutions—particularly education—and touch every aspect of our lives. Business sees the opportunity, and it is driving ahead full speed to realize this vision to adapt to, and profit from, the realities of the new information economy. We may speak glibly of the "knowledge revolution," but what does it mean if knowledge is becoming the resource adding the most value to business and the economy? What can business do to profit from the knowledge revolution?[1]

But if Davis and Botkin's image of a failed education system looming in the background is at all valid, then it is all the more important that those who occupy the "foreground" should make sure that we do not repeat the failures of the past. Education has been called to task for its failure to show any positive effects. Students who pass tests, graduate, and take jobs, only to have their employers find out that they are not equipped with the most basic of skills, are a scandal in this society. And partly because of that scandal, any important educational or developmental enterprise in America will be dogged by demands that we demonstrate our effectiveness. Both because of an increasingly competitive business climate and because salaries, as Davis and Bodkin observe, are "increasingly linked to performance,"[2] sooner or later companies and their leaders will be scheduling Judgment Day to see if the hours and money spent on education and development have paid off.

In addition, there is the purpose of this book—to distinguish corporate universities from the old training and development model. Corporate universities are not just glorified teaching departments designed to develop individuals because schools are not producing the products that businesses need. Corporate universities have an even more vital mission—to ensure change and progress at the level of corporate culture. Today's business must go from being a mob of functioning individuals to being a learning organization, and then to being a collective, "thinking" mind. This demands more than an expanded training and development model. It demands that corporate universities become a microcosm of the future organization itself. It means that they must become thinking organizations that think globally, holistically, in nonlinear ways, and it means creating new ways of defining and measuring outcomes.

Why We Do What We Do

When the concept of guaranteed employment died, we hardly even noted its passing. It was slowly and inexorably replaced by what we called the "new social contract," which went a bit like this: Employees must bring value to the organization, and they must determine what that value will be. In return, the organization will help to ensure that that employee stays not employed, but employable. This means providing either the funding or the education or both to continuously rebuild and improve an employee's skills. We found that this was a good way to attract and retain workers in a tough labor market. It enhanced their morale, and we believed that that would improve productivity, etc., etc.

In addition, the old calculation that, because of ever-changing technology, an employee's skills would become obsolete every five years has itself become obsolete: That number is down to every two to three years and counting. College degrees, including MBAs, now have a shelf life that is increasingly becoming shorter. So we have seen our mission as keeping companies and employees current and productive by keeping their knowledge and information upgraded and updated.

In a way, the increasing need for what we do has become part of the accountability problem, as our attention has been focused on delivering goods that are changing daily to clients whose needs are shifting equally rapidly. So the service of education and development makes us significant partners in the enterprise. But delivering the goods is one thing and assessing the quality and usefulness of the deliverables is another, and if no one can tell whether the goods got delivered and whether they were effective, then the whole game is lost.

Why We Need to Measure

Now, let's acknowledge that we "know" all this; we certainly have developed the philosophical underpinnings needed to justify the existence of employee development programs and corporate universities. We can make the case. A FEDEX commercial and a corporate university charter have one thing in common: They claim to deliver the goods. But FEDEX goes the corporate university one better: It provides a means to prove to you that it in fact did deliver the goods and did so yesterday at 2:15 P.M. It is the argument of this chapter that if learning professionals are going to stay in business, we have to act more businesslike. The academic model in America is under attack, and with few exceptions this has to do with its failure to show the kind of accountability that businesses routinely must demonstrate: ensuring quality, usefulness, ROI, and profitability.

Think of the alternatives: If we continue to be lulled by a sense of security falsely passed on from the very academic environments that are coming under intense scrutiny for accountability, defending ourselves philosophically but not on the basis of proof of purpose and ROI, our enterprise could very well start looking like a cost center or support staff that could be outsourced or eliminated in difficult economic times.

At the same time that we worry about this dark scenario, we should recognize that versions of this worry are well known and widely publicized by practitioners and writers on the subject. It isn't that the subject has not come up; it is, instead, that we haven't found a solution. In the literature review that follows, we will examine published reports of research efforts in which the authors have certainly attempted to go beyond the philosophical and make a real business case for the effects of training. Sadly, we will also find that those efforts have largely been unsuccessful.

Knowledge That Stacks Up Versus Knowledge That Adds Up

We are discovering that the way we have talked about the problem is part of the problem, and that part of the solution is to talk about it differently. Any survey of practitioners and institutions who are debating training and development issues will turn up discussions of terms and labels, operational definitions, categories, and so on.

An example is that of the nation's business schools as they deal with the quandary of how to measure their effectiveness in an increasingly competitive market. The question of whether the student is a product or a customer influences the way we measure learning. For years, academia has measured learning based on papers, examinations, reports, and attendance. But do these really measure learning? Or do they, as the critics say, simply stack up and accumulate facts? Knowledge that stacks up is very different from knowledge that adds up. When we consider the customer to be the company that "buys" or hires this student (who then becomes the product of the educational system), it changes the curriculum, the deliverables, and the measurement of the quality of those deliverables.

In addition, academics have measured teaching effectiveness by student evaluations at the end of each course. Critics argue that these are popularity or "satisfaction" polls that do not measure student learning; they cite cases in which students had a hard or difficult educational learning experience that they did not particularly enjoy, but from which they learned much. Our literature review found many reports indicating that corporate learning centers borrow this model from academics quite routinely. But they do not seem to provide a more persuasive case than the academics have done that it in any way approaches a reasonable definition of learning.

Knowing About "Knowledge," Learning About "Learning": What We Really Mean

Before reviewing the published literature on assessment of training, I should remind the reader that the purpose of this chapter is not just to lament the problem but also to contribute to solving it. Accordingly, a specific set of proposals for change will follow the review. In order for the reader to see the review as setting the stage for and anticipating those proposed changes, it is appropriate to offer a definition of the kind of learning I'm talking about: learning that adds up, instead of just stacking up. For now, I will use a general and approximate definition, since the full definition requires laying out the actual operational program. That is yet to come. For now, we will think of learning as two things that are closely linked: the acquisition of knowledge and the actual use of that knowledge for increased productivity in the workplace. Productivity in this sense is also bidimensional, consisting of *efficiency* and *effectiveness*. Can we ensure that the learning we promote accomplishes this? Yes, we can. Does the literature show that we have done that? No, it most certainly does not.

Review of the Literature

Of course the very phrase *review of the literature* reeks of the academic; it reminds one of plodding summaries of obscure, not-very-interesting articles from that least fascinating form of literature on earth, the journal. But I hope you will take the time to peruse this review, because the conclusions it comes to are surprising and perhaps controversial. For what the review turned up was not the usual array of materials demonstrating a thriving field full of successes and interested in the odd failures. Instead, it seems to point to a field on the verge of a crisis, a field that vaguely knows that its credibility is in question, but doesn't know just how bad things are. I think you will find it to be an interesting review, perhaps one that you will want to disagree with. But even in the event that the review overstates the case, it faithfully represents a large body of recent literature from sources central to the game, and the picture that emerges suggests a code-red emergency.

This review of recent published literature on assessing the results of training surveyed training, business, management, and educational sources published from 1999 through mid-2001. The usual review of the literature of a field turns up the good and the not-so-good, the noble and the ignoble, highs and lows, the "agony and the ecstasy" that are common to most human endeavors. But this is not just any human endeavor: It is the area of trying to know whether all or any of our efforts to advance business through training work or not.

The review covers the last three years of professional periodicals and research journals on any subject that was related to assessing the effects of training. In addition, it scrutinizes the available books in the field and reports our interviews of people involved in corporate universities. The available literature includes hundreds of similar articles, so what is reported here is an extensive, but also representative summary.

Omitted were many of the hundred or so studies that used paper-and-pencil tests, self-reports, standardized tests, etc. (That includes almost all of them, with some of the rare exceptions noted here.) The best, most rigorous writing on the subject is here; unfortunately, it is not very good and not very rigorous. And many writers wander hopelessly between saying, "Here's what we ought to do, but nobody does this because it's impossible or too expensive or too time-consuming" on the one hand, and saying, "Here's what we should do," but not attempting it and then dropping the subject of whether anybody else could ever scale this ideal mountain they have created on the other. The review of this literature does not turn up a sort of normal-curve distribution of successes and failures; instead, it illuminates a kind of wasteland, where the norm is failure.

Most of the literature on assessment of training hinges, explicitly or implicitly, on Donald Kirkpatrick's four levels of evaluation.[3] These levels provide a convenient way of talking about different kinds of results of training, so this review employs them as well. Kirkpatrick's levels are:

❏ *Level 1, reaction.* "As the word reaction implies, evaluation on the level measures how those who participate in the program react to it. I call it a measure of customer satisfaction."[4]

❏ *Level 2, learning.* "Learning can be defined as the extent to which participants change attitudes, improve knowledge, and/or increase skills as a result of attending the program."[5]

❏ *Level 3, behavior.* "Behavior can be defined as the extent to which change in behavior has occurred because the participant attended the training program."[6]

❏ *Level 4, results.* "Results can be defined as the final results that occurred because the participants attended the program. The final results can include increased production, improved quality, decreased costs, reduced frequency and/or severity of accidents, increased sales, reduced turnover, and higher profits."[7]

One thing Kirkpatrick achieved: His "level 4" criterion looms large, either explicitly or between the lines, in the thinking of virtually every recent writer on the subject of training assessment. As Henry VIII said about wine, one looks at it, one smells it, one drinks it, and one *talks* about it; our writers certainly do all four with level 4. The reason for this, of course, is obvious: The criterion "can we demonstrate rigorously that *this* training benefited this organization more than it cost?" is the ultimate ROI criterion. But beware of a lofty standard that is not achieved; it has a way of becoming an indictment of failure. Our examination of three years' literature, including hundreds of articles on training and its effects, finds virtually no verifiable report of a training effort that reached the ideal of the Kirkpatrick level 4. And disappointingly, even those studies that attempt a run on levels 3 and 4 employ "research" and assessment methods that are antiquated and widely considered invalid by related fields. Houston, we have a problem.

Such an unexpectedly dismal finding is worthy of a couple of disclaimers. There may be in-house, proprietary studies of training effects that actually achieved Kirkpatrick's level 4 that have not been reported in the published literature. If so, the field at large would benefit from knowing about these studies. Second, there are a few studies in the literature that claim to be exceptions to the "wasteland" judgment we have made; so, as we survey the thicket of white flags erected over failed attempts on the part of the field to demonstrate ROI, we will also consider the few claims of success. Maybe some have succeeded, but we simply haven't seen them.

We have divided this review into sections:

❏ Studies that conclude that you can't get to level 4
❏ Studies that claim that they achieved level 4
❏ Studies that get to level 4 and then backfire
❏ Studies that go for level 4 and fail
❏ Transference studies, level 3

You Can't Get to Level 4 from Here

Let us first consider some writers who conclude that achieving both level 4 and also a connection between the achievement and the effects of training is impossible and might as well be abandoned. No less a commentator than Ron Zemke, senior editor of *Training,* editorializes that training should be recognized as necessary, somewhat like support staff, and that trying to justify it by attributing profitability to it is asking too much.[8]

A parallel skepticism about demonstrating broadly positive effects of training comes from John P. Dalton of Forrester Research of Cambridge, Massachusetts.[9] He argues that only a fraction of (on-line) training even attempts to measure effects, with the result that much training represents waste. His three-point program for improving this situation addresses the problem of achieving demonstrable effects by suggesting that training be aimed only at goals that are capable of being assessed. In other words, if you can't demonstrate results in terms of the training goals you have, then change your goals to focus on what you can demonstrate—goals that are narrowly conceived, with training that is narrowly focused.

A survey of United Kingdom business training efforts by Patton et al.[10] represents a massively impressive study of a whole nation's business efforts to train effectively. Among its conclusions, based on its survey of hundreds of companies, is that it has not been possible and it may not ever be possible to demonstrate a direct causal connection between the effects of particular training and the profitability of a company.

These sources that doubt the plausibility of achieving anything like Kirkpatrick's level 4 are arguing, directly or indirectly, that it is an impossible standard to reach, and that we had better think of something else by which to judge our training efforts.

They Got to Level 4; Unfortunately, They Forgot to Take Pictures at the Summit

A few authors actually claim to report studies showing that training effects directly cause increases in ROI; we now consider three of them. First, a highly interesting study of training effects in Ireland represents another major effort to sum up the training situation of a whole country. Barrett and O'Connell[11] are actually interested in a different, but related question: Does "specific" training (training that focuses on the needs of the organization) have a greater effect on ROI than "general" training (training that focuses on the development of and benefits to the individual). Interestingly, they come to the opposite conclusion from Forrester, i.e., that a greater positive effect for the organization comes from the more "general" training that develops the individuals.

But our concern here is: Did that more general approach actually achieve a demonstrable effect that we can confidently say benefited the organization significantly? These authors say yes, and they make the claim that "increased profitability" was the direct criterion used to judge the results of general versus specific training. It is tempting to take this at face value and conclude that this is a promising exception to our general gloominess about defending the results of training. However, there is a problem, one that stalks virtually every good report of positive results in the field: The authors' method was to survey "managers" about the effects of training, but apparently the survey, as reported, did not ask the respondents to describe details of their method of assessment.

In other words, Barrett and O'Connell don't know how these "managers" arrived at their conclusions, and neither do we. Of course managers are going to have opinions about the link between profitability and training. But without some criteria that are specific and replicable, the speculations of Barrett and O'Connell are of that most dangerous kind: speculations as wide as a whole nation. Unsupported editorializing by a hundred managers just multiplies our validity problem by 100.

Moving from the macro to the very micro, consider an attempt to demonstrate training's effect on the bottom line. Prechelt and Unger[12] report on a study comparing two different approaches to software training that was able to show a criterion of success different from profitability, but arguably very close to it. In this case, training effects were assessed by means of something that appears to be a quasi-experimental design, and the criterion of success was concrete: namely, how well did the software work that was created by the students who experienced two types of training.

I read this article after scanning some hundreds of published reports, and this was the first I had found that had a kind of "workability" or "utility" criterion of success. It is very impressive, but this study takes Forrester's advice to an extreme. You can demonstrate the effects of training on the bottom line when the training is focused on some goal that is very close to and measurable by the bottom line itself. We could define "training" this narrowly if we chose, in order to assess its effects, but that truncated view of training would exclude training aimed at changing many effects in the organization and training aimed at broad cultural shifts that are expected to ripple out through the organization as a whole.

Bendick et al.[13] are confident that measurable benefits to the organization can be traced to the effects of diversity training. These authors are interested in a comparison of types of diversity training, and they argue that an emphasis on a "business" rationale for diversity works best. Their national survey of companies argues for the effectiveness of a diverse workforce, and their reporting of some case studies of different approaches to training in diversity suggests indirectly that their favored method of training produces greater profitability. But the connection is indirect, and the article, like virtually every other piece in the literature, does not deliver specifics. At about the moment when you would like the authors to get specific about criteria for success, specific about the rigors of their study, and specific about how someone could test their claims by trying what they tried and measuring the results similarly, the writing drifts off into nonspecificity, the kind intended both to leave the reader with a warm feeling and also to conclude before anybody demands to know what we're *really* talking about here.

To say that these studies are representative of what our review turned up is to overstate the case. Actually, these are the *best* "got-to-level-four" studies we found. What is representative about them is the reasons for their failure, reasons shared by every other study we found that claimed to be a success: Either the criteria for success are so specific (the company needed more workable software and it had expert engineers to assess workability) that the case is exceptional and unrepeatable, as most companies have goals and assessment techniques that are much less specific, or the successes are reported so generally ("managers" told us that a particular kind of training increased profitability) that we get no report of any concrete measures that made credible causal connections between training and ROI beyond the personal opinions of unnamed, unqualified respondents to surveys.

To sum up this section: These are the best studies that claimed to make a connection between training and benefits to the organization overall, and their limited, highly specific successes accompanying general failures point to a Kirkpatrick's level 4 as a latter-day Mt. Everest that still has never been scaled.

When They Got to Level 4, There Wasn't Any There There

One of the frankly weirdest experiences in reviewing this literature was to read the studies that actually picked out a significant, concrete criterion for success that might have put them in the level 4 success column, but the study boomeranged and produced results opposite to those intended.

Riordan[14] was interested in whether a variety of on-the-job socialization tactics employed by the organization would combine to create positive work attitudes and less turnover. The trainers employed a collective model of job training and compared their results against the effects of a different training approach on other employees of the same company. Among the criteria of training effectiveness were some paper-and-pencil tests of self-esteem and positive job attitudes, plus records of subsequent employee turnover. Like dozens of studies this review encountered, this study found that the collective style of training improved the self-esteem and attitude scores but catastrophically and almost laughably resulted in *greater* turnover.

Bingham and Scherer[15] present a training effort that actually resulted in potentially more sexual harassment in the workplace. Not only did this study backfire, but the increase in the problem of sexual harassment was almost perfectly causally related to effects of the training. Some criteria, such as employees' perceptions of what constitutes sexual harassment, seduction, relational imposition, or gender harassment toward a subordinate, were unchanged. Even worse, male program participants ended up being much less likely to perceive certain kinds of sexual behavior as coercive and a lot more likely to blame the victim than those males who had not received the training. The authors introduce "reactance" theory to explain this result: The training was perceived as a crackdown by administration that the employees didn't agree with, so they reacted in the *opposite* way to what was intended.

These bizarre results of a couple of studies (and there were a few more) suggest that the closer we get to a real link between training and a high-level criterion of benefit to the organization, the more difficult this link is to demonstrate. They also suggest that sometimes, when we do make the causal link we think we want, we discover a darker truth: that training can make things a lot worse, and that without valid assessment, we may not know the damage that has been done.

They Talked the Talk, but Then They Stumbled the Stumble

Countless studies that we read gave some sort of lip service to a level 4 criterion for the success of training, then changed the subject and settled for less. Angrist and Lavy[16] report the application of a regression-statistic method to studying the effects of in-service training on children's education. The multiple regression approach is consistent with the authors' claim that the definition of an "effective teacher" is complex and should be studied multidimensionally, but in choosing a measure of the effects of the teacher training on students, they select the more unidimensional criterion of student scores on standardized math and reading tests. It does not occur to these authors that if teachers are complex, then the effects of teaching need to be measured in an equally complex fashion.

One of the most egregious examples of a published report in which the implied aspirations fall very short of the results as reported is an article whose title asserts that "companies are using 'metrics' to justify e-learning's impact on strategic business goals."[17] This article throws "metrics" around as though to imply rigorous quantification, but the "metrics" turn out to be undisclosed proprietary measurement devices, and "we coulds," like increases in sales when training is given by e-learning rather than in a classroom. These authors didn't get around to doing it, but they "could." And then the "metrics" turned out to be self-reports four months later of how much salespeople *thought* the improvement in their performance was worth in dollars to the company. This article seems to be a case of a company selling its wares; when the abstract is found in a database, it looks like research, but the contents are self-indicting, cloaking the reality of insignificant criteria and results in the glow of empirical-sounding language. But that knot on the head of this article comes from bumping up against Kirkpatrick's level 2 ceiling and finding it to be very hard, indeed.

Another discouraging attempt to connect training to bottom-line results is seen in Chandler and McEvoy.[18] These authors wanted to show that TQM training plus a group-based incentive program is more effective (more profitable) than TQM training without the incentives. But profitability was assessed by a report from CEOs of the small companies studied, and the criterion was not an *increase* in profitability, but simply one report of profitability, "adjusted" for company size. The obviousness of there being many possible causes of profitability scarcely needs to be mentioned, except as a comment on the credulity these authors must attribute to their readers. And we report this only that we all might be amazed and appalled that such stuff constitutes the "literature" of our enterprise.

It Ain't Level 4, but It Ain't Bad

A few studies in this review get so far as to find some "transference"—that is, to discover that trainees' behavior in the workplace seemed to be altered as a result of training. This is not to say that benefits to the company were demonstrated, but that at least the trainees themselves showed some change.

May and Kahnweiler[19] tested the effects of two different types of training: training followed by a "mastery" session and training without the extra session. The subject of the training was "active listening," and the authors employed a standardized 360-degree test (peers, subordinates, and boss) four weeks later, as well as open-ended interviews that were coded and compared. The mastery practice training worked better on knowledge criteria measured by a pencil-and-paper test, but after four weeks the 360-degree assessment showed no difference. This is one of the very few 360-degree assessments found in this literature; unfortunately, as we have seen with other studies, the more rigorous and promising the assessment technique, the more adaptable to less significant and less global sorts of changes it seems to be.

A study on socialization in the workplace by Klein and Weaver[20] includes among its many self-reports a self-report on transference; that is, it asks respondents to report how much they estimate their training transferred. Respondents were at least able to discriminate among criteria of socialization as they self-reported, which lends some credence to the authors' claims that some dimensions of socialization are better trained by one method rather than another. These authors would have made a stronger contribution to the literature, however, if they had included a comparison of the self-reports to something more objective, such as a 360-degree assessment; that way, they would know more about actual transference and also more about whether their carefully crafted self-report questions actually got any objective and accurate information.

Finally, the study by Richman-Hirsch[21] is interesting because it got prominent placement in the *Human Resource Development Quarterly* and the honor of a major critique published by the editors of that journal.[22] Richman-Hirsch attempted some assessment of the transference effects of training and found only weak results, even though the subject matter of the training was simple and specific (i.e., greater use of eye contact). So this is a not very successful attempt to study an academic question comparing two theories of training, but one trying to measure a few empirical, concrete effects in the workplace.

The discussion by the critic, Brethower, makes the whole thing interesting, however, because he politely damns the study for not going to level 4, never says how this should be done, except to refer the reader to some theoretical material by a third author, and then changes the subject and berates Richman-Hirsch for the lack of complexity in her approach. The reason for the significance of this exchange is that it represents an archetypal, perfect example of how we talk the game of assessing effects of training on the organization, but just at the moment when we might be specific as to how, we change the subject—because evidently we don't know how.[22]

Reviewing the Review: What's Wrong with This Picture?

To begin with (let's say it outright), this review presents a picture of a field that, by any reasonable standard, is deep in a crisis of significance, validity, and usefulness. The emperor's clothes are transparently, pathetically failing to cover the subject. This review is accurate as to the literature; if it is accurate as to the field, then the crisis is dire, as we have said. If there are rays of hope anywhere, they lie in effectiveness studies that are not appearing in the major journals and publications of the field, and that represents a different, but almost equally significant problem.

But to say that we have not gone to the level of assessment that we agree is necessary but that, according to this review, is actually *never* achieved hints at the systemic problem underlying it all: We don't know how to do the job. And there is another problem behind that one: We don't understand the *research* that would help us understand the *job* that would help us understand the *effects* we're supposed to ascertain.

One example of the problem with research is this field's dependence on self-reports. This smacks of a field that has no grounding in the rigors of behavioral or social science research methods. Social science research long ago abandoned any hope that subjects of studies, trainees undergoing training efforts, patients in therapy, or anybody else would be able to tell a researcher in an unbiased way whether the manipulation of education, training, experiment, or therapy had had any effect or what that effect was. In addition, many research studies have found that self-reports not only are inaccurate, but sometimes provide information opposite to the actual effects. That research shows that bias masquerades as objectivity in very sincere subjects, who then blurt out well-intentioned, sincere, but false results. The same research has identified sources of bias such as norms of self-presentation (subjects' desire to give the answer they think will make them look OK to the researcher), the tendency to confirm the hypothesis of the study (subjects try to figure out the "right" answer and give that one), and of course the tendencies to please the boss, protect your job, and keep out of trouble. These tendencies are palpably, obviously, and catastrophically present in every study in the published literature that this review has examined—that is virtually *every* study, and they number in the hundreds.

And if you still don't believe that self-reports are pervasive enough to invalidate the entire field, consider the attempt of some researchers[23] to make self-reported, quasi-experimental studies more rigorous. These studies certainly could use some more rigor, as they depend on subjects' self-report for the "pretest" and the "posttest" data. But Robinson and Robinson,[24] in their widely published training methods book, argue for a "then" condition. This is a technique that involves using a self-report posttest to generate a "then" condition, which is then treated as a pretest. The way this works is, instead of asking before training "how often do you . . . ?" Robinson and Robinson suggest asking people right after training, "Before training, how often did you . . . ?"

Robinson and Robinson have found that these "then" numbers come out lower than pretraining self-assessments, presumably because trainees now have a better understanding of what is meant[25]—and, of course, a lower pretest makes the effects of training look more impressive. The obvious criticism of all this is that self-reports are self-motivated. It is almost a research cliché that subjects in studies obey norms of self-presentation that lead them to respond to questionnaires and interviews in such a way as to make themselves look good, contribute to the success of the study, and please the researcher.

The posttraining "then" questionnaire that tends to lower self-assessments is almost laughably suspect for two reasons. First, the greater "awareness" of subjects may not be about what was meant and their own pretraining naiveté, but instead may be due to their realizing that they were going to be measured ("posttested") later and that they had better leave themselves some room to look as if they changed in the way they were supposed to. And second, the trainers and researchers themselves are likely to be biased in favor of lower self-assessments before training so that they themselves will appear more successful as trainers. Robinson and Robinson become their own perfect example of this, as, apparently without reservations or recognition that this might be even a little controversial, they claim that the "then" assessment is a good way to increase rigor and validity.

The literature of this field is disturbingly unanimous to the point that the very research that would get us to better methods and rigorous assessment is itself eaten up with boneheaded biases and ancient invalidities that keep it and us from getting anywhere.

Maps on the Road to Nowhere: Books on Training

Robinson and Robinson: *Training for Impact*.[26] This book recognizes that assessment is vital to a demonstration of the effectiveness of training and includes several chapters on posttraining testing. However, it assumes that the goal of all training is skill transference and says specifically that the more global an objective is, the less testable it is. So the scenario is, train for specific skill/behavior changes (these authors often call these "discrete behaviors or skills"), then use specific tests to look for the "transference" of the training, which is measured in increased frequency of trainees' execution of the "discrete" skill or behavior. There are techniques suggested to make this more accurate, including making self-reports based in scenarios, critical incident reports or simulations, cross-checking paper-and-pencil self-reports with paper-and-pencil assessments by peers or superiors, observing people on the job with a trained judge or two (the authors declare that this is time-consuming and expensive, and so they don't do it much themselves, except to cross-check paper-and-pencil measures), and so on.

Their discussion of design suggests using control groups to compare differences between the trained and the untrained, but the criteria are still frequency and self-reported success of specific skill transference. As to more global, attitudinal changes ("nonobservable results") sought by training, the authors state flatly that the trainee himself or herself is the only source of data. For this, they recommend one-on-one interviews in which the trainee describes what he or she would do in a particular situation, and the interviewer compares the result to the contents of training. As to values and beliefs, they recommend making up your own paper-and-pencil instrument with questions like, "I believe the most effective way for people to work effectively in our organization is to be cooperative, not competitive," responded to via a strongly agree–strongly disagree scale. But this is even worse than most self-reports: With these kinds of questions, the employee doesn't need to remember any of the contents of training to know what the "right" answer is.

Robinson and Robinson give an example of a case in which two groups of trainees were asked one of these value questions to which there was a "right" answer, according to the training and the desires of the client. One group increased its agreement with the value issue, but another group decreased its agreement; the authors indicate some difficulty in interpreting this result but report that they were able to use the information to warn the client of a "problem" with the group whose favorable value decreased. A more plausible reading of these results is that the training failed, and failed so badly that it made one group actually resist the corporate value it was supposed to promote. Robinson and Robinson unwittingly make this argument: Trainer bias can invalidate even a seemingly simple and objective skill-transference training, but even more so when the objective is attitude- or value-driven.

Finally, in a chapter on assessing operational results, Robinson and Robinson point out the difficulties of causally linking specific training to the general results of the organization. Their best hope is that if training addresses a specific problem or need area, the company will already have criteria and assessment mechanisms in place that are sensitive to changes in the area: less employee turnover, less waste, and increased productivity, for example. But every example they give is one in which the company's assessment mechanism was utilized, and there is virtually nothing here in which the trainer takes primary responsibility for creating a way to assess the effects of training. And if ROI is to be found at the operational level, they think it's nearly impossible to assess.

Summing up Robinson and Robinson: They shoot low and hit it—so low that they're blind to the invalidating bias that they themselves describe. This book is discouraging for any trainer who sees the task as creating a culture shift in the organization and assessing its value, because these authors believe that this is impossible and provide a "method" that will make sure they're right.

Giber et al.: *Best Practices in Leadership Development Handbook*.[27] This is a report of training in several companies using a particular approach, that of Linkage, Inc. Apparently, the discussions all are based on self-reports and have other obvious invalidities. The Colgate-Palmolive study claims that it assessed all four levels of effects of training, but if it assessed them, it did so by surveying participants of the study (imagine, if you will, the problems of asking the trainees how much their value to the organization increased). Motorola paid for a study in which business effects were assessed by sending out an e-mail to participants' managers, but the e-mail broadly hints that many managers will have already found the training to have had positive business effects, and also invites responses by e-mail *only* from those who are prepared to report positive findings! Several of these studies used 360-degree assessment instruments, but of course they assessed the most slippery of "soft" or personal criteria and were satisfied with that. Why shouldn't they be, when the authors had gone so far as to bias the results, according to their own report?

Here's another observation on these and other studies: Authors argue that management commitment to the training is essential to make it work. But then they assess the effects of training by surveying these same managers, whose commitment, if it's there at all, is almost certain to bias them in favor of it.

Shapiro: *Training Effectiveness Handbook*.[28] This book falls into many of the same research/assessment traps as the rest of the literature but stays focused on the author's own program, which is difficult to read and not very illuminating. Perhaps if you buy the program, the author will clarify the assessment and also his difficult book.

Gerber, comp.: *Evaluating Training*.[29] This anthology is a compilation of old *Training* articles that bear on the assessment of training; however, the most relevant, bottom-line-related, level 4 articles are full of we-could-do-this-and-it-would-be-neat but do not give many specifics on how to accomplish this ideal.

Kirkpatrick: *Evaluating Training Programs,* **2nd ed.**[30] This book is a short essay on the four levels of assessment, followed by about a dozen reports of assessed training efforts. But again, these are good companies, the reports are earnest, and the specifics are impressive, up to a point. The point beyond which they're not impressive is the point of assessing skill transference (level 3) and benefits to the company (level 4). At levels 1 and 2 they provide impressive attitude instruments, they have lots of ideas about measurement and validity, and so on. But when they move into levels 3 and 4, they become (1) once again based on participant reports and managers-of-participants' attitude measures and (2) very vague (management determined that these results were "worth 3 million," but they don't tell you how—not even close, not even a hint).

Finally, as we consider methods books, let us consider the holy-of-holies:

Phillips: *Handbook of Training Evaluation.*[31] This is the best source on how it *could* be done. It has chapters that detail a much longer list of "hard" or quantifiable criteria of measurement than is given anywhere else in recent literature, as well as arguing that these hard criteria can be assessed using data and assessment mechanisms that are already available in the organization. In addition, he devotes a chapter to an extensive list of "soft" outcomes of training and then makes the argument for and provides a method of estimating the dollar value of both hard and soft outcomes, so that ROI can be calculated in terms of dollars.

There are chapters on assessing the real costs of training, training assessment designs provided in terms of their similarity to research designs, and data analysis of experiment-related research designs.

This is a great book on "here's what you *can* do"; the odd thing is, one doesn't see anybody in the published literature taking its advice. The recent published studies in periodicals are not even close to this level of thoroughness and rigor. Compared to what actual training assessment studies accomplish, Phillips seems pie-in-the-sky. The author makes it sound plausible, but in spite of how reasonable it sounds, it's far away from what people are actually doing; this may be in part because the approach advocated here requires a lot more time and planning and rigorous assessment than most people want to or are able to plan for.

Summing Up the Literature, Moving to a New Approach

Clearly the literature on assessment of training varies widely, from the dismal to the ideal. Unfortunately, the ideal does not seem to appear anywhere in the actual. The ideal appears in a pure form in the Phillips textbook, but the actual studies themselves are characterized more by the dismal, the invalid, the we-really-don't-know-whether-we-had-any-effect-or-not.

So it is now time to shift our attention to the happier task of proposing solutions and new directions. The method used in the following discussion will be important to consider a new way of talking and thinking about the problem, a new model that aims to do justice to all the aspects and possible outcomes of corporate education and points to more plausible and effective ways of assessing those effects.

Of course, any new model must acknowledge and respond to Kirkpatrick. As we have seen, Kirkpatrick's model of the four levels has become an industry standard, and it has certainly made the field think hard about rigor and accountability. However, our literature review suggests that some of the problems may be with the model itself. Level 4 has come to be viewed by some as a perfectionist ideal, able only to indict those that fail, without promoting any successes. The remains of studies that failed to scale its heights are littered around its base camps.

An important clue to the problem may lie in the fact that Kirkpatrick is a *training and development* model. It is time to recognize that corporate universities must be a different animal, one whose purpose is to consistently, effectively, and efficiently enhance the culture of an entire organization. Training and development models tend to participate in the old, comfortable assumptions from academia that exclude wondering about whether we're necessary or expendable. Of course, we're necessary; after all, we're *training and development*. Furthermore, the structure of the corporation has often supported this, burying training departments deep in the human resources wing, where they were cozy and academic (and also unquestioned).

It is time for corporate universities to step up to the difference and choose a new course. In other words, if corporate universities perceive themselves to be different, not just glorified training departments, then they must actually *be* significantly different. Otherwise, the choice is to outsource training or to go back to being buried deep inside the human resources department, bringing in off-the-shelf courses, sending your folks out to various and sundry programs that not only don't complement each other but can actually conflict, then bringing your folks back into the environment after they have been "developed" and letting them suffer the massive frustration of having new skills that can't be used in the old culture. If you have actually chosen to travel the path of a *corporate university,* then you must recognize that your mission includes not just keeping up with a few technological changes, but rather advancing and altering the whole culture of your organization to adapt to a world in flux. This means developing a sophisticated view of the big picture of change, and it means treating yourself like other top executives by giving yourself the same respect and rigor that all other leaders are given—by proving and communicating your worth.

Proposed Changes in the Measurement Model

I propose using the Kirkpatrick model as a launching pad but going beyond the training approach to a more holistic, complete model, one oriented more toward corporate universities and the more influential mission that we argue for throughout this book. At the same time, we propose an approach that is more *plausible and rigorous* in terms of assessment tools available for measurement. In other words, a good corporate university model should deal accurately with the actual dimensions and effects of corporate development, but also deal *realistically* with appropriate tools and methods to assess those effects.

Accordingly, I propose the following methods of assessment.

Level 1, Participant Satisfaction: What Does the Student Think of the Training?

Well-known pencil-and-paper instruments that assess this level exist, but it is important to remember to measure what you really want to know and not to give excessive credence to results from this level. All too often a development session that left people in a mental spin because it challenged their worldview was panned by participants because the educator/facilitator made students uncomfortable or did not use PowerPoint. Let's be *very* clear: You may want to know about "satisfaction," but it does not measure *learning*. I'm not even sure that we want people to feel satisfied at the end of a development program. If the purpose of development is change, then people will by their very nature strain against it. We have been unable to find any research that significantly correlates participant satisfaction with any of the other forms of measured results, such as attitude or behavior change. Sometimes, if we consider the participants as the *products* of the training, perhaps making them uncomfortable can even be a good thing.

In addition, there is a danger in asking about people's satisfaction prematurely. Business professors will argue that the results of their teaching shouldn't be measured until well after their courses have been completed. What key learnings people needed and used and what made a difference in their careers can be measured only long after the completion of a course.

Level 2, Cognitive Acquired Knowledge

Here we split Kirkpatrick's level 2. Our level 2 deals with accumulated content or cognitive knowledge. To assess this dimension, we can continue to utilize the academic model of testing—multiple-choice and/or essay exams. These existing assessment tools can adequately answer the question: Did the participant acquire new information, facts, vocabulary, and formulas, at least in short-term memory? It is important to note that this measures only the acquisition or "stacking" of information, not "learning," which we define as the use and application of knowledge.

Level 3, Technical Skill Acquisition

At this new level, we place the most basic of behavioral changes, those that are easiest to measure accurately. Did volume increase as a result of new skills training? Did safety improve as a result of learning new ways of doing things? Is the participant able to program or use computer software? Most technical areas of expertise have tools for assessment that are valid and are in place now. We know how to assess whether new software does the job, whether a pilot can demonstrate increased skills on the simulator, or whether a repairperson can effectively troubleshoot a piece of equipment.

Level 4, Attitude and Perception Change

At this point, corporate universities must launch themselves from the Kirkpatrick platform to greater rigor and more noble and global outcomes. Training and development pays entirely too little attention to measuring attitude. The various specialties in behavioral science—psychology, sociology, influence, and persuasion, to name a few—have long known that attitudes and behaviors are closely linked. Imagine what would happen if marketing specialists failed to prove the effects of their work, were never asked to do so, and/or did not know how to measure the effects of their work on consumer attitudes and buying behavior. How long do you think they would keep their jobs?

The literature review on corporate training, however, shows that a situation much like this one exists in our field. For example, it identifies several failed studies whose authors expressed disappointment at their inability to see positive change in the area of attitude or perceptual change. Trainees stayed where they were, or trainings backfired and made things worse. The review makes it clear that to change attitudes and perceptions, to get people to see things differently, we must leave the fields of education and training and development and introduce the social and behavioral science fields of influence and change, moving away from educational design and assessment tools and drawing on social science research techniques. This means that development programs are a form of "treatment," educators are change agents, and the intention of development is to create the kind of change that we hope adds up to something. Our literature review suggests that efforts to change attitudes have fallen into the trap that Abraham Lincoln feared: passing off "as progress what was really just change," and "dispensing only knowledge when we should be dispensing wisdom."

Furthermore, we cannot afford to be ineffective in this area:

> What does attitude or belief change buy the change agent? Potentially a lot, because these internal changes often set the stage for later behavior changes."[32]

Furthermore, these authors point out, attitudes are deeply embedded in the human system and represent a sort of key or opening to the system that, once changed, can make way for systemic changes in other components as well.

> The interconnectedness of attitudes, cognitions, feelings, intentions, and behaviors into organized systems has a very important implication. It means that change in any one component may lead to change in another. A change in belief may cause revision of the attitude. A new atti-

> tude, as already suggested . . . may ultimately lead to new
> behaviors (or . . . a reverse process is possible in which
> behavior change may cause attitude change). . . . Attitude
> systems—within and between each other—are orga-
> nized, such that changes in one facet of a person often
> cause changes in other facets.[33]

It is well known in the social sciences, however, that standardized and
pencil-and-paper attitude measures are an unreliable method of predicting
specific behaviors. The connection between attitudes and behaviors has
been a source of ongoing study for decades but has been poorly tested by
many researchers because of overly simplified attitude measures. Fortunately for our purposes, a new generation of attitude assessment tools has
emerged that apply strategies and tools of narrative analysis to what people
say about a topic during a conversation, interview, group session, or other
occasion where their narrative can be recorded and analyzed objectively. It
is important to note that the nature of narrative data (participants' opinions,
beliefs, and attitudes about certain concepts) is drastically different from
that of self-report data (opinions about themselves) and drastically different
from essay tests (answers measuring data recall and application).

> A large number and variety of psychological variables can
> be measured through content analysis: needs, values, atti-
> tudes, stereotypes, authoritarianism, ethnocentrism, cre-
> ativity, and so on.[34]

Zimbardo and Leippe agree, saying that content analysis techniques
can be useful for analyzing a person's narrative to measure "such dimensions as complexity of thought, evaluative consistency of thought, and
knowledge of a topic."[35] Content analysis is arguably more revealing of the
complexity of attitudes because it gets around the problems of tests made
up in researchers' language that misses the subjects' own constructs. It is
important to use content analysis when "given certain theoretical components of the data themselves, the subject's own language is crucial to the
investigation."[36]

Narrative analysis software can make this analysis and assessment technique not only easier to use, but also more objective and valid as well. In
one narrative pre- and postassessment, we found that beliefs about leadership changed as a result of a thirteen-month leadership action-learning de-

velopment program for fast-track high-potential managers in a succession-planning model. We simply asked, "Define leadership and leadership behaviors." Participants' predevelopment narrative themes clearly showed that they thought leadership behaviors included treating people fairly, listening, communicating, and so on (almost all soft-skill and interpersonal behaviors). But in our analysis of postdevelopment narratives, participants had clearly changed their beliefs, adding an equally important external focus of knowledge and application of business acumen, making difficult decisions, setting direction, understanding strategy, knowing the competitive environment, and being able to look further into the future.

This is one of the first demonstrations of significant attitude change among business development participants that we have seen anywhere, and it brings with it the dual credentials of being measurable and empirical, while also being generated in the very words of participants themselves, not those of trainers or researchers. If Zimbardo and Leippe are correct, we can now expect most of these participants to behave differently and, in addition, to maintain different expectations and understanding of their leaders.

We emphasize that in the present era of American business, it is now possible for the first time both to change attitudes (utilizing a research-validated social scientific model) and to accurately assess pre- and posttraining attitudes and make reliable predictions from attitude data using a software-based analysis of participants' own narratives. Again, we stress that the nature of narrative data (participants' opinions, beliefs, and attitudes about certain concepts) is drastically different from self-report data (participants' opinions about themselves) and drastically different from essay tests (answers measuring data recall and application).

Level 5, Individual Behavior Change

Assuming that the mission of a corporate university is that of change agent, we again quote the social science experts in attitude change. "Ultimately, the goal of an influence agent is to change the target's behavior."[37] Our level 5 is similar to Kirkpatrick's level 3, which states, "Behavior can be defined as the extent to which change in behavior has occurred because the participant attended the training program."[38] Consequently, we must accurately and effectively measure the change in the individual participants' behavior. As we argued in the previous section, the most common method of measuring behavioral change is through self-report data, but self-report data are simply not a reliable or valid way to measure behavioral change. In fact, social scientists have long known that this method is absolutely preposterous. So what do we do to measure more effectively? Aside from the simple ways to measure that are easily quantifiable (fewer sick days taken by the individual, more phone calls answered by the individual, fewer complaints about the individual, etc.), the best ways we have of measuring behavioral change are through videotaping and different types of 360-degree evaluations. These measures *are not valid*, however if we do not have pre- and posttraining measures. In what used to be called soft-skill training (which we now call "the really hard" skill development), measuring effects is essential but has historically been an embarrassment.

Pre- and posttraining videotaping is permanent and visual proof of learning. When the trained changes are behavioral rather than cognitive in nature, this method is the only one that can actually prove effective outcomes. In developing improved decision-making skills, team effectiveness, meeting management, facilitation behaviors, and executive presence, for example, we videotape the participants before the learning program and several weeks after the program (we do this several weeks later in order to determine the permanence or "stickiness" of the change). Neutral evaluators are then trained to evaluate and quantify any differences. The setup, of course, must be rigorous enough to permit unobtrusive measures and coding criteria to ensure reliability and validity. This is not a complicated or costly method. It can also be simplified so that it is quite efficient, as well. Considering the cost of delivering and attending such programs, the minimal dollar and time costs of measuring the effects are well worth it.

Although we strongly recommend the use of 360-degree instruments, the criticism of pre- and postlearning measures of these tools is worth paying attention to. These tools are designed to evaluate the strengths and weaknesses in the perceived behaviors of the subjects according to the people who are the recipients of the behaviors. The program for the participant is then to develop him or her through classroom and coaching treatments, assuming that the weaker behaviors (those evaluated as needing improvement) will improve. The main concern in this design is that the people filling out the postlearning questionnaires may not be the same people who filled out the prelearning questionnaires; the concerns revolve around two different populations filling out the survey instrument. In other words, the people who decided that you needed to improve are not the ones who get to decide *if* you improved. Looked at objectively, there is a faulty assumption in these concerns. The purpose of a 360-degree instrument is supposed to be an objective measurement that determines other people's perceptions of you—not those of specific people, but of the population in general. If the prelearning evaluators would rate you differently in the postlearning evaluation from the way another neutral population would rate you, we can interpret this in only three ways: (1) The results say more about the original evaluators than they do about you; (2) what you need is relationship management, not behavioral change; or (3) there is something wrong with the measurement design. This can easily be overcome by using the rigors of a "nonequivalent group" research design.

Level 6, Individual Behavioral Change Regarding Application of New Knowledge

This level starts to get at the cultural change aspect of development. Our level 6 applies to the more advanced development programs intended to build problem solvers, decision makers, supervisors, managers, leaders, specialists, experts—in other words, thinkers. At this level, a potent way to measure individual change regarding the application of knowledge can be very behavioral in nature: active versus passive learning. Action learning projects, which are assigned to participants in longer-term development programs, are intended to measure the application of new knowledge, especially in ways that can enhance the organization that is bearing the developmental costs. If the participants are required to calculate potential or actual ROI as a result of their action learning projects, we are then able to quantify the value of the new learning. In most of the leadership programs we have conducted, however, we have found a serious lack of skills regarding the ability to calculate ROI or cost versus benefits. If employees cannot calculate these simple formulas, they run the risk of not being allowed to have ideas or to further or implement those ideas. The problem we are addressing here in this chapter regarding training and development is rampant as we go deeper in organizations in general.

First and foremost, people in all areas of business must have a basic understanding of cost/benefit analysis. We cannot assume that individuals or groups can make informed decisions without using this basic tool. But to ensure progress, not just change, we must also reframe our definition of risk and ROI. Historically, risk has been calculated in terms of simple cost/ benefit analysis: If the project outcome fell within the benefit side of the equation, it was considered a success. We propose a new definition for "successful outcome," one that redefines the word *benefits*. Benefits cannot be defined solely as saved or earned dollars. For a progressive organization, a "thinking" organization, this definition is too narrow. There is an old story about an R&D team that was sent off to invent a special kind of widget. Historically, the company had given bonuses to teams that were able to successfully complete their projects. This team invented the specified widget but found that it could not reasonably be taken to market because it would be too expensive to manufacture and would not replace what was currently on the market. The company then said, "Thank you very much" and denied the team its bonus. The R&D team cried foul. Going back to the leadership, the team members explained that they had done what was asked, and that what they had done was of value because of the knowledge gained. They had learned that it could be done but would not be, so they needn't worry about the competition or spend any more time on this project. To make a long and probably mythical story short, the company rethought its position and gave the R&D team two bonuses, one for inventing the product successfully and one for teaching the company that transferable knowledge is a successful outcome. In our action learning projects, knowledge or learning gained as a result of the project that can be demonstrated to be transferable and able to be used to improve other situations (there is a specific formula for this) is considered ROI and is considered a successful outcome.

Another, very simple change in the way we define the outcome of a simple calculation of costs and benefits can help. The action learner determines the cost/benefit formula in the proposal for her or his project. If the program is then implemented and the results fall within the predicted cost/benefit range, the project is considered a success because the cost/benefit range was predicted accurately, even if the outcome falls closer to the cost than to the benefit. This is one more way of recognizing that knowledge is another form of ROI if that knowledge can be transferable.

Redefining the way we calculate risk and ROI will move us toward a more risk-friendly environment—a "thinking" organization. The more we can do this and measure the results, the more we can move the culture as well. Ironically, corporate universities, if their mission is truly to change the culture, can alter and improve the culture powerfully yet simply by changing the way they measure the results of training and development programs. To become a thinking organization, we must learn to more effectively . . . think.

Level 7, Critical Mass Change

Corporate universities like CB Richard Ellis's CBREU are trying to make a bigger difference. Their development programs are designed to create a critical mass so that there is a large enough group of people who have the new worldview and the new skills to move the entire organization. In the case of corporate universities, therefore, the target is not just the participant himself or herself, it is the organization's culture in general. Kirkpatrick circles around this vaguely in his level 4 definition: "Results can be defined as the final results that occurred because the participants attended the program. The final results can include increased production, improved quality, decreased costs, reduced frequency and/or severity of accidents, increased sales, reduced turnover, and higher profits."[39]

Our level 7 is a very simple step that adds and/or averages the accumulated data within all of the previous evaluation steps. For corporate universities whose purpose is to create corporate culture change (which, it is hoped, is what Lincoln meant by progress), this is a critical form of measurement. A pre- and postlearning narrative that measures the aggregate would easily measure corporate attitude change. This measurement costs about $5 to $20 per person maximum. To date, CBRE, for example, has developed 1,000 people worldwide at the mid to upper levels. The cost of the final measurement is small, considering that it proves ROI and effect. Then, in pilot tests of newly formed pilot teams, a simple cost/benefit formula could be developed and the final analysis could be calculated.

Level 8, Culture Change

To show rigorous, comprehensive level 7 results, you would need to triangulate results from multiple levels, such as (1) cumulative results from attitude change scores; (2) cumulative results from behavioral change scores; (3) cumulative results from cost/benefit analysis outcomes; and/or (4) cumulative results from cognitive knowledge gained scores. Triangulation is a concept and a simple statistical formula that seeks multiple ways to answer the same question. If there is agreement among the answers, then you can assume that you are onto something—that the individual answers are more valid. You are testing one result against another. If you arrive at differing answers, they cast doubt on each other and on the methods you used to arrive at the results. This is similar to going to at least three doctors for independent opinions regarding a diagnosis. If they agree, you can assume that they confirm each other. It gives you more confidence that you have arrived at a "truth." If you finally triangulate the various results you have found in the areas of knowledge, attitude, and behavior, for example, you will have a comprehensive measurement of results that can show large-scale organizational change.

To recap and simplify, here is a brief description of each of the levels we use:

Level 1: Participant satisfaction. Self-report measures of participant satisfaction.

Level 2: Cognitive acquired knowledge. Pencil-and-paper multiple-choice or essay tests to measure accumulated information.

Level 3: Technical skill acquisition. Pre- and postlearning measures and observations of specific, technical skill behaviors.

Level 4: Attitude and perception change. Pre- and postlearning narrative design content analysis to demonstrate attitude and belief change.

Level 5: Individual behavioral change. Pre- and postlearning video and/or 360-degree evaluations using nonequivalent group design.

Level 6: Individual behavioral change regarding application of new knowledge. Calculated ROI on action learning projects to measure behavioral change and application of learning.

Level 7: Critical mass change. A combination of pre- and postlearning data within levels 1 through 6 to show cumulative and general results at each level.

Level 8: Culture change. Triangulation of measures of cognitive, attitudinal, and behavioral changes to cross-check the reliability and validity of all three.

Conclusion

Einstein once said, "Perfection of means and confusion of ends seems to characterize our age." A word of caution is necessary here before we conclude. We have attempted to give the reader a new, more rigorous, yet cost-effective way to measure the effects of employee development and changes in corporate culture. To defend our existence, corporate universities and chief learning officers must be held to the same rigor as other corporate departments and executives. As developers of human capital, we must not shy away from what looks complicated, and, even more important, we must not shy away from what might be considered negative results. I have argued here that knowledge gained has a positive benefit when it comes to the difference between what is just change and what is truly progress.

At this point, at the risk of seeming to contradict this entire chapter, I would like to close with a contrary thought. We must prove the need for our existence; we must calculate the value we bring. If we are going to measure, we should, of course, measure rigorously, measure what we really need to know, and learn from our results. It is equally if not more important, however, that we keep our focus on what truly matters. Human development does not always lend itself to perfect mathematical formulas or even statistics. We must be careful, therefore, to avoid getting caught up too much in our own paradigm, our own perfection of means, and forgetting the immeasurable value of learning in and of itself. The mind that has been exposed to ideas is not like a rubber band—once expanded, it does not snap back to its original shape. The purpose of an education, regardless of how it is obtained, is actually not to *know,* but to *think.* This may be what Lincoln meant by the difference between knowledge and wisdom. The purpose of thinking is to analyze, to assess similarities and differences among situations, to be able to detect variations and exceptions, to make creative and effective decisions based on this analysis, and to act on those decisions in effective and ethical ways. It is nearly impossible to measure the mistakes we do not make because of what we have learned. Einstein also once said, "Not everything that counts can be counted, and not everything that can be counted counts."

10

Measuring ROI in Corporate Universities

Death of the Student Day and Birth of Human Capital

Matt Barney

The bottom line is what matters to your CEO. Corporate universities need to shift their focus to the bottom-line issues that matter. This means becoming both physicians diagnosing business pain and investment bankers looking at what solutions will have the best payoff. Those of us who have made this shift know that sometimes learning solutions are needed—but not always. As Tom McCarty pointed out in Chapter 4, an understanding of organizational goals and gaps is the foundation of metrics for modern corporate universities.

The new rallying cry for corporate universities is creating value. Your corporation has thousands of different investment options. Learning is just one candidate. At the time of this writing in late 2001, the global economy is skirting recession. Thousands of employees are losing their jobs, and corporate university budgets are being cut. Why? Because in the past we have managed training as an entitlement. For executives, this translates to a cost without discernible value. Some training leaders have an almost religious belief that more training is always better. Their corporate universities offer catalogs of courses, much as Club Med offers guests the options of swimming, snorkeling, and gourmet cuisine. Training metrics also follow this Disneyland model. Success in an entertainment-centered corporate university means that lots of students attended lots of classes, loved the cookies, and enjoyed the instructor's jokes.

Rarely is training used as a strategic weapon. Business leaders are cutting training budgets today because the costs of training are crystal clear, but the value is murky. Rarely do corporate universities get around to measuring anything more than the first of Kirkpatrick's levels. Return on investment (ROI) is almost never examined. ROI has often been rejected as too difficult or impossible to attribute exclusively to training. At the same time, without any information about value creation, is it really surprising that training budgets are slashed?

Rethinking Corporate University Metrics

Measures are the starting and end points for a new corporate university. Where are business results bad? What's causing these bad results? Is employee performance part of the cause? Where are investments required to close the business gap? By helping our executives answer these questions, we diagnose and solve critical business problems. To do this, we have to turn Don Kirkpatrick's and Jack Phillips' evaluation models upside down (see Figure 10-1). We also need to rethink the first few levels of their models, based on the latest research. This will give us a new model that will help us become human capital asset managers.

Before I go into human capital asset management, I will review the landscape of corporate training metrics. This will help us understand where we've been, so we don't repeat our past mistakes.

Old-School Metrics

Traditionally, corporate universities have placed a large amount of emphasis on metrics dealing with class satisfaction and volume. The focus has been on the quantity of training and on students' pleasure in learning. Unfortunately, these do not predict whether the learner will perform better[1] or help the business.[2] Performance, not satisfaction, is the fundamental goal of the new corporate university.

Figure 10-1.   Turning Kirkpatrick and Phillips upside down.

5. ROI

4. Business Impact

3. Performance

Don Kirkpatrick

2. Learning

1. Predictors of Performance

Most trainers focus exclusively on end-of-class satisfaction measures. Unfortunately, cumulative research has shown that satisfaction measures do not predict improved employee performance.[3] Class satisfaction is important only in predicting whether students will want to take future classes. If traditional "level 1s" don't predict employee performance improvement, then they can't possibly predict business impact or ROI. External training vendors that want to sell more training will still want these "smile sheets," since they predict whether people will want to come back. But for the modern corporate university, traditional level 1 evaluations are largely useless. Sure, you don't want to bore your learners to death, particularly if they are senior executives. But the emphasis needs to be on ramping up

199

the performance that constrains business goals. Business performance improvement and early warning signs of ROI are the metrics that matter.

In addition to class satisfaction measures, another commonly used measure is course volume. Volume metrics like "student days" or "cost per student day" are even more common than class satisfaction "smile sheets." Trainers have fallen in love with student day metrics for years. We count them, compare them, and feel good about how many student days we've produced. Our love affair with student days is so intense that when new technology, such as e-learning, comes along, instead of creating new metrics, we continue to measure in hours.

Why do we measure student days? We believe that student days or student hours are a measure of the quantity of value we have produced for the company. We feel good about producing more student days every year, feeling that more is always better and that it shows growth. Does it really? Do our organizations always benefit from more student days?

RIP (b. 1980–d. 2001)

Several years ago, experts working with a "human performance technology" frame of reference argued that the student day was not meaningful.[4] Strategic business result gaps should define what types of employee performance enhancement are needed in the first place.

1. To begin, who produces time? In the past, understanding class duration helped us to understand the amount of resources we needed in order to teach courses. Cost per student day was a simple metric that became an industry standard that could be used to measure efficiency in "producing" student days.

But is this really consistent with how business defines efficiency? The semiconductor industry manages cost-efficiency by taking a global look at the total amount of resources it takes to produce the transistors on a chip. Cost per chip per layer is a standard industry benchmarking metric used to compare production efficiency across companies. This is sensible, because computer chip factories produce transistors. They seek to maximize the number of quality transistors with the fewest possible resources. However, cost per minute or per day is not a meaningful measure of a factory's performance, because factories do not produce time. No one produces time.

If cost per day or per hour is not meaningful to them, why should it be meaningful to us? Courses are one of several ways to produce improved employee and business performance. Motorola University is starting to measure cost per employee performance shift and ROI because they are much more reflective of organizational-level value creation.

2. Minimize cost or maximize hours? In the past, people believed that focusing on a cost per day metric would drive cost efficiency by directing training organizations to minimize the numerator of the equation: the cost. But this measure also creates an incentive to create training that is longer than needed. The denominator (the student day) can be expanded to get a better cost per day metric, without taking into consideration whether longer is better for the business. Similarly, this measure creates an incentive to stuff the largest possible number of students into each instructor-led class when the costs remain the same, or to offer low-quality, inexpensive e-learning offerings when cost is the biggest driver. In these ways, the cost/time measure motivates the learning professional to reduce training's ability to help the business because longer classes and weak educational offerings destroy value. Minimizing cost per unit of time also inadvertently minimizes ROI.

In reality, time is money. The more time it takes for students to learn, the less productive they are. This opportunity cost is reflected in what finance calls the time value of money. Money (capital) that the company spends on creating long classes and sending students to classes that are longer than needed is money that should have been invested elsewhere. If time is a cost to the business, then cost per day is irrelevant—it is cost divided by cost.

3. Real cost. Training organizations usually consider their own budgets in the cost estimate. But if you ask your CFO, the bigger cost to the business is having valuable employees away from their work, burning travel and living dollars—especially when the learners are executives. These costs are typically not included in the cost per day measure because they are incurred by the business (not the training department) or because the qualitative aspects are perceived as more difficult to measure.

4. Static versus dynamic time. At the same time, costs that were once fixed are now variable. In the past, when all courses were taught in a face-to-face environment, every student spent the same amount of time in the class. With the dawning of e-learning, assessments can be used to tailor instruction to the unique needs of each student. Each student can have a variable instructional path that achieves the same performance goals. E-learning is helping to highlight how nonsensical cost per hour, day, or minute measures are because each learner takes a different amount of time to complete learning objectives. While some trainers in the industry have tried to use an e-learning equivalency multiplier, the cost per day measure is still fundamentally flawed, since its base is cost, not value.

Birth of Human Capital Metrics

The bottom line is that satisfaction- or volume-based approaches attempt to measure the wrong parameters. Student satisfaction and course volume measure superficial aspects of learning. Volume deals with the quantity, as opposed to the quality, of formal instructional activity. Satisfaction isn't related to impact. The purpose of almost any human resource system change is to improve employee performance. This can be done through learning—books, e-learning, instructor-led training, communities of practice, and nonlearning interventions—incentive compensation, selection, or automation.

In training, we pretend that our cost per day or cost per hour metrics are measuring our efficiency. In reality, they are not because the purpose of training is not to produce time. Training produces performance shifts or behavior and attitudinal change. The only employee performance shifts that matter are those that help your corporation accomplish the strategic goals Tom McCarty discusses in Chapter 4.

Motorola University has developed a new model that understands the interrelationships between measures that give early warning signs about whether the business is likely to get a return on its human resource system investments. Motorola does this holistically—not just for training, but for all aspects of human resources that drive employee performance and can cause the business pain. At the same time, unlike other companies that do ROI only after the fact (and rarely at that), Motorola uses ROI as an investment banker does—before and after initiatives.

Practical ROI

The approaches to using ROI developed by Kirkpatrick and later by Jack Phillips[5] are typically implemented after the fact, long after training is complete. This focus is, in part, responsible for the fact that existing ROI measures are scarcely used in real companies. Businesspeople consider the ROI of investments before and after making them.

The most important measures for training involve the outcomes they produce on the business. As mentioned before, the approach that is used at Motorola University turns the traditional Kirkpatrick and Phillips levels upside down by first focusing on the value of business metric gaps. We do this in a way that borrows the latest ideas from a number of different disciplines (solution sales, finance, project management, and psychology) to transform the traditional corporate university. We call this the Motorola University (MU) Performance Gap Analysis Model (Figure 10-2).

Step 1: Diagnose Business Pain

The Performance Gap Analysis Model starts with understanding the type and financial size of business gaps. Examples of business metric gaps include cash flow problems, shortfalls, and slow cycle times. We start with the metrics that are keeping your CEO from sleeping soundly at night. Ideally, they should be derived either from setting new strategic objectives, as described in Chapter 4, or from reviewing current initiatives in service of an existing strategy. We work together with the business to monetize (put into dollars) what those business-level metrics are worth. For example, suppose your executive team has a goal of acquiring 20 percent of the total available market but as of today has acquired only 5 percent. By looking at the financials of competitors, marketing knows that the total available market is worth $20 billion. If your business only has $1 billion of the total (5

Figure 10-2.   MU Performance Gap Analysis Model.

| 1. Business metric gap—$ |
| 2. Business gap closure date |
| 3. Performance |
| 4. Performance drivers |

percent of total available market) and you're looking to get $4 billion (20 percent of total available market), then you have a $3 billion business gap ($1 billion—$4 billion). The key to making this analysis successful is to collaborate on the analysis with your leaders. The numbers have to be theirs—they have to believe them. The importance of this first step cannot be stressed enough. It is critical to collaborate with your executive sponsor on this step. If your client doesn't understand the business metric gaps and believe the dollar value of solving the problem, the rest of your ROI analysis will lack credibility and validity. Figure 10-3 shows an example of monetizing a business performance gap.

At the same time, you need to understand the date by which the business must have the improvement. This should be derived from the strategic goals. Suppose in this example that the strategic objective of securing 20 percent of the market is to be complete by Q4 of 2002. This means that all the efforts to improve market share must secure the additional $3 billion of business no later than December 31, 2002. Both of these metrics will be critical to framing the particulars of the investment opportunity—whether or not learning is one of the causes. Figure 10-4 shows the lead and lag indicators of time. Time is a critical component of the modern return on investment analyses described later in this chapter. Again, it is critical that your client derive this date from its strategy, so the date is believable and meaningful.

Step 2: Analyze Employee Performance

The second step is to troubleshoot the root causes of the gap. Using techniques from organizational diagnosis and performance analysis,[6] we look

Figure 10-3. Business gap in dollars.

Worldwide opportunity, 2001	$20 billion
Desired win rate (20%)	$4 billion
Current win rate (5%)	$1 billion
Equals $ value of the business problem	$3 billion

$$(\$20 \text{ billion}) \times (15\%) = \$3 \text{ billion}$$

for symptoms of what is causing the business gaps. Sometimes, but not always, the root cause is employee performance problems. To determine whether employee performance is one of the causes, we look for data that will give us clues. The sources of data for this analysis can include customer satisfaction data, business process data, performance appraisals, or organizational surveys. We want to solve only real problems that are causing the business metric pain.

Once we are sure that employee performance is one of the culprits, we work with our business leaders to understand how much of the business gap is due to employees. Continuing the previous example, Figure 10-5 shows the result of a fictional collaboration on understanding why we have a market share gap. Note that this process involves consultation and collective decision making about the relative contribution of different root causes. From all the available data, you and the business leaders agree that the biggest cause (60 percent) is the unreliability of our product. Competitors have products that are significantly more reliable, and our customer satisfaction surveys suggest that this is the main reason why they are buying from our competition.

Second, our costs are 35 percent too high. Costs represent 20 percent of the reason why the business gap is looming.

Figure 10-4. Business gap closure date.

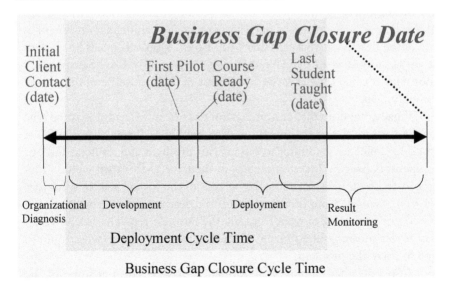

205

Figure 10-5. Causes of business gap.

Actions	Owners	% Impact on Goal	Status	Completion Date
Increase product reliability to 99.999%	T. Fusakawa	60%	On track to be 1 month early	04 Sep 01
Decrease cost by 35% by leveraging supplier management	G. Hernandez	20%	Current cost reductions at $200M (30%)	22 Jul 01
Improve solutions selling performance of sales force to be at 85% Top Box	M. Kennedy	10%	New driver identified. Solution project plan ready in 2 weeks	14 Jun 02
Increase new high-bandwidth technologies to 100 Gig/sec	S. Patel	10%	25 Gig/sec prototype successful	31 Dec 05
Totals		100%		

Next, suppose our salespeople are product and quarterly quota focused, as opposed to being solution and customer loyalty focused. Because of their product focus, they do not attempt to understand the needs of the customer and position our products relative to the customer's unmet needs, and in contrast to competitors. In our customer satisfaction surveys, our salespeople get an average of only 25 percent of customers rating them as one of the best. Motorola calls this "Top Box." Motorola needs 85 percent of all its customers to perceive our sales team as Top Box. Salespeople's poor performance appears to be 10 percent of the root cause of the overall $3 billion gap.

Finally, we note that customers don't see how we're going to be able to take them to the next generation of technologies. They have significant "lock-in" once they commit to buying our products and services, and our competitors have better technologies in their R&D labs than we do. This appears to be the cause of about 10 percent of the overall gap. In summary, we have examined the data along with our leaders and collaborated on a shared understanding of what's causing the business gap. This is a powerful way to get meaningful estimates of ROI before we choose what route to take to solve the problem.

Also note that employee performance may be creating some of the root causes. For example, are employees using good statistical quality methods to ensure product reliability? Is the financial performance of inventory managers causing the cost gap? Or perhaps our marketing team is not pricing the products appropriately, causing our prices to be too high? Are our scientists able to invent the future in the same way as our competition? Each of these may be an additional opportunity to identify areas in which the corporate university may be able to add value.

Step 3: Determine Performance Drivers

Third, we need to dig into why employees are not performing. Performance appraisals, organizational climate surveys, process data, and interviews can help uncover the root causes for employee performance gaps. When sifting through the data, we look for clues as to whether the work environment, process design, motivation, skills, or capacities seem to be responsible for the performance gaps. This step is critical to understand whether learning is part of the problem, and if so, how big a driver it is. Figure 10-6 lists the various performance drivers and possible solutions. It is important to note that even if knowledge and skills gaps are causing the business performance gap, training may not always be the best solution. Certain knowledge and skill drivers take a long time to develop or are very expensive to train (e.g., Ph.D. molecular biologists). For these areas, hiring new employees might give your company a better ROI. Alternatively, if you need a large volume of scarce knowledge or skills, you might achieve a better ROI by acquiring companies with a bunch of employees who possess these capabilities rather than trying to train for those skills. At the other end of the spectrum, the knowledge gaps may be for jobs that have mundane and repetitive tasks. It may be better, faster, or cheaper for your organization to automate these tasks.

Once we have a handle on the performance drivers causing employee performance, we also try to understand the relative size of the drivers. This helps us understand how much of the overall dollar value of the business gap we should invest in any particular learning solution. Figure 10-7 takes us through the example with these next estimates. In this example, customer knowledge and solution sales skill is causing 22 percent of the overall employee performance gap.

Step 4: ROI

Taking these steps together gives us a powerful, credible way to causally link learning to business results. It also helps us frame the size and speed of

Figure 10-6. Driver-solution links.

Driver	Possible Solution
Environmental	Culture change
	New tools
	Automation
	Provide access
Process	Redesign
	Hire more people
	Automate
Motivation	Reward right behavior
	Show performers the value of their work
	Performance management
Skills/Knowledge	Communities of practice
	E-learning
	Instructor-led education
	Hybrid e-learning and classroom-based
	Job aids
	Performance support tools
	Hire people with the knowledge and skills
	Automate
Capacities	New recruiting and selection system
	Career transition employees without capacity
	Redesign job

the investment. Together with cost estimates, these data allow us to estimate the ROI of different options before investing, and ultimately calculating our actual ROI. Figure 10-8 shows the basic ROI equation. It involves the ratio of benefit to overall investment. Importantly, it emphasizes that any investment should produce a return above the capital cost, or else it may not be worthwhile to make the investment. For example, corporations have to pay interest on bonds in order to get cash to invest. This interest is a component of the cost of capital. We should seek to get better returns on our investments in training rather than merely recovering this cost. In our

Figure 10-7. Performance drivers and solutions.

Driver	%	Possible Solution
Environment • Sales force is an average of one day of travel from customers	5%	Relocate sales force so it can be an extension of customers' team
Process • Lead qualification process is too slow	15%	Business process redesign
Motivation • Paid to reach quarterly targets, not long-term relationships/outcomes	33%	New solutions—selling/customer loyalty–based compensation and performance management system
Skills/Knowledge • No access to global customer intelligence (data on current and future needs across customer locations) • Product sales proficiency, not solution-oriented consultative sales	10% 12%	Create Web-enabled strategic customer data mines (e.g., companysleuth.com) and customer solutions communities of practice Teach solutions skills for sales force whose 360-degree feedback scores fall into "require development" category
Capacities • Traits not systematically sought after in hiring process	25%	New realistic job preview and prehire assessment

Figure 10-8. ROI calculation.

Equation:

$$\frac{\text{Benefit} - (\text{Investment}) - (\text{Investment})(\text{Cost of Capital})}{\text{Investment}}$$

Example:

$$\frac{50{,}215{,}018 - (900{,}000) - (900{,}000)(15\%)}{900{,}000} = \frac{50{,}215{,}018 - 900{,}000 - 135{,}000}{900{,}000} = 6{,}260\%$$

equation, the costs and the cost of capital are removed from the top of the equation and divided by the overall investment to produce the ROI percentage.

To calculate the benefits, we rely on the data we created with the business to establish the size and causes of the business gaps. Figure 10-9 shows how the business gap, performance, and performance driver data are combined to estimate the overall benefit of the investment. However, the potential benefit is just an opportunity. We have to execute or alter em-

Figure 10-9. Benefit calculation.

Value X Effectiveness = Benefit

What's the scorecard gap worth in dollars?

X

What % is due to human performance?

X

What % of performance is a knowledge or skill gap?

Did we shift performance the entire distance the business required? (Manager's ratings)

X

In the time frame the business required?

Shareholder value-added estimate

---

ployee performance no later than the business gap closure date, in order for the company to get a benefit. By understanding the portion of benefit that we can create, we can be sure to frame our overall improvement effort at a level commensurate with the need.

To make this clear, let's pull together all the data from the previous example; this is shown in Figure 10-10. Our overall business gap was $3 billion, and we discovered that many different factors were responsible for this business gap. Ten percent was due to our salespeople performing poorly. Looking through the data and interviewing folks who know about sales performance, we determined that 22 percent of the root cause of the employee performance gaps was lack of solution sales skills and customer intelligence. To calculate the value, we multiply these numbers together. $3 billion 10 percent 22 percent gives us a total value that we could possibly create of $66 million. We have this $66 million opportunity only if we actually shift sales performance from 25 percent Top Box all the way to 85 percent Top Box. At the same time, we must shift employee performance no later than December 31, 2002. Timely performance shifts are what the effectiveness part of the equation addresses. If we are not fully effective at shifting performance on time, then we may create only a portion of the total value possible. For example, look at the text under the effectiveness

Figure 10-10.   Calculation example.

Value X Effectiveness = Benefit

What's the scorecard gap worth in dollars? 15% gap = $3 billion
What % is due to human performance? **10%;**
25%-85% = 60%

What % of performance is a knowledge or skill gap? **22%**

Did we shift performance the entire distance the business required?
Top Box is now 80%
55/60 = **91.7%** of desired performance improvement

In the time frame the business required? Goal: by 12/31/2002
Actual: 15 days late
100%-(15/90) = 100%-16.7% = **83%**

Shareholder value-added estimate

Value = **$66** million × **91.7%** Top Box goal × **83%** on-time= **$50,215,018**

part of the equation in Figure 10-10. You'll recall that we originally discovered that only 25 percent of our employees were rated Top Box by our customers, and that we needed this to be at 85 percent. If, after training, our employees were rated Top Box by 80 percent of our customers, then we shifted employee performance 91.7 percent of the total distance we wanted (55/60). Suppose we did this 15 days late, based on our original project plan of 90 days. In effect, we were 83 percent on-time. Together our performance and schedule metrics suggest that we were able to create a portion of the total $66 million worth of value. $66 million times 91.7 percent times 83 percent gives us more than $50 million worth of benefit that we created for the corporation in addressing a critical business need: market share improvement.

But we also need to know how well we did in creating these benefits relative to costs (Figure 10-8). We know from our finance controller that the corporation's cost of capital is 15 percent and that we came in $100,000 under our original budget of $1 million. We take the benefit figure that we created in the previous analysis, $50,215,018, and subtract the total investment and cost of capital. Our total investment was our budget, $900,000, and the cost of capital is just the cost of getting that $900,000, or $900,000 15 percent. We divide this number by the total investment and discover that the ROI was a whopping 6,260 percent. You should expect bigger-than-usual ROI estimates for investments in employees, since they're traditionally underexamined as an investment opportunity. Advanced research from finance is showing that physical and financial capital investment returns are substantially smaller than the value of intangibles like human resources.[7]

Comparing Options

Before you engage in an improvement project, you can use this sort of analysis to estimate the ROI of different options. When doing this, it is important to estimate the total investment the corporation must make to get the benefit, not just your training budget. This includes the time that learners are off the job, opportunity costs, and travel expenses. To add the most value, and gain credibility with your executives, it is also critical that you compare the ROI of learning and nonlearning solutions, such as hiring, contracting, or automating the work.

Lead and Lag Indicators

Once we have established the ROI business case, we use metrics that give us early warning signs that we are on track to producing an ROI. We call these signs *lead* indicators because we manage these metrics ahead of the lagging business results and ROI that we are after.

To generate our world–class lead indicators, we conducted a series of studies at Motorola University. First, we looked comprehensively at the models from research that summarized the state of the science.[8] We validated our own assessments based on these models and looked for the dimensions that best predict employee performance shifts.[9] We compared models based on the previous literature and on Occam's Razor (a principle that suggests that simpler is better). The study was conducted across more than 10,000 students in more than 1,000 courses in more than 20 different countries in which Motorola does business. The results are summarized in Figure 10-11. The solid arrows show links that we tested in our study.

The lead and lag model in Figure 10-11 is a powerful way to understand the "upside down" Kirkpatrick and Phillips model in Figure 10-1. The earliest leads that tell us whether learning is or is not working we call "predictors of performance." Five scales, or sets of questions, measure whether a class will improve the employee's performance: relevancy, transfer climate, instruction and design effectiveness, learner motivation, and preparation to transfer.

The performance gap and consequent ROI analyses establish business and job relevancy. Supervisors and coworkers create a supportive work

Figure 10-11. Leads and lags.

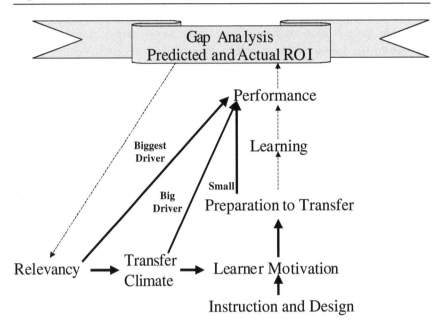

environment for transfer, before the learner starts a class, if it is relevant to helping the business. If the ROI is compelling and clear, managers will emphasize the importance of the training and communicate that there will be rewards for improving performance (or that rewards will be withheld for no improvement). Managers will seek out opportunities for learners to practice and give them feedback on how they are performing, before and after the training. Similarly, coworkers may need to coach or support the employees' job performance. The manager and coworkers together provide a powerful support system that influences whether the learner takes the training seriously. We call this area "transfer climate."

Transfer climate works in conjunction with excellent instructional design and teaching (instruction and design) that together drive the learner's motivation. Learner motivation deals with whether the learner puts forth the effort required to acquire the new skills. Motivated learners pay close attention to the instruction and take learning in the training event very seriously. Finally, our Preparation to Transfer scale deals with whether the learner sets goals for using the training, and whether learned skills were practiced during the class.

Big and Small Leads

The three most important predictors of performance may be surprising, given that trainers have traditionally focused on instructional systems design. Motorola University research[10] suggests that the single biggest predictor of training transfer is course relevancy—by a very large margin. The business gap analysis determines the performance that needs improvement. Courses that are relevant to business and job goals are most relevant. Similarly, courses that work business objectives into their instructional objectives seem to have the biggest payoff.

The next most important driver of training transfer is transfer climate, followed by, to a small degree, preparation to transfer. Even though they do not directly predict transfer, the learner motivation and instructional design scales are helpful because each of them affects the other metrics. Transfer climate, together with instruction and design, drives learner motivation. Learner motivation, in turn, predicts whether students take steps to get ready to use the training, such as setting goals and practicing (preparation to transfer). Together, all these indicators show how training transfer can be measured and managed in the context of the business results sought. By examining pilot classes with this lead-lag model, we can catch defects in time to still get an excellent ROI.

In taking a diagnostic approach to defining business gaps, we turn Kirkpatrick and Phillips upside down by starting with the business case for change. We look for indicators that tell us what aspect of employee performance may be causing the gaps. This frames the initiatives we undertake in order to improve individual and organizational performance. The lead indicators—predictors of whether the training intervention is working—are the early warning signs that we use to predict whether our project is on track to hit our ultimate lag indicator: return on investment.

Conclusion

Rather than using traditional training evaluation metrics, corporate universities now are adopting a consultative and holistic business-partnering approach. Engagement begins by diagnosing the root cause of business gaps. Using business data (e.g., market research, finance) about what the identified gaps are worth in dollars, we collaboratively estimate the percentage of the gap that can be attributed to employee performance. Next, we estimate the portion of the employee performance gap that is due to knowledge or skills that training might address.

By establishing the potential value of the training with credible financial estimates—both value and cost—we build strong relationships with business clients, because we can collaboratively estimate ROI before we ever build a module or teach a class. Our experience at Motorola University has been that this approach to defining where training is (or is not) needed and whether it worked is exactly what our business clients desire. It treats learning solutions as one facet of investments in human capital, to be managed with respect to return, no different from technology or physical capital investments.

This approach is inspired by the new ideas for managing people as a human capital asset.[11] We believe that using such a human capital approach can help training professionals gain credibility with CEOs and other executives who have critical business problems that we can help solve. It is also a powerful, business-focused way to finance your training department, based on the value it will add to the business. The cost per student day and student satisfaction approaches are dead and buried because they promote lengthy, expensive classes without making the primary connection to business need. Let the student day rest in peace—long live human capital measurement!

Special thanks to Jill Brosig for contributions to an earlier version of this chapter.

International Perspectives

11

Corporate Universities
in Europe

Annick Renaud-Coulon

Corporate universities were originally created in the New World, but they are increasing their presence throughout Europe. While the first corporate universities appeared on the Continent in the 1970s, there has been a notable increase in the number of universities since the 1990s—especially since 1998.

Describing this phenomenon and analyzing the perspectives within this region of the world can pose a number of challenges:

❏ The first is derived from the very definition of Europe, which is not a politically and culturally united region, but rather a collection of nation-states with separate cultures and developmental stages and with extremely different areas of competition. Even if the European Union (currently composed of fifteen member states) succeeds in creating a European zone, it will still be confronted with numerous problems related to its increased size. Since Europe has never had political uniformity, the Continent consists of a socio-economic and culturally complex ensemble. One of the visible signs of this is the lack of a harmonized education system. Educa-

219

tionally, the cultures in the north are very different from those in the south. It is also evident that western Europe does not have much in common with the cultures of the former Soviet Union, although the geography and history of those countries is situated in Europe.

The worldwide study that I completed on corporate universities[1] demonstrated that their emergence is undoubtedly linked to the political, economic, cultural, and educational contexts of the companies that promote and finance their existence. It is consequently difficult to provide a concise and satisfactory description of the European realities that describe and explain the corporate universities' raison d'être on this continent. Moreover, approaching this phenomenon in a microeducational and microeconomic manner remains very dissatisfying. My best course was therefore to engage in an exercise that is similar in nature to an Impressionist painting: that is to say, to look at small tasks that together offer a complete view, although one that is imperfect if one looks too closely. Not all of the European countries are represented here, since the experiences of certain corporate universities could not be incorporated for various reasons: Interviews were not possible because of the time period, management was unavailable, or organizations were in a period of transition. However, although this sample may not be exhaustive, it is nevertheless of great interest, since it includes more than thirty prestigious companies in nine European countries or other entities: Denmark, France, Germany, United Kingdom, Italy, the Netherlands, Russia, Spain, and Switzerland.

❑ Another difficulty, shared by all of the countries and researchers, is the nature of the corporate university phenomenon. A fluid, hybrid, and vague concept, it does not easily lend itself to a definition that is precise, unique, and definitive. As was discussed in the introduction, this situation is certainly not limited to Europe. My definition for the purpose of my recent study reads as follows: "educational units developed within organizations to serve their global performance." This definition covers a wide spectrum of entities that are at times experimental laboratories, research and development centers, and what I call *applied economic spaces*, where one sorts out real organizational problems (being exposed to the increasing demands and constraints of world markets) and where one "sells" business solutions.

❏ Finally, there is a last difficulty: Since they represent a living, organic phenomenon, corporate universities do not allow themselves to retreat into immutable truths. Everywhere in the world, they spread and reinvent themselves, and some die from a lack of support and or overly ambitious strategies. In other words, we cannot deal with corporate universities as a hard or soft science; they are an empirical phenomenon that renders all generalizations and statistical data quite rash because they are inevitably full of errors.[2]

One may then ask, to what degree does Europe embrace corporate universities, since when, and in what manner? Can one predict that one day these structures will enjoy a nice future and will penetrate into numerous companies and distant places in eastern and southern Europe that have scarcely heard of corporate universities? This chapter addresses these questions.

Anchored in Old Educational Traditions

From Papal Universities to Corporate Universities

In Europe, the Middle Ages gave birth to ecclesiastic educational institutions under the papal authority (universities born from the fusion of Catholic, monastic, and private schools). Before a relatively autonomous educational system was set up in the nineteenth century, both universities and state-owned establishments multiplied, primarily in Bologna, Paris, and Oxford throughout the eighteenth century. However, it was the Industrial Revolution that brought recognition of educational institutions financed by corporations, such as the Solvay School in Nancy, France. The beginning of the twentieth century therefore brought the emergence of a concept that would lead to the corporate university, as schools financed by corporations participated in the great historical growth period *(la belle époque)* enjoyed by Europe until World War I.

Differing Rates of Emergence Throughout Europe

Not all of the European countries have been seized by corporate university fever in the same manner:

❑ Among those countries studied, France is in the leading position, with more than thirty corporate universities worthy of the name, set up during the 1980s (Thales and Axa, for example). Many more are in the process of being created at the beginning of the twenty-first century. There are several reasons that contribute to France's success in this area. The first is the existence of a law, adopted in 1971, requiring employers to dedicate 1.1 percent of total wages to continuing education. These funds were quickly used to benefit managers and technicians rather than nonqualified workers. This resulted in the early creation of educational structures for management and the development of a true learning culture within French companies.

A second, less well known reason is the partition maintained between the higher education system and the corporate world. In contrast to the United States, where relations between the higher education system and companies remain strong, the French system favors the extremely prestigious universities or *grandes écoles* (Polytechnique, Écoles des Mines, École Centrale, Écoles de Commerce, etc.), which are too isolated from and remain virtually unknown to the rest of the world. Employers do not find the necessary competencies, especially international competencies, in young graduates because the educational system is overly academic and far removed from business realities. They have therefore set out to develop substitute strategies by creating corporate universities on the principle that "one cannot be better served than by oneself."

❑ The balance sheet contains more nuances in other European countries. Great Britain is in second place (with less than twelve corporate universities); Germany is in third place (with between five and ten), followed by the Nordic countries (Sweden, Finland, Denmark), and the Netherlands, each of which has up to five. Other countries, such as Belgium and Portugal, do not yet have any corporate universities.

❑ Finally, with regard to the former communist bloc, Russia (which was also included in my research) has a dozen internal education structures. Apart from Gazprom and Alfabank, a majority of these structures are technical education centers. Corporate universities still do not exist in the former Soviet bloc countries of Poland, Romania, Hungary, the Czech Republic, Slovakia, etc.

European Specifics for Corporate Universities

The Term *University* Is Still Reserved for the Academic World

Companies in the United States dare to use the term *universities* to name this phenomenon. Although the United States is confronted by deficiencies in its secondary education system, higher education in that country is a superior system, recognized as one of the best in the world. The term *university* was used by 53 percent of our sample—of those, the majority (68 percent) were in the United States.

It seems, therefore, that Europe is showing a certain modesty in the use of the term *university* other than in reference to higher education. Among the thirty corporate universities studied in Europe, fourteen carry the "university" name, five use the term "center," four use "institute," three use "academy," and one is called "school of business." Still others use a name linked to their location, such as Unilever's "Four Acres," or a title that does not make reference to an organizational structure, such as Siemens Management Learning or Vivendi Universal Management. In comparison with the United States, therefore, Europe remains conservative in its use of this term. In certain countries, this is due to reluctance on the part of the government (such as in Great Britain and Spain) or to universities' reaction to the semantic duplication.

"The word *university* is contrary to the practical and pragmatic business spirit and we use it often for marketing reasons," emphasizes Siemens Management Learning in Germany. A spokesman from CenterParcs in the Netherlands estimates that "the notion of university is not pertinent, dismissed as a 'difficult' connotation, and that it is too pretentious" in a country where the national culture is completely marked by modesty.

On the other hand, the European companies that chose the term university explain their reasons as follows:

❏ For its old meaning referring to a place for exchanging knowledge and competencies (DaimlerChrysler, Germany)

❏ For its "universal" character and its common understanding in international relations (Suez, France)

❏ For the idea of greatness and superior education, and to illustrate its ambitions in the area of research (ISS, Denmark)

❏ To create awareness of the necessity of enrolling oneself in a process of continuing education and as a brand image vehicle (ST Microelectronics, France)

❏ Because it expresses the idea of a "living" transmission of knowledge with a view to action (Bayard Presse, France)

❏ Because it evokes the idea of internal and external knowledge exchange (Caisse des Dépôts et Consignations, France)

❏ To make a strategic link from knowledge transfer to knowledge creation (Heineken, the Netherlands)

In short, companies like McDonalds and Motorola set the tone for the phenomenon in using the term *university*, and Europe cannot remain a stranger to this for too long, even if the term is used in a different manner.

A Very Widespread Elitism

In general, the European corporate universities have an audience that includes executive managers (twenty-four of the thirty surveyed), managers (nineteen of thirty), and young potentials (thirteen of thirty); only five open their doors to all employees. This characteristic does not appear in the same form in other parts of the world. For example, of the thirty corporate universities surveyed in the United States, twenty have expanded their audience to include all company employees. In effect, the higher percentage of universal access in the American corporate universities studied was explained by the larger participation in e-learning, which permits a wider reach worldwide than classroom instruction.

An Openness to the World That Remains Incomplete

Only five out of thirty European corporate universities open their doors to customers, and just three out of thirty open their doors to suppliers. This is, of course, a very small sample, but the finding is fairly significant, since openness to partners in corporate universities is generally found in those that carry a responsibility for optimizing the value chain—in other words, corporate universities with close links to business strategies.

Limited Use of Rewards, Diplomas, or Accreditation

While the American corporate universities use various combinations of rewards without hesitation, including certificates and awards of all types, the Europeans seldom make use of this practice, since they view it as somewhat childish. Certificates and awards are still regarded as sacred documents whose legitimate delivery belongs to the academic world.

DaimlerChrysler, for example, has specified that it does not expect an accreditation system. In other words, its university partner establishments do not deliver any diplomas (MBA or others) to participants in the DaimlerChrysler University professional program. This is not the mission of the corporate university: Its goal is to develop the talents within the company in order to satisfy the company's objectives.

The tendency to avoid degrees and certificates is not universal. In Great Britain, Bae Systems Virtual University delivers the British Aerospace Certificate in Management within its Integrated Development Framework program. In Finland, ISS has conceived its own distance learning MBA program in association with a Finnish university, and a similar system has been introduced in Sweden. In Italy, Isvor-Fiat works jointly with its university partners to deliver diplomas that are often custom made. In France, ST University, in partnership with two engineering schools, has developed a Master's in Microelectronics Technology and Manufacturing program that corresponds to a master's level of education and is recognized by the French Conférence des Grandes Écoles. Much like Gazprom in Russia, Heineken University in the Netherlands delivers a diploma to every participant in its seminars. One cannot draw too much from these last two cases, however, since these documents serve as certificates of attendance rather than the effective recognition of acquired knowledge and competencies.

A Less Pronounced Taste for Standardization and Formalization

European corporate universities are not tempted very much to standardize their products or services, or by the global use of common tools. In the latter case, the only exceptions include Siemens Management Learning, which created the Business Impact Projects (BIPs), and Heineken University, with its Heineken Business Challenges (HBCs).

While some corporate universities present offerings with skillfully researched names, such as Axa (France) with Telemaque and Columbus; Suez (France) and its programs Discovery, Explorer, Focus, and Semaphore; Pinault Printemps Redoute (France), which has Uknow, Unext, and Umap; Sodexho (France), which offers Entrepreneur 1 and 2; and the Body Shop (United Kingdom) and its offering, Project Quest; these offerings are generally focused on internal education, and they do not take root outside the organization.

In the same way, the educational approaches or the conceptual foundations that support corporate university methods give little consideration to rigid conceptual structures. For example, "change management" remains a simple theoretical and generic approach for describing a vision or ambition. It is never seen as a body of knowledge or an ensemble of professional practices, as it is in the United States. In other words, Europe likes the concepts in which projects are joined, but it avoids the tools and well-oiled machinery that give the impression of limited maneuverability or a lack of freedom to think. If the European companies have, for example, arrived at a degree of standardization, it is due more to the effect of international commerce than to their own natural tendencies.

Select Partnerships with Universities Preferred Over Many Alliances

Corporate universities in the United States have the reputation of being created and delivered in partnership with the university world, and the same tendency exists in Europe (eighteen out of thirty surveyed). However, in Europe this seems to be a matter of specific contracts rather than long-term alliances, with the exception of Nestlé, which has a close and historical link to IMD (Institute of Management Development) in Lausanne, Switzerland. Moreover, some prefer the option of entering into partnerships with carefully chosen name universities rather than with university structures, which are deemed to be costly institutions with limited freedom. This is the case of Bayard Presse, Schneider, Suez, and Thales in France, and of Unilever in the United Kingdom.

Some companies wonder about the opportunity to find and particularly how to approach such partnerships. "On the subject of content, the universities sometimes have difficulty in adapting themselves to the problems of the company. They are not always capable of adapting to the pedagogical philosophy, either. A seminar is as much a life experience as it is a place where one acquires content. Based upon the experience of the participants, interaction should represent almost 50 percent of the time period. This does not correspond to the classical academic approach. The university institutions are producers of generic knowledge and consultants are even better at transmitting and adapting knowledge to a business environment," states the president of a major European corporate university.

An Interest in Châteaus and Human Contact

The Europeans have an attraction for physical infrastructures that bring people together. Axa, Cap Gemini Ernst & Young, STMicroelectronics, Thales, and Suez (France); Isvor Fiat (Italy); CenterParcs (the Netherlands); Union Fenosa (Spain); Unilever (United Kingdom); and ABB and Nestlé (Switzerland) all own physical facilities that include a "campus" much like that of an academic university (often in a place remote from the city, in calm green surroundings favorable for study and reflection). This is called a *logique château*, because some universities are literally installed in châteaus from the eighteenth century (Axa, Cap Gemini Ernst & Young, and Suez, for example) and because several, such as Cap Gemini Ernst & Young (300 rooms), Thales (180 rooms), and Unilever (73 rooms), contain large numbers of hotel rooms.

Almost all of the universities studied, even those calling themselves "virtual," organize seminars in residence. Many include conferences, breakfasts, afternoons, workshops, leader clubs, study trips—in summary, physical meetings between people. It is often specified that face-to-face interaction is preferred because it permits the sharing and discussion of ideas in addition to the creation of friendly relationships (around dinner and good Bordeaux wine, as exemplified by Axa), and because it is the foundation of mutual trust for creating interactivity and dialogues. Siemens specifies that workshops rather than seminars serve as theaters for discussion and common reflections favoring interaction among participants, followed by work projects and evaluation of results. Thus, in Europe, corporate universities unquestionably favor the type of work that permits human contact. These corporate universities not only favor the strategic mission of integration by culture, but also allow future employees to create a network for the long term. It is very difficult to create these relationships by distance learning.

A Limited Interest in E-Learning

Some of the corporate universities studied were quite advanced in the practice of e-learning:

❑ The Towards One Bank program has already conducted more than 60,000 hours of e-learning and has placed more than eighty-five programs online via the branch network personal computers of the University for Lloyds TSB.

❏ DaimlerChrysler has developed a considerable content package with an important intranet platform through DaimlerChrysler University Online.

❏ Isvor Fiat has deployed impressive technologies (a corporate television channel transmitted via satellite across a variety of countries, Web solutions, and videoconferences).

Other findings regarding e-learning:

❏ Siemens democratizes access to knowledge and encourages self-directed learning, requiring the learner to take responsibility for his or her learning.

❏ Cap Gemini Ernst & Young offers great flexibility in allowing learners to manage the learning time at their own convenience.

❏ Nestlé has established a certain homogeneity of information and knowledge within groups prior to the session to ensure that everyone starts on the same page.

❏ Schneider, where e-learning is planned centrally, has realized a better operational implementation of knowledge. This company emphasizes the interactive and play aspects of e-learning, which makes the medium more interesting than the more static format. This aspect is also present at Siemens.

❏ Some find a means of monetary savings through e-learning, especially in regard to travel costs. Fewer trips, reduced teaching fees, and lower accommodation costs can be sources of savings that derive from e-learning programs.

Aside from the above-mentioned universities, however, the great majority of companies still remain cautious about e-learning. It seems that e-learning is more easily introduced into North American and Asian cultures than into other cultures, especially Latin ones.

Financial Organization Plays Only a Small Role in Success

Almost without exception, European corporate universities are organized as cost centers. Only the Axa and Thales universities in France, British

Telecom Academy in Great Britain, and Isvor Fiat in Italy state that they are profit centers. In general, most European corporate universities have an independent legal structure as suppliers of education in which the company's organizational model is based upon operating business units with maximum financial autonomy.

The others are organized as cost centers that characteristically work within the context of an allocated budget set by corporate headquarters. The important financial aspects are easily captured, since the budget allows evaluation of investments and consequent developments; however, they do not appear to be determinants of success for European corporate universities. The budget dedicated to these universities' functioning is not an element for which management demands a return on investment.

Few Standardized Evaluations

In order to assist their evaluation methods, the universities have a tendency to help one another with conceptual approaches. While twenty-two out of twenty-five American corporate universities use a formal evaluation system, and thirteen of these use the Kirkpatrick model, only three European corporate universities use this model: Isvor Fiat, Unilever, and ST Microelectronics. Many responsible European corporate universities had not heard of this model, and the others did not find its features effective for implementation.

That having been said, practically everyone proceeds with at least an evaluation of teaching results in comparison with previously set learning objectives. This is evidently the most essential and convenient aspect for a majority of these corporate universities. With regard to the universities' measures of productivity and efficiency, only Heineken University measures the "perceived quality" as seen by its beneficiaries. As for business impact, this evaluation piece is still barely defined in Europe. It is difficult to objectively measure the many changes in the management of a business and to attribute these results to university actions.

Future Perspectives

The traits specific to corporate universities that were observed during my research make it clear that a European model certainly exists, and it will be interesting to observe its evolution in the coming years. A question still remains as to whether this model will continue to distinguish itself as being uniquely European, or whether it will be homogenized by benchmarking studies and other methods, leading to standardization and erasing of the pertinent differences. In light of the way in which American managerial methods are having difficulty developing lasting roots within European corporate universities, I think that the corporate universities from the Continent will keep most of their characteristics.

In all probability, the globalization of ideas should continue to multiply in Europe (including the east and the south), thanks to information technologies and the development of commercial exchanges. With success relayed by the media and the Internet, I predict an overly strong infatuation with educational units and a new type of economics from the heads of multinational corporations, but also within smaller organizations operating in domestic markets and even those in local and territorial communities, and state and administrative sectors. However, the trend for corporate universities to contribute to the global performance (economic, financial, commercial, human, and social) of firms and institutions should favor their development.

In other words, we should encourage organizations to enter a new phase in which corporate universities will be a source of competitive advantage designed to manage companies' intellectual capital. Then corporate universities could really be considered as *the link that is missing in the educational chain*. This is truly the major issue that faces European corporate universities today.

Corporate Universities in Australia and Southeast Asia

Ian Dickson

The colonial past still resonates within Australia and Southeast Asia, and this may partially explain the slow acceptance of the concept of the "corporate university" and the relatively few regional corporations that claim to use this model to shape their corporate education functions.

University systems in the region are based on European models established by the colonial administrations some hundred years ago. Consequently, the concept of a university is colored by these perceptions; in fact, in many countries the term *university* is protected by law and granted to an educational organization that meets certain requirements set down by government.

For example, in Australia, a country formed in 1901 by a federation of six British colonies, an educational institution can be designated a university only by an act of Parliament. There are thirty-six universities, each of which is closely monitored by the federal government to ensure that it meets the set of stringent criteria that have been laid down. Consequently, the term *university* implies an institution that generally meets the criteria laid down by the government. Although the general public neither knows nor understands the details of these criteria, a company using the term *corporate university* would be treated with a mix of responses ranging from humor to contempt—none of which has the positive connotations associated with the term in the United States. It is not a marketing ploy or a statement of excellence, nor would it be seen in the Australian context as an appropriate use of the word *university*.

A similar response would be found also in Asia—although the existence of private tertiary institutions (many with recognized high standards) has softened this perception—where the reputation of a university as an educational institution of high-level teaching and research based on the accepted disciplines is jealously guarded by established universities.

However, organizational training and education functions that in North America would be called a corporate university do exist. In Southeast Asia, many countries are conservative in their training and development strategies, relying heavily on traditional face-to-face training. As elsewhere, e-learning is increasingly being used as an alternative distance learning strategy as the availability and use of the Internet increases. The concept of the corporate university in these countries is relatively new, although some of the larger local companies have well-developed corporate training functions that would qualify for the title "corporate university" if they were situated in America. These training entities often carry the title of "institute" or "college." For example, in India large national corporations have training departments that are often housed in their own corporate offices. Some examples of corporate training campuses are the Tata Management and Training Centre at Pune, the Mudra Institute of Communications and Advertising, and the UTI Centre in Mumbai. Nirma has established the Nirma Institute of Technology and the Nirma Institute of Management in Ahmedabad. Although these institutions have many of the characteristics of a corporate university, it is not clear that this model has been influential in their development.

The establishment of corporate universities in Southeast Asia is being driven by international companies that have established corporate universities elsewhere in the world. For example, McDonald's University has recently been established in Hong Kong, and the PRUuniversity of the Prudential Corporation Asia is one of the region's largest corporate universities.

Many Southeast Asian countries have embraced the communication revolution, and countries like Singapore are building communication networks to make the Internet available to virtually every home and business.

Australia, on the other hand, has a long history of innovative, flexible corporate learning. Perhaps because of the nature of universities, the policies and support of governments, and the age and sophistication of distance and flexible learning techniques, many Australian companies show a history of innovation and cooperation with educational institutions that has not been evident elsewhere. Consequently, Australian companies are less inclined to embrace an on-line training culture, as they are comfortable with a variety of flexible on-the-job training strategies and use a blended approach to the delivery of training. As can be seen from the case studies described later, many Australian "corporate universities" incorporate the best of corporate training and university education.

Role of Government in Corporate Training

Many governments in the region have been proactive in the development of their workforces through government policy and financial assistance.

As might be expected, the Singaporean government is very proactive in the development of the country's workforce. Recognizing that in order to maintain its current strong economic growth, the small island nation must increase the expertise and productivity of its people and the government, the Ministry of Manpower (MOM) has a mission to develop a "globally-competitive workforce to support Singapore's vision of a knowledge-based economy" (http://www.gov.sg/mom). One of its six strategies is lifelong learning. The Ministry of Trade and Industry is also involved, and an agency of this ministry, the Productivity and Standards Board (PSB), assumes the important catalyst role of initiating and encouraging various training schemes among companies. For most schemes, the PSB will partner with training providers from the private and public sectors to meet the needs of the industry.

Australia has a well-developed competency-based vocational education system, financially supported by the federal government and underpinned by nationally accredited awards.

In early 1990, the Ford Motor Company of Australia partnered with its unions and Victoria College (a degree-granting college of advanced education) to develop and deliver a flexible 24/7 degree program in technology management to support its first-line supervisors while the company underwent a significant restructuring. This program had a number of features that would be still considered innovative today:

❏ Learning objectives and content were closely linked to Ford's business objectives.

❏ Learning and assessment were based around the participant's work-place.

❏ The program included 24/7 laptop communication with tutors, students, and resources and on-demand individualized testing.

❏ The program included university accreditation with an articulated set of awards (university certificate, diploma, degree) that allowed participants to enter and leave the program with credit as their career dictated.

❏ The program included recognition of prior learning.

As a result of this program and strong lobbying from Ford Australia, the federal government introduced a unique, federally funded system for creating university places (admission into universities) designed to cater to corporate programs such as Ford's. The Commonwealth Industry Placement Scheme (CIPS) provided university places through corporations for their employees that were funded 60 percent from government funding and 40 percent from the participating corporation.

Although subsequently discontinued, this scheme encouraged close partnerships between corporations and universities, the effects of which are still seen today. This close cooperation and partnership between universities and corporations characterize many of the Australian-based corporate institutes, with a number of them incorporating university resources and awards into their corporate training profile. Case studies are given later in the chapter.

Distance Education Tradition

Another contributing factor that encouraged close cooperation between the corporate sector and educational institutions was Australia's distance education tradition and infrastructure.

Prior to the development of the Internet, distance education was not well developed in Southeast Asian countries, whose culture of respect for the teacher encouraged face-to-face instruction. Australia, on the other hand, with its small population and large landmass, has a tradition of distance education and learning that stretches back more than a hundred years. Although early distance education usually involved unsophisticated correspondence programs, the 1970s saw the development of high-quality print-based distance learning strategies that were influenced by the Open University in the United Kingdom. This approach, whose underpinnings included a strong, disciplined instructional design, resulted in learning materials that delivered truly individualized stand-alone instruction that did not require an instructor to intervene unless requested by the student.

A number of universities, including Deakin University, Charles Stuart University, and The University of Southern Queensland, became centers of excellence and acquired considerable infrastructure for developing, delivering, and administering distance education programs around the country and internationally. This infrastructure, intellectual property, and expertise became a valuable community resource that corporations tapped into to meet their organizational development requirements.

The late 1980s and 1990s saw the development of closer associations between corporate training arms and universities, utilizing the distance and flexible delivery resources of the educational institutions. The catalyst was economic. The late 1980s were difficult economic times for Australian companies, and Australian industry went through a process of rationalization. Companies that survived this period downsized considerably, began outsourcing noncore functions, and looked for innovative ways to cut costs and increase productivity. Training and staff development was (as usual in times of economic stress) a prime target.

The Ford program described previously was a result of such a restructuring process. Ford recognized the need to provide its first-line managers with the skills and knowledge they needed in order to operate in the new Ford structure and culture and achieve the company's objectives and vision. Ford partnered with Victoria College (now a part of Deakin University), leveraging off that institution's education expertise and infrastructure. The flexible design and delivery of the program allowed the company to keep training close to the workplace, thus minimizing the amount of time off the job and encouraging the transfer of the skills and knowledge into the workplace—a challenge that faces any training program and that often is not achieved. The innovative Ford Foundation Studies Certificate proved to be very effective in supporting the organizational restructuring, won many industry training awards, and is still in place more than ten years later.

Over this period, the relationship between Ford Australia and Deakin University has broadened and deepened. It has reached the stage where Ford Australia has outsourced its entire training function to Deakin University through DeakinPrime. (DeakinPrime is the commercial center within Deakin University that provides education and training services to organizations.) Deakin has taken on the role of "master vendor" and manages all the training functions for Ford Australia. Appropriate governance structures are in place to ensure that the company retains strategic controls that link the training to the corporate objectives. This is truly a corporate university. All programs are monitored for quality by Deakin University through DeakinPrime to ensure that they are educationally and pedagogically sound, appropriately and validly assessed, and, where possible, linked to Deakin University awards. The integration of university resources into Ford training is so extensive that at any stage in a Ford employee's career there is a development program leading to a vocational or university award available to him or her.

The relationship extends beyond training and development into research and community services (Deakin hosts an automotive museum at one of its campuses in partnership with Ford Australia).

The Ford program was one of the first programs in Australia or Southeast Asia that creatively utilized the resources of a university for corporate learning. The partnership had a dramatic effect on Deakin University and its operations and structures, including:

❑ *Articulated awards that cater to the needs of corporate learning.* Corporate learning is short, focused, and designed to deliver results to the business. Traditional university degree programs are long and provide a depth and breadth of knowledge and skills that are often inappropriate for a business setting. In response to their corporate partner's needs, Deakin developed a set of articulated awards leading to a degree in management at the undergraduate level and to an MBA at the postgraduate level. The smaller awards (university certificate, diploma, graduate certificate in corporate management), available only through an organizational setting, are designed to recognize corporate learning. The content of these awards is driven by the needs of the organization, and learning can take place in the context of the organization. Deakin course material that is specially designed for corporate learning can be incorporated into the company program, or internal company programs can be included in accredited Deakin awards, provided they meet the accreditation requirements of the university.

Employers can offer their employees university recognition

for the education and training they receive through the company, and an individual employee can enter traditional Deakin University courses with maximum credit transfer. This unique award structure helps to balance the learning needs of the organization and the individual career development needs of the individual. Many companies use this award recognition as an employee retention strategy.

❏ *Accredited programs designed specifically for organizational learning.* Although MBA courses and materials are appropriate for middle and senior management, undergraduate courses were found to be inappropriate for lower and first-line management development, which requires a more applied and pragmatic learning environment. In close collaboration with its industry partners, Deakin developed a range of accredited courses for corporate learning that are available only through an organization. These programs draw heavily on the Ford experience and have underpinnings of print-based flexible learning materials that allow an organization to deliver the programs where, when, and how best suits their business. The programs are highly applied and use the workplace as the major case study, and all assessment uses workplace-based projects that demonstrate that the participant understands the skills and knowledge and can apply them in the workplace. Some programs use a full competency-based instructional model.

❏ *Capture the company's internal intellectual property.* Deakin has entered into partnerships with organizations in which it uses its instructional design expertise to capture an organization's internal knowledge and convert this into an education and training product. Deakin has developed programs in tire technology, timber technology, and procurement, to name a few. These programs can be incorporated into the award structures described previously.

❏ *Development of learning materials to meet specific training needs.* Deakin-Prime has developed learning programs and materials at levels other than those generally offered by universities—entry-level programs and programs in team leadership, personal skills, and self-development, to name a few. In these cases, companies utilize Deakin's instructional design expertise to develop university-quality programs to meet their particular staff development needs. Where possible, these programs are linked to Australia's vocational award system, and Deakin is now a certified provider in this system.

❑ *Establishment of a center to manage organizational education and training and deliver it to organizations.* As a result of its growing partnerships with organizations, Deakin established Deakin Australia (now DeakinPrime) in 1993 (http://www.deakinprime.com) as an independent center within the university to design, deliver, and manage education and training for organizations. DeakinPrime is a business-to-business entity whose CEO reports directly to the president of the university. It is not affiliated with any faculty or school, and, although the authority to manage and deliver selected accredited corporate programs has been delegated to it, it has no academic authority; that resides with the university's faculties and schools.

DeakinPrime is the window to Deakin University resources for organizations, and its structure and relationship to the university and faculties have removed the structural barriers that typically inhibit and frustrate organizations when they try to work closely with a tertiary institution.

The case studies described in the next section illustrate how a close partnership with a university can produce innovative and efficient "corporate university" structures within corporate training groups.

Case Studies

The Coles Institute

The Coles Myer Group is the largest retail organization in Australia, with 56,000 employees and more than 430 stores located around the country. The Coles Institute was established in 1999 to meet the training and development needs of staff within the Supermarket Group of Coles Myer.

The Original Vision. The mission of the Coles Institute is:

> *To provide seamless integrated training education and development programs which enable all Coles' employees to reach their full potential and Coles Supermarkets to achieve its business objectives.*

The Institute was set up as a partnership between Coles and Deakin University and was the first "corporate university" established in Australia.

The programs delivered by the Coles Institute through the partnership between Coles Supermarkets, DeakinPrime, and Deakin University is driven by Coles's business objectives, linked to Coles's identified competencies, and delivered in ways that meet the training needs of the organization and the people involved in the programs.

The Coles Institute focuses on two groups:

❏ Coles Supermarkets—providing flexible education and training programs in all areas of its operations to meet the needs of its people.

❏ The people of Coles Supermarkets—their training, their development, and their future.

All existing and future education and training programs have come under the central management of the Coles Institute.

The Coles Institute is managed by the Coles Institute Steering Committee through the director of Coles Institute and the national Coles Institute manager. The policy, direction, and decision-making processes of the Coles Institute are set and governed by the steering committee. The committee includes senior management representatives from Coles Supermarkets and Deakin.

The Coles Institute management team, which reports to the steering committee, includes employees from Coles Supermarkets and from Deakin, representing the national office and each state, is responsible for implementation of the steering committee requirements through the director of Coles Institute and the national Coles Institute manager.

DeakinPrime is the single point of accountability, as required for the Coles Institute, and acts as its learning broker—sourcing, supplying, administering, customizing, and integrating accredited and nonaccredited, internal and external, education and training programs, as required.

Because of the close partnership between Deakin University and Coles, accredited programs have been integrated into the institute's offerings. Many of these accredited programs incorporate programs that were specifically designed for Coles. This is represented in Figure 12-1.

The partnership between the two institutions ensures the quality and

Figure 12-1. Coles Institute learning framework incorporating university and vocational awards.

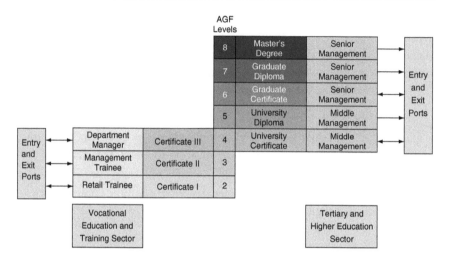

relevance of the institute's programs. An added benefit perceived by Coles is that the offering of high-quality accredited programs to employees through in-house training and education programs facilitates staff retention and recruitment.

The Coles Institute was planned to be implemented over a two-year period.

The Operating Reality of the Coles Institute Two Years On. It is interesting to review what has been achieved in the light of the vision just outlined. Many of the objectives have been achieved, but, as expected, the institute has evolved to adapt to the changing commercial environment and what was realistically achievable in the organization.

The level of understanding of the Coles Institute within the business has grown. All new staff are first exposed to the Coles Institute via their induction. Existing staff are exposed through regular features about the institute in the national communication magazine *Wavelength*, through a range of Coles Institute-branded development programs, and through regular Coles Institute graduation ceremonies held around the country.

The operations of the governance committees have been altered only slightly from the original vision. In the first eighteen months, meetings of the steering committee were held every six to eight weeks. The committee now meets quarterly.

The vision of the institute has been put under increasing business pressure. As increased expectations for Coles Supermarkets' performance within the corporate group are applied, Coles Institute is experiencing increasing pressure to cut expenditures. Consequently, links between the investment made across a range of Coles Institute initiatives and the business bottom line that would support the spending of increased dollars on developing staff have not yet been clearly established. This has been recognized and is currently being addressed.

The institute management team has changed completely in the two-year period. Initially it was composed of employees from Coles Supermarkets and Deakin, representing a cross section of functions and states for Coles and representing a range of expertise within Deakin; now it is composed of employees from the national office and from each state, with appropriate Deakin expertise depending on the issues being discussed. The effectiveness of this group has increased as resources have been allocated for agreed-on specific business objectives and ownership of these objectives is located firmly with individual staff. Coles's staff have been driven to deliver on their responsibilities and are appraised on the achievement of their suite of specific objectives. This dedication to achieve brings with it pragmatism and a clarity of roles that is well understood by the business.

A major drawback resulting from this ownership is a reluctance (owing to prioritizing of time and other resources) on the part of managers to provide long-term support for the business through the Coles Institute and its activities. Although the steering committee is responsible for creating the vision and future strategic direction, in reality the committee relies heavily on the Coles Institute management team and the national HR executive to provide direction.

This group's role and its influence on setting strategy are best illustrated by the diagram in Figure 12-2. The role of the director now is to challenge the status quo and to provide ideas about future direction and strategies, drawing on the expertise and experience of Coles and Deakin University. A major issue is that this role is not easily fulfilled by someone who is not *of* the business and who has no direct business accountability. The lack of role definition for the director of the institute has emerged as one of the major challenges to be addressed in the future.

Figure 12-2.

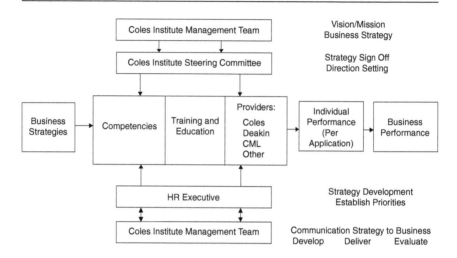

PRUuniversity[1]

PRUuniversity is the corporate university of Prudential Corporation Asia, a well-known financial company spanning twelve countries in the region and six different languages. The university was established in early 2001 and was modeled on successful corporate universities in North America. It was established to support a critical element of Prudential's HR strategy: "to build a compelling and distinct competitive proposition so that our people will want to join, stay and develop their careers with the company."[2] The university is integrated into the company's HR structures and benefits, ensuring that recognition is given to choice, flexibility, and diversity within the company.

PRUuniversity has many of the trappings of a traditional university. It awards internally accredited certificates and diplomas and intends to award degrees in the future. It uses a blended delivery approach for its programs that includes examinations. The aim is to offer programs in four languages: English, Japanese, Simplified Chinese, and Traditional Chinese.

Considerable effort has been made to ensure that the programs offered are business-oriented, employee-centered, and seen by management and staff as a high-value proposition. Senior management sponsors programs to ensure:

- ❏ Business relevancy
- ❏ Suitability for staff development needs
- ❏ Appropriate quality and standards
- ❏ Up-to-date, relevant content

The curriculum covers three areas:

- ❏ Technical skills
- ❏ Management skills
- ❏ General skills/life skills

A core curriculum is prepared for each job family in the company. All programs are being developed internally. Any external programs will need to meet the university's stringent requirements in order to be accepted.

The university is truly international and spans all countries in the region in which the company operates. The head of faculty is based in Hong Kong, and access to the university is through the PRUuniversity Web site on the company intranet. Each country has a designated faculty member, certified by the university. The university is overseen by a "learning council" made up in part of subject matter experts who are responsible for each business campus.

The university administrator is based in Singapore, and administration and enrollment are managed via the intranet and e-mail. All enrollments must have the approval of the line manager. There are many student support services, including an on-line student "union," a merchandise store, a bookstore affiliated with Amazon.com, and a language lending library.

The university is seeking affiliation with outside organizations and universities and currently offers seven diploma programs in conjunction with professional associations in India.

Professional Associations

The corporate university movement has historically focused on corporations and government entities, but the same principles can be applied to large professional associations that provide education and training to their members and the wider profession.

As many associations experience a decline in membership, nondues revenue is becoming increasingly important to associations trying to support their members throughout those members' careers and to become less reliant on membership fees for revenue. The provision of education and training services has become a major source of this nondues revenue.

Professional associations are not well developed in Southeast Asia. However, Australian professional associations are significant providers of professional education and training. For example, the Australian Society of Certified Practicing Accountants is responsible for Australia's largest distance education program (the CPA Certification program), with tens of thousands of students in Australia, New Zealand, and throughout Southeast Asia.

Almost all significant professional development programs delivered through professional associations lead to a professional certification with the aim of maintaining standards within the profession. Australian professional associations deliver the courses that lead to certification and conduct the certification examinations. The associations are at pains to ensure that these two functions are separate, thus avoiding any conflict of interest. This is in marked contrast to the usual American model, where the professional association administers the certification examination and other vendors offer courses and programs to prepare candidates for the examination. The Australian system gives the association access to the total value chain and the resultant revenue stream. Certification programs and examinations are significant sources of nondues revenue for Australian associations.

To reach the maximum number of professionals in the most cost-effective way, almost all of these programs are print-based distance programs and the association usually has a close relationship with a university. As the preeminent distance education university, Deakin University dominates the market, but other universities such as Charles Stuart and Macquarie are also involved. Some programs are being transferred online (the APESMA MBA in Technology Management, discussed in a case study on page 246, for example), but a surprising number of students prefer the print-based learning approach with its flexibility and are resisting the change. A further factor is that print-based distance programs are considerably cheaper to develop than on-line products.

The relationship between the association and its university partner varies from partnership to partnership, but in all cases the association lever-ages the university's existing infrastructure and expertise. In many cases the university partner provides some recognition and credit transfer into existing university programs. In a few cases (Association of Professional Engineers, Scientists and Managers of Australia; Australian Human Resource Institute), the university partner has accredited the association's programs.

All of these programs have strong education and professional governance structures, to which the university partner makes a significant contribution. At a minimum this governance would involve:

❑ A high-level management committee structure that provides management oversight and sets the strategic direction of the program; and a subject committee for each course in the program. This committee contains association and university representation, subject matter expert(s), instructional designers, and representatives from relevant industries.

❑ Relevant internal association committees; for example, Committee on Continuing Education, Committee on Professional Practice, etc.

The partnerships have some common features. Typically, the association provides professional direction and oversight, markets and sells the program, ensures that it meets the needs of the association's members, and is instrumental in the identification of subject matter experts and committee members. The university provides education and management services that could involve:

❑ Design and detailed specification of the curriculum, including the program content, learning outcomes, instructional strategy, media usage and assessment approach, proposed delivery platform, and any additional services.

❑ Development of the program and learning materials. This could include the ongoing management and review of course content.

❑ Examination administration. Many distance institutions have established an international examination infrastructure that can be utilized by the association.

❑ Program administration. Once again the association would leverage off the existing university educational administration infrastructure.

❑ Fulfillment. Many providers of print-based distance learning have developed a sophisticated infrastructure and outstanding project production management systems. For example, Deakin has the capability to distribute substantial amounts of material to students located anywhere in the world.

❑ Evaluation. The university provides monitoring and evaluation of the programs and delivery modes. The evaluation enables the association to continuously improve the program and maintain its credibility and competitiveness in the market.

❑ Project management.

Certification courses delivered through an association are of university quality, drawing from the recognized disciplines, but with content dictated by the needs of the association's members.

Case Studies

This section offers two examples of large programs that are partnerships between an association and a university in Australia.

Association of Professional Engineers, Scientists, and Managers (APESMA). Many engineers enter management during their careers and turn to postgraduate programs to provide them with the skills and knowledge required to be a successful manager. APESMA found that many of its members were dissatisfied with traditional MBA programs, as they did not address management in technological environments.

In response to its members' needs, the association entered into partnership with Deakin University to develop a postgraduate diploma and MBA in technology management designed for engineers and technologists. The program is a joint award offered by APESMA and Deakin University.

Since the commencement of the Graduate Diploma (Technology Management) in 1989 and the MBA (Technology Management) in 1992, more than 12,500 Australian and overseas students from more than 5,000 organizations have participated in the program, making this the largest management program in the Australasian region. The APESMA/Deakin University MBA currently has participants from over fifty countries.

The governance of the program is rigorous, as it must conform to the accreditation requirements of the university and the standards of the professional association. A high-level management committee with representation from the association, the profession, and the university oversees the program and determines its strategic direction. Industry input into the course content, structure, and direction is seen as critical. Industry input is provided through the professional committee structures of the APESMA.

This industry input is vital to the relevance of each course. Therefore, a review committee has been established for each course. Each review committee typically consists of:

❏ The APESMA program director for the MBA program

❏ A Deakin University representative

❏ A subject matter expert

❏ An instructional designer

❏ Two industry nominees

Each review committee provides advice to the subject matter expert and instructional designer regarding the content of each course.

This governance structure is integrated into the university's accreditation procedures, thus satisfying the quality requirements of both organizations. APESMA also offers the Doctorate of Business Administration (DBA) degree and certificate courses in first-line supervision in partnership with other institutions; these programs are also subject to similar governance structures.

The APESMA/Deakin programs are delivered through proven distance-education techniques managed jointly by Deakin University (through DeakinPrime) and APESMA. Participants receive extensive, professional learning materials and are not required to attend formal lectures at any stage of their studies. This makes their studies truly portable, and they can continue even if they relocate geographically or change employment. Although it was initially a print-based distance program, the course is currently being converted into an on-line program.

The partnership between the association and the university has held to both professional and academic recognition, including:

❏ The program has national and international accreditation.

❏ In 2000, the program was validated as an award that meets the requirements of the United Kingdom Quality Assurance Agency.

❏ The program is accredited by the Hong Kong Council for Higher Education.

❏ The Institution of Professional Engineers, New Zealand; the New Zealand Institute of Architects; the Australian Computer Society; the Royal Australian Chemical Institute; and the Institution of Engineers, Papua New Guinea, also endorse the program.

The APESMA/Deakin MBA program has been a major contributor to the extraordinary increase in the number of engineers participating in management education. This number increased from 2 percent ten years ago to 14 percent currently. The APESMA/Deakin MBA program accounts for 50 percent of this increase.

Through intelligent marketing, the MBA has served to assist APESMA in attracting and retaining members and has become a significant source of nondues revenue for the association.

The Australian Human Resources Institute. The Australian Human Resources Institute (AHRI), established in 1943, is the leading member-based association for people working within the human resources profession in Australia. It is a large association, with a national membership of more than 13,500 individuals.

The association made a substantial commitment to the professional development of its members in 1995 by contracting Deakin Australia, the corporate arm of Deakin University, to develop and manage a Professional Diploma of Human Resources. This program was developed at a first-year postgraduate level, and although it had AHRI professional recognition, it did not have university recognition.

This issue was addressed in 1997, when AHRI and Deakin entered into a partnership to develop a Graduate Diploma in Human Resources that had both professional and university certification. The Graduate Diploma is an accredited award of the university.

This distance learning postgraduate program was developed through a partnership between AHRI and Deakin's Bowater School of Marketing & Management and offered as a joint program. The intellectual property is shared, and the revenue distribution reflects this ownership. Deakin recognizes AHRI's professional diploma, and graduates of this program are granted 50 percent advanced standing in the Graduate Diploma program. These education programs provide a valuable service to AHRI members, have become an industry standard, have allowed the association to take a leadership role in the development of HR professionals, and provide a significant nondues revenue stream for the association.

Both programs have strict academic and administrative governance structures with representation from AHRI, Deakin University, and DeakinPrime. The programs are supported by extensive short course, seminar, and conference schedules.

The partnership (expressed through contractual arrangements) recognizes the inherent strengths of the stakeholders. AHRI, as the peak professional body in Australia, is responsible for the marketing and professional integrity of the program. It has a direct relationship with its members as well as a network of professional decision makers and provides an enviable marketing channel. The programs are marketed through the association rather than through the university. Further, the members' expertise provides prospective authors material with a practical emphasis, ensuring that the material has an adequate balance of theory and application appropriate for practicing HR professionals.

Deakin University provides the academic oversight for the programs and has the credibility and the accreditation to confirm the quality of the programs. The university qualification, coupled with professional certification, is valuable to many HR professionals.

DeakinPrime is the interface between the academic component of the university and the profession, as represented by AHRI. Its role is the project management of the programs and the facilitation of the transfer of information. It also serves as a single point of accountability in student administration matters between the two organizations.

The partnership has not been without its problems, problems that are common when a market-oriented organization such as AHRI works with a more conservative university. Issues such as ownership of intellectual property, access to student details, branding issues, and the inability of rigid university procedures to respond to market requirements are ongoing sources of conflict. In 1999, after several years of substantial financial losses, the institute was placed into voluntary administration. In early 2000, Deakin University purchased the assets of the organization. This has presented the parties with a unique opportunity to develop procedures that address the problems just described. The programs being offered continue to grow in terms of numbers of students and professional standing. However, many of the operational and philosophical differences between the university and AHRI still remain.

Conclusion

The development of corporate universities in the region has been heavily influenced by cultures, by the traditional university systems in place, and certainly in Australia by the highly competitive economy and the strong history of distance and flexible tertiary education. The Australian experience shows that it is both possible and beneficial for organizations and universities to work in close partnership, combining their differing but complementary resources, to bring applied education and training to the workforce.

Conclusion
Whither Corporate Universities?

Mark Allen

T he foregoing chapters have been designed to describe the current state of affairs in the corporate university world. This conclusion takes a different tack. Given what we know about corporate universities, what we can observe of the trends, and what people are saying, I will attempt in this chapter to predict the future—to discern where corporate universities are going and where they will be in five or ten years.

These predictions center around five key dimensions: (1) the growth of corporate universities, both in America and around the world; (2) the use of electronic delivery formats; (3) the growing number and types of partnerships; (4) the migration toward more strategically oriented corporate universities; and (5) the increasing use of measurement and evaluation in corporate universities. Each of these issues is explored in this chapter.

The Growth of Corporate Universities

There is no question but that the number of corporate universities throughout the world has been growing rapidly over the past decade. As mentioned in the introduction, Meister estimated that the number in the United States in 2001 was in excess of 2,000. Her estimate was 800 in 1995, 1,200 in 1997, and 1,600 in 1999. The growth of corporate universities in this country (at least, according to Meister's estimates) has been remarkably linear—an increase of 400 every two years, or about one new corporate university every workday. While it is not clear which definitions of corpo-

rate universities are included in these estimates or how accurate the estimates are, it is evident from these estimates, from the growing number of
conferences relating to the topic, and from personal observation that there
has been remarkable growth in the number of corporate universities over
the past decade.

In order to examine whether this growth will continue, the reasons
for the growth should be examined. Certainly the concept of the corporate
university is a popular one. Organizations tend to like the idea of having
their own university, and decision makers are often quick to give their
approvals. Once installed, corporate universities tend to take root rather
quickly and to become a part of the structure and culture of their parent
organizations.

In attempting to glimpse five years into the future, there are three
possibilities: fewer corporate universities, about the same number of corporate universities, or more corporate universities. That there will be fewer
seems unlikely. A reduction in the number of corporate universities would
occur only if organizations made a decision to shutter their corporate universities or if the organizations containing these universities ceased to exist.
There has been little evidence that organizations are souring on the idea of
corporate universities and are closing them. Economic conditions may
cause some organizational retrenchment (and training and development
have often been among the first casualties of these cutbacks). But as corporate universities come to be viewed more as a strategic lever and an investment than as a luxury and a cost, the likelihood of significant declines
diminishes. It is also conceivable that an economic downturn will eliminate
numerous organizations in the American economy. However, corporate
universities tend to be housed in the larger, more stable corporations and
in large nonprofit and governmental organizations. The smaller companies
and more technology-oriented companies that are likely to be hardest hit
by recession are the least likely to have a corporate university in the first
place. And if we believe the premise that a corporate university is a device
to aid organizational success, then we should conclude that those companies that have embraced the notion of the corporate university are those
that will be best positioned for future success.

A prediction that the number of corporate universities in existence
five years from now will be about the same as the current count is neither
bold nor likely to be accurate. In order for this to occur, the new entrants
must be cancelled out by departures. Based on the tendency of corporate

universities not to disappear and the tendency for new universities to be created, this is unlikely.

Therefore, the logical conclusion is that there will be an even greater number of corporate universities five years from now than there are now. Looking internationally, the information in Chapters 11 and 12 supports a prediction of continued growth throughout the world. In America, it is likely that the corporate university movement has not yet peaked. Therefore, the question is not whether there will be more or fewer—it is how many more there will be.

Regardless of whether you believe the estimates, there is no doubt that there has been tremendous growth in the number of corporate universities over the past decade. While I believe that this growth will continue, it is unlikely to continue at the same rate as in the past. Many of the largest and best companies already have corporate universities. Many of those that do not are not sizable enough or may lack the financial resources to start a true corporate university—one that is tied into the strategic intent of the organization.

If there are indeed two thousand corporate universities in America, many of them are little more than renamed training departments. I think the trend for companies to establish entities that are corporate universities in name only will diminish. Organizations are discovering that other than receiving a little internal public relations boost, there is little advantage to having an entity called a corporate university that does not truly add value. As more is written about what a true corporate university is and how it can benefit an organization, fewer organizations will bother to create corporate universities that exist in name only. And some of the existing corporate universities that are merely a concept or a training department will abandon the appellation.

However, this reduction will be offset by some real growth. Again, as more is written about true corporate universities and their benefits, many organizations will embrace the concept. I think there will be genuine growth in the number of true corporate universities and a reduction in the number of name-only corporate universities.

I also think that some of the name-only corporate universities will experience some growth and learning and will evolve into true corporate universities. So while the overall number of corporate universities in the United States is unlikely to continue to double and redouble over the next decade, there is likely to be continued slow and steady growth. Moreover, there will be real growth in the number of corporate universities that truly fit the definition—those that really serve to enhance the organizational mission by being tied into the strategy.

The Use of Electronic Delivery Formats: Putting the Learning Back Into E-learning

The greatest buzz in the corporate university world is around the use of electronic delivery formats. Many organizations are wrestling with the decision of how much technology to incorporate into their corporate universities. Some companies are boldly announcing that they are planning, in the near future, to deliver 100 percent of their offerings via an e-learning format; these organizations proudly proclaim that they are running a virtual university. Others promise that a majority of their offerings will be delivered using technology.

The arguments for e-learning can be seductive. You can deliver the same educational program to hundreds, even thousands, of geographically dispersed employees without having to incur travel costs, either to transport learners to a classroom or to bring an instructor to the employees. Distance learning technologies can efficiently deliver training over time and space to many. And, the argument often goes, after an initial investment in the technology, the costs of delivery can be much lower than continually paying "stand-up" instructors to offer classroom delivery. Numerous vendors offer products ranging from hardware to software to courseware to turnkey solutions.

Over the past several years, there has been extraordinary growth in the amount of programs in corporate universities that are delivered electronically. While this growth may continue over the short term, within a few years the pendulum will swing back and there will be a reduction in e-learning and an increase in classroom delivery.

The main reason why I am certain that the use of e-learning will diminish is that there is often very little learning in e-learning. Much of the discussion about e-learning revolves around the "e" and very little around the learning. Next time you hear people discussing an e-learning initiative, see if the conversation is about actual learning—what happens inside a learner's head—or if it is about technology—what happens on a learner's computer. All too often, discussions about e-learning contain terms like *bandwidth, platform, courseware,* and *state-of-the-art server*—none of which have anything to do with workers gaining knowledge and skills. Technology can offer a fabulous delivery medium, but it is foolish to focus so much of the discussion and so many of the resources on delivery without giving the quality and goals of the underlying educational initiative the same level of scrutiny. It is akin to a manufacturer concentrating on the trucks that will deliver its product rather than on the product itself. Remember, learning is a change that happens inside the head (or the heart) of a learner—it is not something that happens inside a computer. So be careful about using the term *e-learning* to describe a delivery format—reserve the term for describing a situation in which someone actually learns something.

While we know a great deal about technology, we still know relatively little about how people learn using technology. Other than in a few specialized applications, there is no evidence that people learn better using technology than they do in a classroom with a talented instructor and a group of peers. I have actually heard technology vendors brag that their products can simulate the classroom environment so well that using them is almost as good as being in the classroom. Why invest millions of dollars in technology that, at its best, is not quite as good as the current state of affairs? While distance learning technologies can be an *efficient* means of delivering educational products to many potential learners, there is little evidence that this is an *effective* delivery format.

Educators have known for decades that learning occurs in three domains: the cognitive, the affective, and the psychomotor. The cognitive domain refers to our intellectual side. Emotions, values, and beliefs come into play in the affective domain. The psychomotor domain involves physical activities. I have surveyed hundreds of students over the years, and most agree that their best learning experiences have occurred when their affective domain was engaged. When we are in a learning environment and our emotions and values are touched, we tend to embrace learning more enthusiastically. I am not sure if the best way to a man's heart is through his stomach, but I am certain that the best way to a learner's brain is through the affective domain.

This is where distance learning technologies become problematical. A gifted classroom instructor can engage learners' emotions, values, and beliefs. Although not impossible, it is much more difficult to engage a learner's affective domain when that learner is sitting alone in a room in front of a computer screen.

Additionally, many corporate universities have already discovered that distance learning solutions are far more costly than was originally envisioned. They are just starting to learn that, in many cases, the learning benefits are not as great as they had hoped. Over the next few years, the trend toward transforming corporate universities into virtual universities will abate. The growth in distance learning solutions will diminish.

This isn't to say that technology cannot help a corporate university achieve its mission. While I am skeptical about most distance learning programs, some are of high quality—that is to say, they help employees learn. While these are in the minority, when done properly, technology can help people learn. Brandon Hall describes some of the methods that can be used to enable technology to enhance learning in Chapter 8. It is essential that technology be approached with an eye toward enhancing learning, not merely distributing education.

Some of the best technology solutions are those that are designed to *enhance* classroom learning, not *replace* it. These so-called hybrid solutions are designed to give the educator (and the learner) the best of both worlds: effective classroom instruction and learning that is enhanced by technology. In some cases, this involves a "wired classroom"—a situation in which a group of learners are in a classroom with an instructor, but there is a considerable technological presence. In other cases, learners get together periodically in classrooms but use technology to continue their course work during the intervals between classroom meetings. This could involve learners interacting with technology on an individual basis, class members using technology to communicate with one another asynchronously, or virtual class sessions in which groups of students meet with one another (and maybe even the instructor) in real time using text, audio, video, or a combination thereof. These hybrid solutions allow instructional designers to create programs that permit learning to happen interactively in classrooms while being enhanced by the best that technology has to offer.

In sum, I think the move toward eliminating or reducing classroom instruction in favor of virtual corporate universities will abate. Technology will not go away—there are certainly great applications that can be used to help corporate universities achieve their goals. However, these applications will come into play in hybrid solutions, which I believe will represent the dominant use of technology in corporate universities in the years to come.

Partnerships

As discussed in Chapter 5, there are many ways in which a corporate university can develop partnerships. I think we will see very few large, "full-service" corporate universities over the next few years—creating them is too difficult and not necessary.

By definition, corporate universities are educational entities that are part of organizations whose main purpose is something other than education. Therefore, it is not always feasible (or wise) for the organization to attempt to do everything that a strategically aligned corporate university needs to do. There are many other organizations that can assist with everything from needs assessment to program design, and from program delivery to evaluation. While all of these functions are important, it is not always necessary for the corporate university to attempt to develop the expertise to perform them in-house.

Bear in mind that when I refer to partnerships, I am not referring to outsourcing. Many corporate universities use vendors to provide various services, but the type of partnerships I am referring are long term and mutually beneficial. Rather than hiring a vendor to provide a service, corporate universities can work with traditional universities, consulting companies, technology providers, or even other corporate universities in relationships that last for years. While money may change hands, there may also be reciprocal delivery of services. The organizations will get to know each other's issues and processes, and this familiarity will enable educational opportunities to have a higher level of customization and personalization than off-the-shelf vendor products.

While not every corporate university will undertake partnerships, I think we will see many embrace this concept. It will be common to start associating various corporate universities with their university or technology partner. And while some of these partnerships will falter, I think we will see many that continue for years.

The Migration Toward More Strategically Oriented Corporate Universities

If there is one theme that has been echoed by many authors throughout the various chapters of this book, it is that in order for a corporate university to be effective (and to truly be a corporate university), it must be tied into the strategic intent of the parent organization. Even if there is continued growth in the number of name-only corporate universities, I think we will see the organizations with "real" corporate universities get serious about linking their corporate universities to the organizations' strategic intent.

This will have ramifications that will permeate the organization. First off, strategically oriented corporate universities will no longer be housed in the human resources department. Rather than being an HR function, strategically oriented corporate universities will be closer to the seat of power, often residing in the chairpersons's office. One way to determine how close a corporate university is to an organization's strategy is to look at whom the corporate university director reports to. If the head of the corporate university reports to the vice president of HR, that corporate university is often a step or two removed from the core of the organization. If the head of the corporate university reports directly to the CEO, that is a clue that the university is tied in closely to the direction in which the organization is trying to head.

Another indicator is to look at the offerings of the corporate university. If most of the activities are centered around job training, the corporate university is providing an operational assist, but not a strategic one. If there is considerable work in executive development, then the corporate university is one step closer to guiding the organization toward its intended future. And if the corporate university is actively involved in culture change and strategic alignment, then you know that it is tied in closely with the organization's strategy. If the corporate university has responsibility for knowledge management, succession planning, and possibly even the recruitment of new employees, that also signals ties to corporate strategy.

Another way in which corporate universities can assist in advancing organizational goals is through new employee orientation. Often dismissed as a routine HR function, this task, when done properly and coupled with savvy recruitment and hiring, can go a long way toward shaping an organization. If it's merely an introduction to the health insurance plan and a tour of the facility, then it's a missed opportunity.

The MGM Grand Hotel in Las Vegas saw the value of strategically using the corporate university to align people with the organization's vision. While most large companies grow over time and have their corporate university evolve, the MGM Grand opened its doors in 1993 and on its opening day was the largest hotel in the world. In order to prepare for that opening, more than eight thousand workers had to be hired and trained. Rather than just screening applicants, offering job skills training, and giving a tour, the MGM Grand decided to create a corporate university that would, above all, provide a forum for the acculturation of MGM Grand employees (or, as they are called at MGM Grand, "cast members"). And thus the University of Oz was born.

The first job of the University of Oz was to orient these eight thousand new cast members to the MGM Grand's culture and mission. Whereas most organizations start small and have a culture that evolves over time, the MGM Grand started large and created its own culture through conscious decision making. The company had decided on a culture that emphasized fun—for both guests and cast members. All of the cast members spent their first six hours at the University of Oz becoming immersed in the company's culture and mission.

The founding executives of the MGM Grand Hotel decided that if their property was to distinguish itself among the crowded field of Las Vegas hotel/casinos, it would have to do so through its people. They created the University of Oz as the lever to help them create and sustain a culture.

After the orientation of the initial eight thousand cast members, the University of Oz has continued its task of acculturation. It has also added the usual array of training and development classes. An interesting wrinkle to the University of Oz is its awarding of an internal degree—the Th.D. Th.D. means Doctor of Thinkology (movie fans will recall that this is the degree that the Wizard of Oz awarded to the Scarecrow). Cast members who complete a specified course of study at the University of Oz are awarded the Th.D. and receive a diploma and can proudly wear the designation on their name badges. Both the acculturation function of the University of Oz and the internal degree are designed to aid in employee retention. After working hard to earn a Th.D., the recipient has a great deal of prestige—within the walls of the MGM Grand. Outside, it's merely a conversation piece on a résumé.

Thus the University of Oz not only serves to create and sustain a culture, but also is the primary lever in the effort to retain employees. Since the gaming business is so labor dependent and there is such high turnover, retention is a crucial issue. The MGM Grand Hotel effectively uses its corporate university to help it achieve its employee retention goals.

And so I believe the next few years will see a greater reliance on corporate universities to advance strategic initiatives. This movement will be driven not from the corporate universities themselves, but from the slow realization among senior executives that corporate universities are more than just another HR function; they are a potentially powerful force for moving the organization—what Tom McCarty in Chapter 4 calls a "strategic lever."

Greater Reliance on
Measurement and Evaluation

My final prediction is that as corporate universities become more aligned with organizational strategy, there will be more frequent and more effective evaluation of corporate universities as a whole and of their individual programs. As Laree Kiely contends in Chapter 9, evaluation is crucial for corporate universities, not only to justify their existence, but in order to let everyone know if the corporate university is doing the job it is intended to do. When that job is to support the organization's strategy and mission, it is essential that the leaders of both the corporate university and the organization know that the corporate university is performing its function.

Measurement needs to be tied into the design of the corporate university and its activities. The goals of the corporate university should be clearly articulated. Failure to do this is the biggest flaw in attempts to evaluate—if you don't know specifically what you were trying to do, it is very hard to precisely measure whether you've done it. If you can't specifically state your goals, then you can't measure your success. The flip side is that if you do clearly articulate your mission, then you should be able to measure it. And the metrics should be specifically laid out in advance of launching activities. Too often, corporate universities dive into their activities and then, once those activities are under way, try to find ways of measuring and evaluating them. Evaluation methods need to be built in at the outset. Before doing anything, corporate university leaders need to decide what they are trying to do, how they will do it, and how they will measure it. The greatest barrier to corporate universities' being successful in supporting corporate strategy is the failure to specifically address all three of those questions before starting to offer programs.

Typically, measurement frightens people. It's too hard. It's too expensive. For God's sake, it involves *statistics!* However, as both Laree Kiely in Chapter 9 and Matt Barney in Chapter 10 point out, there are many realistic and feasible methods of performing evaluation. More important, there is no point in investing millions of dollars in a corporate university if you do not know whether it is doing its job.

Measurement can often be simple if the mission is straightforward. In the example of the MGM Grand Hotel, one of the main jobs of the University of Oz was to assist in employee retention. When, after its first five years of existence, the hotel had the lowest turnover rate in its industry, the

University of Oz was considered a success. While sophisticated methods relating cause and effect were not undertaken, the goals were being met, and that was enough for the decision makers to declare a success.

While measurement and evaluation will not always be that simple, it will always be important. I think we will see very few serious corporate universities that do not undertake some form of evaluation. And since the number of organizations that rely on their corporate universities for mission-critical activities will increase, so will the number of corporate universities conducting serious evaluations. And while, as Laree Kiely points out in Chapter 9, the literature is currently bereft of success stories about measurement, we will see an explosion of written accounts in which corporate universities reveal their evaluation methods.

★   ★   ★

As both this chapter and the previous thirteen have discussed, the corporate university phenomenon is an evolving one. I have heard people in traditional higher education (who might feel a tad threatened by corporate universities) predict that within ten years, we will look back at corporate universities as another fad that came and went. While predictions about the future are generally fraught with uncertainty, I am very confident in predicting that the corporate university movement is not going away. As a matter of fact, as corporate universities grow in sophistication, their impact on their parent organizations will intensify. Currently, in many organizations, the corporate university is a novelty or a toy. However, once senior executives realize the potential of this tool, they will not only take their corporate universities more seriously, but also use them more strategically. We will no longer hear about random organizations that have good corporate universities—we will hear about world-class, successful organizations that attribute their success to strong, well-run corporate universities.

Notes

Introduction

1. J. C. Meister, "The Brave New World of Corporate Education," *The Chronicle of Higher Education*, Feb. 9, 2001, pp. B10–B11.
2. E. M. Hawthorne, P. A. Libby, and N. S. Nash, "The Emergence of Corporate Colleges," *Journal of Continuing Higher Education* 31(2), 1983, p. 2.
3. N. P. Eurich, *Corporate Classrooms* (Princeton, N.J.: The Carnegie Foundation for the Advancement of Teaching, 1985), p. 96.
4. B. C. Edelstein and D. J. Armstrong, "A Model for Executive Development," *Human Resource Planning* 16(4):51–68, 1993.
5. G. Thompson, "Unfulfilled Prophecy: The Evolution of Corporate Colleges," *The Journal of Higher Education* 71(3):322–341, 2000.
6. Eurich, *Corporate Classrooms*.
7. M. Rademakers and N. Huizinga, "How Strategic Is Your Corporate University?" *The New Corporate University Review*, Nov.–Dec. 2000, p. 18.
8. P. McGee, "Where Do Training Leaders Come From?" *The New Corporate University Review*, March–April 2001, p. 7.
9. Ibid.
10. Ibid.

Chapter 5

1. R. M. Fulmer and A. A. Vicere, *Executive Education and Leadership Development: The State of the Practice* (University Park, Pa.: The Penn State Institute for the Study of Organizational Effectiveness, 1995).
2. L. Bongiorno, "Corporate America's New Lesson Plan," *Business Week*, Oct. 25, 1993, pp.102–104.
3. M. R. Louis, "The Gap in Management Education," *Selections* 6(3):1–12, 1990; K. Ramaswamy, "Enhancing Business School Effectiveness: A Multiple-Constituency Approach," *Journal of Education for Business* 67(6):353–357, 1992; C. M. Ray, J. J. Stallard, and C. S. Hunt, "Criteria for Business Graduates' Employment: Human Resource Managers' Perceptions," *Journal of Education for Business* 69(3):140–144, 1992; M. W. Aiken, J. S. Martin, and J. G.

Paolillo, "Requisite Skills of Business School Graduates: Perceptions of Senior Corporate Executives," *Journal of Education for Business* 69(3):159–162, 1994.

4. D. Ready, A. A. Vicere, and A. F. White, "Executive Education: Can Universities Deliver?" *Human Resources Planning* 16(4):1–11, 1993.

5. M. Schneider and B. Hindo, "A Mid-career Boost," *Business Week*, Oct. 15, 2001, pp. 110–114.

6. Ibid., p. 111.

7. J. Jampol, "Corporate Universities: Friend or Foe?" *International Herald Tribune*, March 19, 2001, p. 13.

8. J. Traub, "Drive-thru U," *The New Yorker*, Oct. 20 and 27, 1997, pp. 114–123.

9. J. Reingold and L. Bongiorno, "When the Best B-school Is No B-school," *Business Week*, Oct. 20, 1997, pp. 68–69.

10. M. Kaeter, "Cap and Gown," *Training*, Sept. 2000, pp. 115–122.

11. K. S. Mangan, "Top Business Schools Try Collaboration Over Competition," *The Chronicle of Higher Education*, July 6, 2001, pp. A23–A24.

12. Ibid.

Chapter 6

1. American Productivity and Quality Center, *Saturn Site Visit Report* (Houston: APQC, 1997), p. 17.

2. J. C. Meister, *Corporate Quality Universities* (New York: Richard D. Irwin, 1994).

3. J. C. Meister, "Future Directions of Corporate Universities," Unicon Conference, 1996.

4. R. H. Miles, *Corporate Universities: Some Design Choices and Leading Practices* (Atlanta, Ga.: Emory University School of Business, 1993).

5. K. P. Wheeler, *The Uses and Misuses of the Term "Corporate University"* (Fremont, Calif.: Global Learning Resources, 1999–2000).

6. American Productivity and Quality Center Institute for Education Best Practices, *The Corporate University: Learning Tools for Success* (Houston: APQC, 1998).

7. L. Densford, "Corporate Universities Add Value by Helping Recruit, Retain Talent," *New Corporate University Review*, March–April 1999, pp. 8–12.

8. "100 Best Companies to Work For in America," *Fortune,* Jan. 10, 2000.

Chapter 7

1. Laurie J. Bassi et al., *Profiting From Learning: Do Firms' Investments in Education and Training Pay Off? Executive Summary* (Alexandria, Va.: American Society for Training & Development, 2000).

2. Ibid.
3. Corporate Leadership Council, *The Compelling Offer: A Quantitative Analysis of the Career Preferences and Decisions of High Value Employees*, vol. 3, *Workforce Commitment Series* (Washington, D.C.: Corporate Executive Board, 1999).
4. Ibid.
5. Corporate Leadership Council, *Salient Findings on the Career Decisions of High Value Employees* (Washington, D.C.: Corporate Executive Board, 1999).
6. Jennifer Reingold, Mica Schneider, and Kerry Capell, "Learning to Lead," *Business Week,* Oct. 18, 1999, p. 76.
7. Corporate Leadership Council, *Best Practices in Executive Education Programs* (Washington, D.C.: The Advisory Board Company, 1998).
8. David S. Pottruck and Terry Pearce, *Clicks and Mortar: Passion Driven Growth in an Internet Driven World* (San Francisco: Jossey-Bass, 2000).
9. Daniel P. McMurrer, Mark E. Van Buren, and William H. Woodwell Jr., *The 2000 ASTD State of the Industry Report* (Alexandria, Va.: American Society for Training & Development, 2000).
10. Corporate Leadership Council, *Management Training Practices* (Washington, D.C.: Corporate Executive Board, 2001).
11. D. P. McMurrer et al., *ASTD Industry Report.*
12. VisionQuest, a proprietary product of Charles Schwab & Co., Inc., was launched in March 1999 and continues to serve as a conduit for engaging and aligning employees around the company's vision, values, and strategic priorities.
13. D. P. McMurrer et al., *ASTD Industry Report.*
14. L. J. Bassi et al., *Profiting From Learning.*

Chapter 9

1. Stan Davis and Jim Botkin, *The Monster Under the Bed* (New York: Simon & Schuster, 1994), pp. 14–15.
2. Ibid., p. 137.
3. Donald Kirkpatrick, *Evaluating Training Programs*, 2d ed. (San Francisco: Berrett-Koehler Publishers, 1998).
4. Ibid., p. 19.
5. Ibid., p. 20.
6. Ibid., p. 20.
7. Ibid., p. 23.
8. Ron Zemke, "Just Another Shell Game," *Training Magazine*, May 2001.
9. Lynn Miller, "Measure Online Training Efforts for Effectiveness," *HRMagazine,* Oct. 2000.

10. Dean Patton, Sue Marlow, and Paul Hannon, "The Relationship Between Training and Small Firm Performance; Research Frameworks and Lost Quests," *International Small Business Journal,* Oct.–Dec. 2000.

11. Alan Barrett and Phillip J. O'Connell, "Does Training Generally Work? The Returns to In-company Training," *Industrial & Labor Relations Review,* April 2001.

12. Lutz Prechelt and Barbara Unger, "An Experiment Measuring the Effects of Personal Software Process (PSP) Training," *IEEE Transactions on Software Engineering,* May 2001.

13. Marc Bendick Jr., Mary Lou Egan, and Suzanne M. Lofhjelm, "Workforce Diversity Training: From Anti-discrimination Compliance to Organizational Development," *HR Human Resource Planning,* 2001.

14. Christine Riordan, "The Effects of Pre-entry Experiences and Socialization Tactics on Newcomer Attitudes and Turnover," *Journal of Managerial Issues,* Summer 2001.

15. Shereen G. Bingham and Lisa L. Scherer, "The Unexpected Effects of a Sexual Harassment Educational Program," *The Journal of Applied Behavioral Science,* June 2001.

16. Joshua D. Angrist and Victor Lavy, "Does Teacher Training Affect Pupil Learning? Evidence From Matched Comparisons in Jerusalem Public Schools," *Journal of Labor Economics,* April 2001.

17. John Berry, "Corporate Training—The E-Learning Center—Companies Are Using Metrics to Justify E-Learning's Impact on Strategic Business Goals," *Internetweek,* Nov. 6, 2000.

18. Gaylen N. Chandler and Glenn M. McEvoy, "Human Resource Management, TQM, and Firm Performance in Small and Medium-sized Enterprises," *Entrepreneurship Theory and Practice,* Fall 2000.

19. Gary L. May and William M. Kahnweiler, "The Effect of a Mastery Practice Design on Learning and Transfer in Behavior Modeling Training," *Personnel Psychology,* Summer 2000.

20. Howard J. Klein and Natasha A. Weaver, "The Effectiveness of an Organizational-Level Orientation Training Program in the Socialization of New Hires," *Personnel Psychology,* Spring 2000.

21. Wendy L. Richman-Hirsh, "Posttraining Interventions to Enhance Transfer: The Moderating Effects of Work Environments," *Human Resource Development Quarterly,* Summer 2001.

22. Dale M. Brethower, "Invited Reaction: Posttraining Interventions to Enhance Transfer," *Human Resource Development Quarterly,* Summer 2001.

23. Frederick R. Rohs, Christine A. Langone, and Rhonda K. Coleman, "Response Shift Bias: A Problem in Evaluating Nutrition Training Using Self-Report Measures," *Journal of Nutrition Education,* May–June 2001.

24. Dana Gaines Robinson and James C. Robinson, *Training for Impact* (San Francisco: Jossey-Bass, 1989).

25. Ibid., p. 233.
26. Ibid.
27. David Giber, Louis Carter, and Marshall Goldsmith, eds., *Best Practices in Leadership Development Handbook* (San Francisco: Jossey-Bass Pfeiffer and Lexington, Mass.: Linkage Incorporated, 2000).
28. Lester Shapiro, *Training Effectiveness Handbook* (New York: McGraw-Hill, 1995).
29. Beverly Gerber, comp., *Evaluating Training* (Minneapolis: Lakewood Books, 1989).
30. See note 3.
31. Jack J. Phillips, *Handbook of Training Evaluation* (Houston: Gulf Publishing, 1997).
32. Philip G. Zimbardo and Michael R. Leippe, *Attitude Change and Social Influence* (Philadelphia: Temple University Press, 1991), p. 31.
33. Ibid., p. 34.
34. Fred N. Kerlinger, *Foundations of Behavioral Research* (New York: Holt, Rinehart and Winston, 1964), p. 551.
35. Zimbardo and Leippe, *Attitude Change and Social Influence*, p. B-7.
36. Ole R. Holsti, *Content Analysis for the Social Sciences and Humanities* (Reading, Mass.: Addison-Wesley, 1969), p. 17.
37. Zimbardo and Leippe, *Attitude Change and Social Influence*, p. 30.
38. Kirkpatrick, *Evaluating Training Programs*, p. 20.
39. Ibid., p. 23.

Chapter 10

1. T. T. Baldwin and J. K. Ford, "Transfer of Training: A Review and Directions for Future Research," *Personnel Psychology* 41:63–105, 1988; J. K. Ford, E. M. Smith, D. A. Weissbein, S. M. Gully, and E. Salas, "Relationships of Goal Orientation, Metacognitive Activity, and Practice Strategies With Learning Outcomes and Transfer," *Journal of Applied Psychology* 83(2):218–233, 1998; G. M. Alliger, S. I. Tannenbaum, W. Bennett, H. Traver, and A. Shotland, "A Meta-Analysis of the Relations Among Training Criteria," *Personnel Psychology*, 50:341–358, 1997; J. K. Ford and D. A. Weissbein, "Transfer of Training: An Updated Review and Analysis," *Performance Improvement Quarterly*, 10(2):22–41, 1997.
2. M. F. Barney, "Multidimensional Predictors of Training Transfer: An Empirical Study," Technical Report, Motorola University, 2000.
3. G. M. Alliger et al., "A Meta-Analysis."
4. R. O. Brinkerhoff and S. J. Gill, *The Learning Alliance: Systems Thinking in Human Resource Development* (San Francisco: Jossey-Bass, 1994).

5. Jack Phillips, ed., *In Action: Measuring Return on Investment*, vol. 1 (Alexandria, Va.: ASTD Publishing, 1994).
6. G. A. Rummler and A. P. Brache, *Improving Performance: Managing the White Space on the Organizational Chart* (San Francisco: Jossey-Bass, 1995); Brinkerhoff and Gill, *The Learning Alliance*.
7. B. Lev, *Intangibles: Management, Measurement and Reporting* (Washington, D.C.: Brookings Institution Press, 2001).
8. Baldwin and Ford, "Transfer of Training"; P. W. Thayer and M. S. Teachout, "A Climate for Transfer Model," Armstrong Laboratory, Air Force Material Command, Brooks Air Force Base, Texas, AL/HR-TP-1995-0035, 1995, pp. 1–44; Ford and Weissbein, "Relationships"; Alliger et al., "A Meta-Analysis"; L. A. Burkey and T. T. Baldwin, "Workforce Training Transfer: A Study of the Effect of Relapse Prevention Training and Transfer Climate," *Human Resource Management* 38(3):227–242, 1999.
9. M. F. Barney, "Multidimensional Predictors."
10. Ibid.
11. J. W. Boudreau and P. Ramstad, "Measuring Intellectual Capital: Learning From Financial History, *Human Resource Management,* 36(3):343–356, 1997; J. M. DiFrancesco and S. J. Berman, "Human Productivity: The New American Frontier," *National Productivity Review* 19(3):29–36; J. W. Boudreau, B. B. Dunford, and P. Ramstad, "The Human Capital Impact on E-Business: The Case of *Encyclopedia Britannica*," in N. Pal and J. M. Ray, eds., *Pushing the Digital Frontier* (New York: AMACOM, 2001), pp. 192–221.

Chapter 11

1. Annick Renaud-Coulon, *Universités d'Entreprise et Instituts d'Entreprise, Évaluation et comparaison internationale,* ©2001. This study spanned thirty-six countries. In addition to a global analysis, the final paper covers seventy-five corporate university profiles in seventeen countries; it is made up of three volumes and has nearly eight hundred pages. It is available at the Web site www.renaud-coulon.com.

Chapter 12

1. This case study is based on information by Derek Cunard, head of faculty, PRUuniversity, posted on the corporate e-mail group on July 27, 2001.
2. Derek Cunard, e-mail to corporate e-mail group, July 27, 2001.

Index

Index

About the Authors

Mark Allen

Mark Allen, Ph.D., is the Director of Executive Education at Pepperdine University's Graziadio School of Business and Management. He is responsible for designing and delivering executive education programs to corporate clients and alumni. In that capacity he is in charge of the university's Corporate University Partnerships program and has developed alliances between Pepperdine and corporations throughout the United States.

Previously, Dr. Allen was Program Director in Executive Education at the University of Southern California's Marshall School of Business where he developed a variety of highly successful executive education programs. He has also held managerial positions at Kaplan, Integrated Data Concepts, and SRS Publishing.

Dr. Allen has a Bachelor's degree in psychology from Columbia University, an MBA from Pepperdine University, and a Ph.D. in Education from USC. He has published and presented research on corporate universities and nontraditional higher education. Other research interests include the assessment of training and development programs and the evaluation of teaching and learning in postsecondary and adult education.

An award-winning teacher, Mark is an adjunct professor teaching courses in Adult and Lifespan Learning at Pepperdine's Graduate School of Education and Psychology and has previously taught business and management courses at a number of institutions.

He has designed and delivered executive development programs for 3M, Caesars World, the Los Angeles Police Department, Infonet, Safeguard, Samsung, Hughes, Kaiser Permanente, the government of Taiwan, and other organizations.

Dr. Allen lives in Redondo Beach, California, with his wife Dayna and his two sons, Skyler and Dylan.

Karen Barley

Karen Barley is the co-founder and Vice President of Corporate University Enterprise, Inc. (CUE), an educational consulting firm that helps organizations design and manage in-house corporate universities. Incorporated in 1998, CUE is charged with bringing a strategic approach to workforce education in both private and public organizations.

Barley has served clients throughout the United States, Europe, and Asia and has consulted with countless companies and agencies, most recently the Ritz-Carlton Hotel Company, L.L.C., Northern Orient Lines, and the National Institute of Standards and Technology. She has created dozens of corporate universities from scratch for national and global organizations and has served as director of three corporate universities in the federal government.

She holds the copyright on one of the only corporate university planning models and is an international speaker on the subject. Her work with various learning programs has been published and highlighted in the *New Corporate University Review* and other trade journals. She has also completed an independent research project on conceptualizing the corporate university.

Ms. Barley is a founding member and sponsor of the Washington Area Corporate University Consortium, the first regional network of CU practitioners in the Washington, D.C. area. To learn more about Karen Barley and CUE, visit www.cuenterprise.com or e-mail info@cuenterprise.com.

Matt Barney

Matt Barney, Ph.D., is the Director of Six Sigma for Motorola University. Dr. Barney has extensive experience in strategic HR roles at such companies as Intel, AT&T, Lucent Technologies, and Motorola. He serves on the Advisory Board of Knowledge Advisors, Inc., a training measurement technology firm. His current research and consulting involves using interdisciplinary ideas from finance, engineering, strategy, information technology, and psychology to improve overall organizational effectiveness. In particular, he is working on a new approach to valuing human capital.

Dr. Barney has published and presented papers on a variety of topics, ranging from human capital asset management and HR technology to personnel selection and training; and he authors a column in the quarterly journal *The Industrial Organizational Psychologist* entitled "Macro, Meso, Micro." Dr. Barney has also authored three U.S. patents and has others pending. He holds a B.S. in Psychology from the University of Wisconsin-Madison and a Masters and Ph.D. in Industrial-Organizational Psychology from the University of Tulsa.

Ian Dickson

Ian Dickson, Ph.D., has had extensive experience in both the academic and commercial worlds. Dr. Dickson has had a distinguished academic and teaching career, and as Head of School Information and Numerical Science was instrumental in establishing multidisciplinary Applied Science degree programs in Scientific Information Transfer, Health Promotion, Microprocessor Applications, and Technology Management. His work in Technology Management in partnership with the Ford Motor Company broke new ground in university-level, workplace-based learning that established the base on which Deakin University built its extensive partnerships with corporations.

Dr. Dickson was a founding Director of Deakin Australia, responsible for new business development, and as President of DeakinPrime established the business in the United States in 2000. He has a doctorate in Chemistry and an MBA and post-graduate qualifications in education, data processing, and management.

Robert M. Fulmer

Robert M. Fulmer, Ph.D., is a Distinguished Visiting Professor at Pepperdine University and Academic Director for Duke Corporate Education.

He has served as director of corporate management development for Allied Signal, Inc., with worldwide responsibility for management development, ranging from first-line supervision to senior executives.

He is the author of four editions of *The New Management* and co-author of four editions of *A Practical Introduction to Business, Crafting Competitiveness, Executive Development and Organizational Learning for Global Business, Leadership by Design,* and *The Leadership Investment.*

He was previously the W. Brooks George Professor of Management at the College of William and Mary and a visiting scholar at the Center for Organizational Learning at MIT. He also taught Organization and Management at Columbia University's Graduate Business School. For six years, Dr. Fulmer served as director of executive education at Emory University.

Dr. Fulmer earned his MBA from the University of Florida and his Ph.D. from the University of California at Los Angeles. In addition, he has designed and delivered leadership development initiatives in twenty-two countries and on six continents.

Brandon Hall

Brandon Hall, Ph.D., is a leading independent researcher in e-learning, helping organizations make the right decisions about technology. With more than 20 years as a training professional, he is the author of seven widely cited research reports and the groundbreaking *Web-Based Training Cookbook.* His latest reports include *Learning Management Systems 2001: How to Choose the Right System for Your Organization, E-Learning Across the Enterprise: The Benchmarking Study of Best Practices* and *Collaboration Tools for E-Learning: Increasing Completion Rates and Knowledge Sharing.*

Dr. Hall's clients have included IBM, Cisco, General Electric, Motorola, Kraft/General Foods, Hewlett-Packard, Westinghouse, and the U.S. Army. He is the editor of *Technology for Learning* newsletter and has been a columnist for *Inside Technology Training* and a contributing editor to the American Society for Training and Development's *Training and Development Magazine.* As an internationally recognized researcher and speaker on e-learning, he has been interviewed and quoted by *Fortune, The New York Times, The Wall Street Journal, Business Week, Training, HR Executive,* and others. Dr. Hall has written more than 50 articles for industry publications, and he has been a featured speaker at industry conferences, such as ASTD and Online Learning.

Dr. Hall is the lead researcher for Brandon-hall.com and chairs the annual Brandon Hall of Fame Awards, now in its fifth year and the first recognition program dedicated entirely to the e-learning industry.

Laree Kiely

Laree Kiely, Ph.D., is President and CEO of Laree Kiely, Inc.—Organizational Effectiveness Consultants. She has more than 25 years' experience consulting, facilitating, and teaching organizational behavior to businesses internationally. Her areas of expertise include organizational development and managerial behavior, strategic planning, teaming, influence and negotiation, decision making, creative problem solving, and management design.

As a faculty member at the University of Southern California's Marshall School of Business and Director of the Marshall School's Teaching Excellence Center, Dr. Kiely taught in the Executive MBA, executive education, and facilitator and trainer programs. She is also a former manager of Technology Services at First Interstate of California. Among the numerous awards she has received for her teaching and consulting, Dr. Kiely won most recently the 2000 "Best Corporate Intervention" award from the International Society for Performance Improvement. She received her B.A. and M.A. degrees from the University of Colorado and her Ph.D. from the University of Southern California.

Linda H. Lewis

Dr. Linda H. Lewis is Senior Vice President of Learning & Education at Charles Schwab & Co., Inc. In addition to her role as the head of Schwab University, she is also accountable for the design and roll out of numerous HR initiatives and programs companywide.

Lewis has broad-based experience in the public and private sectors, the not-for-profit world, and academe. She holds a doctorate in adult learning and a master's in management and administration. Her array of diverse skills and experience enable her to leverage her academic credentials to address any people-related business need in any environment, national or international.

Formerly Vice President of Strategic Change for Kaiser Permanente, as well as their VP of HR, Dr. Lewis facilitated organizational restructuring, cultural transformation efforts, the adoption of best practices, and the infusion of new practice models. Prior to coming West, she was Vice President of Corporate Education and Human Resources for Travelers.

Lewis's background in financial services is complemented by her ten-year tenure as a professor at the University of Connecticut. As a member of the graduate faculty, with a specialty in adult learning and adult development, she consulted with numerous Fortune 500 companies.

Dr. Lewis is well published in the area of adult learning and is author and editor of numerous books and articles. A former Kellogg fellow, she has received over $3 million in grants to develop innovative programs and demonstration projects. Currently, she serves on several advisory and editorial boards. She spends what little free time she has traveling and working in her gardens.

Thomas D. McCarty

Tom McCarty is the Vice President of Consulting Services for Motorola University. McCarty and the Six Sigma Business Improvement team are dedicated to improving the business performance of Motorola's customers and suppliers through the application of Six Sigma continuous improvement methodology. Their work is focused on partnering with customers and suppliers to launch and sustain Six Sigma business improvement campaigns enabled by Motorola University's consulting and training resources.

Prior roles and responsibilities for Mr. McCarty have included Director of Global Products and Systems Education for Motorola's Land Mobile Products Sector, with responsibility for the design, delivery, and marketing of technical training for customers, and Group Vice President of Training for Motorola's U.S. Distribution Group, where his primary responsibility was sales and customer support training. In addition, he has 14 years of direct sales and sales management experience.

McCarty holds an undergraduate degree in Business Administration from the University of Kentucky and a Masters in Business from Southern Illinois University.

James D. Moore

Jim Moore is an independent consultant working with major corporations to design executive development strategies and programs and to establish strategies and designs for corporate universities. He has served in the Chief Learning Officer role at three major corporations.

From 1994 to 2000, he was director of SunU, the organization that provides education programs to the 40,000 worldwide employees of Sun Microsystems. He was also responsible for Sun's executive development organization, which included succession planning, executive education, and staffing.

Prior to his Sun assignment, he was Vice President—Training and Development for Northern Telecom Ltd. at its Washington, D.C., headquarters, where he led their global education programs and was responsible for executive development.

As Director of Employee Development at BellSouth Corporation, Moore established the BellSouth Management Institute, which helped to reshape the executive management culture at BellSouth. He also created the Global Leaders for the South program, a leadership development experience for public sector representatives appointed by the governors of twelve southern states, and the BellSouth Principals Institute, a leadership development program for public school principals.

Jim holds a Masters of Electrical Engineering degree from the University of Louisville.

About the Authors

Mike Morrison

Mike Morrison, Ph.D., currently serves as Dean for the University of Toyota, a corporate university he helped to launch in the late 1990s. The University of Toyota has quickly established itself as a leading global education institution by offering a comprehensive, cutting-edge curriculum to a worldwide audience.

Dr. Morrison's passion centers on the principles of lifelong learning. An intense research project sponsored by the University of Toyota has revealed timeless, core strategies that are key to maximizing human potential. These strategies are carefully embedded into the University of Toyota's curriculum.

With over two decades of executive-level experience, Morrison has played key roles in strategic planning, human resources, and new business ventures. He holds a B.A. from Gonzaga University, an MBA from the University of Southern California, and a Ph.D. from Claremont Graduate University's Drucker School.

Annick Renaud-Coulon

In addition to studying law, Annick Renaud-Coulon has been a teacher, head of human resources in an industrial organization, a consultant, and head of an enterprise. She currently works as an independent consultant and conference speaker with a network of partners in France and abroad.

Among her other specialties, she consults in the area of change in organizations, both public and private, including the passage from a national to an international environment and from complicated logic to thematic logic. She carries out studies and research, and helps heads of organizations to solve problems in a wide range of situations. Ms. Renaud-Coulon also writes articles and books and conducts seminars and conferences in corporate education and related fields.

She is a signatory of the Manifesto in favor of individual enterprises and member of the Solo Observatory.

Her interventions, investigations, and conferences have allowed her to travel to many countries, including Canada, Hong Kong, India, Japan, Egypt, Morocco, Senegal, South Korea, Taiwan, the U.S., and numerous European countries.